FAITH & FINANCIAL FORTUNE

A CHRISTIAN'S GUIDE TO GENERATIONAL WEALTH

LeRoy L. Deal

ISBN: 978-1-964312-04-0

TABLE OF CONTENTS

FAITH & FINANCIAL FORTUNE

INTRODUCTION

If you've picked up this book, you're likely looking for practical advice on managing your finances and building a secure future. Whether you're a young adult starting your career or a professional seeking better financial management, you're in the right place.

This book aims to blend timeless biblical principles with modern financial wisdom, providing you with a roadmap to achieve financial independence and create lasting wealth.

The Bible offers profound insights into human behavior and ethics, many of which are incredibly relevant today. It encourages diligence, wise stewardship, and generosity—key components of sound financial management. By understanding and applying these principles, you can build a solid financial foundation that benefits not only you but also those around you.

One of the first things I'd like to address is the misconception that wealth is inherently evil. Many people, especially those from disadvantaged backgrounds, have been taught that striving for wealth is wrong. However, it's crucial to understand that money itself is neutral—it's a tool. The issue arises from how it's used. The love of money can lead to problems, but money used wisely can be a powerful force for good. This book emphasizes that building generational wealth is commendable. It's about being responsible stewards, making wise decisions, and using wealth to honor God and benefit others.

An Overview of What's to Come

Biblical Perspective on Wealth: In Chapter 1, we explore what the Bible says about wealth, highlighting passages that emphasize diligence and stewardship.

Financial Blueprint: Budgeting for Success: In Chapter 2, you'll discover the 70-10-10-10 principle—a simple budgeting rule that allocates income for spending, investing, saving, and giving. Practical steps will help you manage your finances effectively.

Building a Solid Financial Foundation: Chapter 3 guides you in assessing your current financial situation, setting SMART goals, and creating actionable plans for success.

Introduction to Investment Vehicles: In Chapter 4, you'll get an introduction to various investment options, giving you a foundational understanding of the tools available for wealth building.

Investing in Stocks for Growth: Chapter 5 delves into stock market investing, offering practical advice on selecting stocks and building a diversified portfolio for long-term growth.

Exploring Options Trading Strategies: In Chapter 6, we dive into more advanced investing with options trading, detailing strategies, risks, and rewards.

Understanding Bonds and Fixed Income Investments: Chapter 7 covers different types of bonds and their role in balancing risk and return within a diversified portfolio.

Exploring Real Estate Investment Trusts (REITs): In Chapter 8, you'll learn how REITs allow for real estate investment without direct property ownership, along with their benefits and risks.

Exploring Tax Liens and Tax Deeds: Chapter 9 introduces you to tax lien and tax deed investing, explaining their potential returns, risks, and the practical steps to get started.

FOREX Investing: In Chapter 10, we explore the foreign exchange market, providing an overview of how to trade currencies and the risks involved.

The Power of Dollar Cost Averaging: Chapter 11 explains the strategy of investing a fixed amount regularly, regardless of market conditions, and its benefits over time.

Leveraging IULs and Velocity Banking for Financial Freedom: Chapter 12 dives into more advanced financial strategies like Indexed Universal Life (IUL) insurance policies and velocity banking, offering ways to enhance financial freedom.

The Entrepreneurial Journey: Starting and Growing a Business: Chapter 13 is for those considering entrepreneurship, providing insights on launching and growing a successful business.

Navigating Challenges and Risks in Wealth Building: In Chapter 14, we discuss common challenges in wealth-building and strategies to mitigate risks and avoid pitfalls.

Financial Planning for Life Transitions: Chapter 15 focuses on financial planning through different life stages—whether starting a family, transitioning into retirement, or navigating unexpected events.

Cultivating a Heart of Gratitude and Contentment: Chapter 16 explores the connection between wealth, happiness, and contentment, and how gratitude plays a crucial role in financial well-being.

Leaving a Lasting Legacy: Planning for Generational Wealth Transfer: Finally, in Chapter 17, we cover the importance of planning for generational wealth transfer, offering strategies for building and preserving wealth to create a lasting legacy.

Throughout this book, you'll find illustrations and diagrams designed to make complex financial concepts easier to understand. Visual aids will help you grasp budgeting techniques, investment strategies, and other key topics more effectively.

My goal is to guide you on a journey toward financial freedom and independence. By following the advice and principles outlined in this book, you'll be equipped to make informed financial decisions, build a solid foundation for the future, and create a lasting legacy for your loved ones.

Remember, this journey is not just about accumulating wealth for its own sake. It's about using your resources wisely, living generously, and honoring God with your financial decisions. Together, we can achieve a balanced and fulfilling life that reflects both financial success and spiritual growth.

Welcome to your financial transformation.

Chapter 1

The Biblical Perspective on Wealth

Wealth is a prominent theme in the Bible, offering timeless guidance on managing resources wisely. The Bible doesn't condemn wealth itself but provides principles on how to handle it responsibly.

Moreover, the Bible emphasizes the importance of stewardship. We are called to manage our resources wisely and use them for good purposes. The parable of the talents (Matthew 25:14-30) illustrates this concept vividly, showing that wise investment and management of resources are commendable.

The Bible views wealth as a tool that, when managed with diligence and integrity, can lead to prosperity and positive impact. It's about how we use wealth, aligning our financial decisions with ethical and spiritual principles.

Proverbs 10:4 states, "*Lazy hands make for poverty, but diligent hands bring wealth.*" This verse emphasizes a fundamental principle: diligence is key to financial success. Consistent effort and hard work are essential for building and maintaining wealth. Diligence involves more than just working hard; it includes being proactive, disciplined, and persistent in managing your finances.

Think of it this way: just as an athlete trains consistently to excel, you must apply the same dedication to your financial life. This means setting clear goals, creating a budget, and sticking to it.

It involves regularly reviewing and adjusting your financial plans to stay on track. It also means seeking opportunities to increase your income, whether through advancing your career, investing wisely, or starting a side business.

Diligence isn't about quick fixes or overnight success. It's about making steady, informed decisions that build wealth over time. By embracing the principle of diligence, you set a solid foundation for financial independence and generational wealth. Remember, the path to wealth is a marathon, not a sprint. Consistent, diligent effort will yield the best results.

1 Timothy 6:10 warns, "*For the love of money is a root of all kinds of evil.*" This verse often gets misunderstood as saying money itself is evil, but that's not the case. The distinction here is crucial: it's the love of money that leads to problems, not money itself. It's important to understand this difference and apply it to your financial strategy.

Money can be used for good or bad, depending on how you handle it. The problem arises when money becomes an obsession or when acquiring wealth becomes your primary focus at the expense of everything else. This unhealthy attachment can lead to unethical decisions, strained relationships, and personal dissatisfaction.

On the other hand, when you view money as a means to achieve your goals, support your family, and help others, it becomes a powerful tool for good. It's about balance and perspective. Use money to create opportunities, invest in your future, and give back to your community.

By keeping your values in check and ensuring that money serves your broader life purpose, you can avoid the pitfalls associated with the love of money and build a healthy, prosperous financial future.

Balancing material wealth with spiritual values is essential for a fulfilling and meaningful life. I believe it's crucial to integrate your financial goals with your core values and beliefs. Wealth, when managed wisely, can enhance your life and support your spiritual and ethical commitments.

However, it's vital to keep material pursuits in perspective. Ensure that your desire for wealth does not overshadow your spiritual and ethical priorities. Regularly reflecting on your values and how they align with your financial decisions can help maintain this balance. For example, when making investment choices, consider not only potential returns but also ethical implications and how they resonate with your beliefs.

By viewing wealth as a means to an end—a tool to support your higher purposes—you can build a prosperous life that honors both your material and spiritual aspirations. This balanced approach ensures that wealth enhances, rather than detracts from, your overall well-being and sense of fulfillment.

The Bible features several figures who were wealthy and used their resources wisely, providing valuable lessons for today. One prominent example is King Solomon, renowned for his wisdom and wealth. Solomon's wealth was immense, yet he is most celebrated for his wisdom and discernment. His story illustrates that wealth, coupled with wisdom, can be a powerful combination for effective leadership and positive impact.

Another example is Abraham, considered one of the wealthiest men of his time. Abraham's wealth included livestock, silver, and gold. Despite his riches, he is remembered for his faith and obedience to God. His story highlights the importance of faithfulness and the blessings that can come from aligning one's life with spiritual values.

Job is another significant figure. Though he initially lost all his wealth, his steadfast faith and integrity led to his restoration, and he ended up with even greater wealth. Job's story underscores the resilience and perseverance needed in financial and spiritual journeys.

These figures demonstrate that wealth in itself is not problematic; it's how it is acquired, managed, and used that matters. Their lives teach us that wealth, when combined with wisdom, faith, and integrity, can be a force for good and a testament to responsible stewardship.

Stewardship, in a biblical context, refers to the responsible management and care of resources that have been entrusted to us by God. It goes beyond mere ownership to encompass the idea that everything we have—our finances, talents, time, and opportunities—are gifts from God. Understanding this concept is foundational to building a solid framework for financial decision-making.

At its core, stewardship emphasizes three key principles: responsibility, accountability, and generosity. Responsibility involves recognizing that we are entrusted with resources that ultimately belong to God. This mindset shifts our perspective from ownership to caretaking, motivating us to manage our finances wisely and ethically.

Accountability means that we are answerable to God for how we use and manage the resources entrusted to us. This accountability encourages transparency and integrity in our financial dealings, fostering trust and credibility in our personal and professional lives.

Generosity is a natural outflow of stewardship. It involves using our resources not only for our own benefit but also for the well-being of others and the advancement of God's kingdom. This can include supporting charitable causes, helping those in need, and investing in initiatives that promote positive social impact.

The parable of the talents (Matthew 25:14-30) illustrates these principles vividly. In this parable, a master entrusts his servants with different amounts of money (talents) before going on a journey. The servants who invest and multiply their talents are praised upon the master's return, while the one who buries his talent out of fear receives rebuke.

This parable teaches us several lessons about stewardship: First, God expects us to use our abilities and resources wisely and productively. Second, stewardship involves taking calculated risks and making strategic investments, rather than playing it safe or being overly cautious. Third, it underscores the importance of accountability—being able to give an account of how we have managed what has been entrusted to us.

In practical terms, applying stewardship means creating and following a budget that aligns with your values and priorities. It means making informed investment decisions that consider both financial returns and ethical considerations.

It also involves planning for the future, including retirement and estate planning, with a mindset of leaving a positive legacy for future generations.

By embracing stewardship in our financial lives, we honor God, build trust and integrity, and contribute to a more just and compassionate society. It's not just about managing money; it's about living with purpose and making a meaningful impact with the resources we've been given.

Biblical Principles of Stewardship

Stewardship, rooted in biblical principles, offers timeless wisdom for managing our resources in a way that honors God and benefits others. Understanding these principles can profoundly impact how we approach wealth and financial decision-making.

1. Ownership Belongs to God: Psalm 24:1 reminds us, "*The earth is the Lord's, and everything in it, the world, and all who live in it.*" This foundational principle establishes that God is the ultimate owner of all things, including our finances. Recognizing this ownership shifts our perspective from possessiveness to stewardship—managing what belongs to God for His purposes.

2. Responsibility for Resources: In 1 Corinthians 4:2, stewardship is described as being faithful with what has been entrusted to us. This involves accountability and wise management of our finances, time, talents, and opportunities. It requires diligence in budgeting, investing, and planning for the future, ensuring resources are used effectively and ethically.

3. Generosity and Giving: Proverbs 11:24-25 teaches, "*One person gives freely, yet gains even more; another withholds unduly, but comes to poverty. A generous person will prosper; whoever refreshes others will be refreshed.*" Biblical stewardship includes a commitment to generosity and giving. By sharing our resources with others, whether through charitable donations, supporting community initiatives, or helping those in need, we participate in God's work of compassion and justice.

4. Multiplying Resources: The parable of the talents (Matthew 25:14-30) also illustrates the principle of multiplying resources entrusted to us. The master commends the servants who multiply their talents, emphasizing the importance of wise investment and strategic growth. Stewardship encourages us to seek opportunities to increase our financial resources through prudent investing and entrepreneurial ventures, aiming not only for personal gain but also for broader impact.

5. Faithful Management: Luke 16:10 reminds us, "*Whoever can be trusted with very little can also be trusted with much, and whoever is dishonest with very little will also be dishonest with much.*" Faithful stewardship involves integrity in financial matters—honoring commitments, avoiding debt beyond our means, and conducting business ethically. It means making decisions that reflect our values and priorities, even when faced with financial pressures or temptations.

In applying these principles, we cultivate a mindset of stewardship that integrates faith with finances. It's about aligning our financial goals and actions with God's purposes, ensuring our wealth serves not only our needs but also contributes positively to society and reflects our commitment to following Christ's teachings.

By embracing biblical principles of stewardship, we not only achieve financial stability and prosperity but also live with purpose, integrity, and generosity. This holistic approach to wealth management fosters a fulfilling and impactful life, grounded in faith and guided by timeless wisdom.

Managing resources wisely is at the heart of biblical stewardship, offering practical guidance for achieving financial stability and building wealth.

Budgeting and Financial Planning: Proverbs 21:5 advises, "*The plans of the diligent lead to profit as surely as haste leads to poverty.*" Creating a budget is foundational to wise financial management. It involves allocating income for essential expenses, savings, investments, and charitable giving. A well-planned budget provides clarity and control over finances, ensuring resources are used purposefully and in alignment with personal goals and values.

Debt Management: Proverbs 22:7 cautions, "*The borrower is slave to the lender.*" Responsible stewardship includes managing debt wisely. This may involve prioritizing debt repayment, minimizing high-interest loans, and avoiding unnecessary debt accumulation. By maintaining a manageable debt-to-income ratio and developing a strategy to eliminate debt, individuals can achieve financial freedom and allocate more resources toward savings and investments.

Saving and Investing: Proverbs 13:11 states, "*Dishonest money dwindles away, but whoever gathers money little by little makes it grow.*" Saving regularly and investing wisely are crucial for long-term financial growth. Setting aside a portion of income for emergencies, future expenses, and retirement builds financial security.

Investing in diversified portfolios, such as stocks, bonds, and real estate, allows assets to grow over time, leveraging the power of compounding returns.

Generosity and Giving: 2 Corinthians 9:7 encourages, "*Each of you should give what you have decided in your heart to give, not reluctantly or under compulsion, for God loves a cheerful giver.*" Biblical stewardship includes a commitment to generosity and charitable giving. By prioritizing giving, individuals participate in God's work of compassion and contribute to meaningful causes that align with their values.

Seeking Wise Counsel: Proverbs 15:22 advises, "*Plans fail for lack of counsel, but with many advisers they succeed.*" Seeking guidance from trusted mentors, financial advisers, and community leaders provides invaluable insights and accountability in financial decision-making. Learning from the experiences and expertise of others can help navigate challenges, identify opportunities, and make informed choices for long-term financial success.

By integrating these principles into everyday financial practices, individuals can cultivate a mindset of stewardship that honors God, fosters financial well-being, and promotes a positive impact on society. Managing resources wisely not only leads to personal prosperity but also enables individuals to fulfill their God-given potential and contribute meaningfully to the world around them.

Let's look at some practical actions we can begin to apply, that align financial decisions with the biblical principles we've just gone through.

Creating and Following a Budget: A clear budget is essential for effective financial stewardship. By outlining income and expenses, individuals can prioritize essential needs, allocate funds for savings and investments, and plan for future goals. Regularly reviewing and adjusting the budget ensures financial stability and helps avoid overspending.

Debt Repayment Strategies: Managing debt responsibly is key to good stewardship. Developing a repayment plan that focuses on high-interest debts first, such as credit cards or student loans, accelerates debt reduction and reduces overall interest payments. Consistent payments and avoiding new debt contribute to financial freedom and enable greater flexibility in future financial decisions.

Building an Emergency Fund: Proverbs 21:20 advises, "*The wise store up choice food and olive oil, but fools gulp theirs down.*" Similarly, setting aside funds for emergencies protects against unexpected expenses and financial setbacks. Aim to save three to six months' worth of living expenses in an accessible account to cover unforeseen circumstances like medical emergencies or job loss.

Investing for the Future: Proverbs 13:11 states, "*Dishonest money dwindles away, but whoever gathers money little by little makes it grow.*" Wise investing involves diversifying assets across stocks, bonds, and real estate to achieve long-term growth and mitigate risks. Regular contributions to retirement accounts, such as 401(k)s or IRAs, harness compound interest and build wealth over time.

Practicing Generosity: Generosity is a hallmark of biblical stewardship.

Setting aside a portion of income for charitable giving supports causes aligned with personal values and impacts communities in meaningful ways. Whether supporting local nonprofits, church ministries, or global initiatives, cheerful giving not only blesses others but also brings joy and fulfillment to the giver.

Seeking Knowledge and Advice: Proverbs 15:22 advises, "Plans fail for lack of counsel, but with many advisers they succeed." Engaging with financial mentors, advisers, and educational resources enhances stewardship practices. Learning about investment strategies, tax implications, and estate planning empowers individuals to make informed decisions and navigate financial complexities effectively.

By incorporating these practical examples into daily financial practices, individuals demonstrate faithful stewardship of God-given resources.

Aligning financial goals with stewardship responsibilities is crucial for one seeking to honor God with their resources while pursuing financial stability and prosperity.

Proverbs 16:3 advises, "*Commit to the Lord whatever you do, and he will establish your plans.*" Begin by identifying core values and priorities that reflect biblical teachings. This foundational step guides the setting of financial goals aligned with personal convictions, such as providing for family needs, supporting charitable causes, and preparing for future responsibilities.

Allocate income across essential expenses, savings, investments, and giving with intentionality.

By prioritizing financial commitments in line with stewardship principles, individuals cultivate discipline and ensure resources are used wisely and responsibly.

Proverbs 21:20 teaches, "*In the house of the wise are stores of choice food and oil, but a foolish man devours all he has.*" Planning for long-term financial security involves saving for retirement, establishing emergency funds, and securing adequate insurance coverage. These measures safeguard against unforeseen circumstances and reinforce financial resilience.

Matthew 6:19-21 reminds us, "*Do not store up for yourselves treasures on earth, where moths and vermin destroy, and where thieves break in and steal. But store up for yourselves treasures in heaven.*" Wise investing involves balancing risk and reward, diversifying portfolios, and aligning investment choices with ethical considerations. By stewarding investments prudently, individuals generate wealth responsibly and contribute positively to society.

Luke 6:38 encourages, "*Give, and it will be given to you. A good measure, pressed down, shaken together and running over, will be poured into your lap. For with the measure you use, it will be measured to you.*" Integrating generosity into financial goals demonstrates a commitment to blessing others and advancing God's kingdom. Set aside a portion of income for charitable giving, supporting causes that resonate with your values and promote social good.

Regularly assess financial goals and stewardship practices to ensure alignment with evolving priorities and circumstances. Seek feedback from trusted advisers and mentors to refine strategies and capitalize on opportunities for growth and impact.

By doing this, you will not only achieve financial success but also live out your faith through intentional and purposeful stewardship of God's blessings. This holistic approach fosters peace of mind, enhances personal fulfillment, and leaves a lasting legacy of integrity and generosity for future generations.

Using wealth for charitable causes is a core principle of biblical stewardship, reflecting a commitment to generosity and making a positive impact on society.

Biblical Foundation of Generosity: Proverbs 11:25 affirms, "*A generous person will prosper; whoever refreshes others will be refreshed.*" Giving generously aligns with biblical teachings and demonstrates a heart of compassion and stewardship. By prioritizing charitable giving, individuals participate in God's work of transforming lives and communities.

Strategic Giving: Effective charitable giving involves intentional planning and strategic decision-making. Begin by identifying causes and organizations that resonate with personal values and align with biblical principles. Whether supporting local community initiatives, global humanitarian efforts, or educational programs, strategic giving maximizes impact and fosters long-term change.

Setting Giving Goals: Proverbs 3:9-10 instructs, "*Honor the Lord with your wealth, with the firstfruits of all your crops; then your barns will be filled to overflowing.*" Set aside a specific percentage or amount of income dedicated to charitable giving as a priority in financial planning. Establishing giving goals ensures consistency and enables individuals to contribute meaningfully to causes they care about.

Impact Assessment: Regularly evaluate the impact of charitable donations to gauge effectiveness and alignment with philanthropic goals. Engage with charitable organizations to understand how contributions are utilized and the outcomes achieved. By measuring impact, individuals can make informed decisions and adjust giving strategies to maximize positive change.

Tax-Efficient Giving Strategies: Explore tax-efficient giving strategies, such as donating appreciated assets or establishing donor-advised funds, to optimize the financial benefits of charitable contributions. Consult with financial advisers or tax professionals to leverage available incentives and maximize resources allocated to charitable causes.

Inspiring Generational Giving: Proverbs 13:22 reminds us, "*A good person leaves an inheritance for their children's children.*" Instill a culture of generosity and stewardship within families by involving children and future generations in charitable giving. Share stories of impact and encourage the continuation of philanthropic traditions to leave a lasting legacy of compassion and social responsibility.

By using wealth for charitable causes, individuals not only fulfill their stewardship responsibilities but also contribute to building a more compassionate and equitable world. Embracing generosity as a cornerstone of financial planning enriches lives, strengthens communities, and reflects a commitment to living out faith through impactful giving.

The Bible provides numerous examples of philanthropy—acts of generosity and compassion that demonstrate God's heart for the welfare of others.

These stories serve as timeless lessons on stewardship and inspire us to use our wealth and resources to bless those in need.

1. The Widow's Offering (Mark 12:41-44): Jesus observed a poor widow who contributed two small coins to the temple treasury, which was all she had to live on. Despite her meager resources, her sacrificial giving demonstrated faith and devotion. This story illustrates that the value of our gifts is measured not by their size but by the sincerity and sacrifice behind them.

2. The Good Samaritan (Luke 10:25-37): In this parable, a Samaritan traveler showed compassion to a wounded man on the roadside, providing immediate care and covering all expenses for his recovery. The Samaritan's generosity transcended cultural barriers and exemplified the principle of loving your neighbor as yourself through practical acts of kindness.

3. Joseph's Famine Relief Efforts (Genesis 41-47): During a severe famine in Egypt and neighboring lands, Joseph, appointed as Pharaoh's steward, implemented a comprehensive plan to store surplus grain during years of plenty. His foresight and administration ensured that Egypt had food reserves to sustain its people during the famine, as well as providing relief to surrounding nations.

4. Barnabas' Generosity (Acts 4:36-37): Barnabas, also known as the Son of Encouragement, sold a field he owned and donated the proceeds to the early Christian community in Jerusalem. His selfless act of giving contributed to the growth of the church and demonstrated solidarity among believers, reflecting a commitment to communal support and care.

5. Zacchaeus' Transformation (Luke 19:1-10): Zacchaeus, a wealthy tax collector, encountered Jesus and experienced a radical transformation of heart. He pledged to give half of his possessions to the poor and repay four times the amount to those he had cheated. Zacchaeus' repentance and restitution exemplify the transformative power of generosity and stewardship in response to God's grace.

6. Paul's Support for the Church (2 Corinthians 8-9): The apostle Paul encouraged generosity among early Christian communities, emphasizing cheerful giving as an expression of faith and gratitude. He organized collections to support needy believers in Jerusalem, fostering unity and solidarity across diverse regions and demonstrating the global reach of Christian philanthropy.

These biblical examples of philanthropy inspire us to emulate generosity, compassion, and stewardship in our financial practices. By learning from these stories, we discover the profound impact of giving on individuals, communities, and the advancement of God's kingdom. Integrating these principles into our financial planning enables us to honor God, bless others, and leave a lasting legacy of faith-driven philanthropy.

Biblical principles of generosity transcend time and culture, offering timeless wisdom for individuals seeking to integrate faith with financial stewardship in today's world. Let's take a look at some practical applications of biblical generosity that resonate with each one of us striving to make a meaningful impact.

1. Adopt a strategic approach to charitable giving by identifying causes that align with biblical values and personal passions.

Research nonprofit organizations or ministries that demonstrate transparency, efficiency, and a clear mission. Consider focusing on areas such as poverty alleviation, education, healthcare, or humanitarian aid where your contributions can make a significant difference.

2. In addition to financial donations, volunteer your time and skills to support charitable initiatives. Many organizations rely on volunteers to enhance their impact and extend their reach. By actively participating in community service projects or mission trips, you embody the spirit of generosity and engage directly with those in need.

3. Explore opportunities for impact investing, which involves allocating capital to businesses or ventures that generate social or environmental benefits alongside financial returns. Impact investments may include affordable housing projects, sustainable agriculture, clean energy initiatives, or microfinance programs that empower disadvantaged communities.

4. Establishing a donor-advised fund allows you to maximize the impact of your charitable giving while benefiting from tax advantages. DAFs enable donors to make contributions, receive immediate tax deductions, and recommend grants to qualified charities over time. This structured approach provides flexibility and strategic planning in managing charitable donations.

5. Align your consumer choices with ethical considerations by supporting businesses that uphold biblical values such as fair trade practices, environmental sustainability, and corporate responsibility. Patronizing socially responsible companies contributes to a more equitable economy and promotes stewardship of God's creation.

6. Share your commitment to biblical generosity with peers, family members, and colleagues. Lead by example through storytelling and testimonies of how your financial resources have made a positive impact in the lives of others. Encourage others to join you in practicing generosity and fostering a culture of giving within your community.

Here are some stories of impactful giving that illustrate the transformative power of generosity and stewardship, inspiring individuals to embrace a lifestyle of purposeful giving.

The Power of Sacrificial Giving: Consider the story of Donna, a young professional who, despite modest means, committed a portion of her income to support an educational scholarship fund for underprivileged students. Through consistent contributions and advocacy, she enabled several students to pursue higher education, breaking the cycle of poverty and empowering future leaders.

Empowering Local Communities: In a suburban neighborhood, a family invested in a community garden initiative to promote sustainable agriculture and food security. Their financial support and volunteer efforts not only provided fresh produce to local families but also fostered a sense of community and collaboration among residents.

Impacting Global Health: Marion is a healthcare professional who dedicated part of her earnings to fund medical missions in developing countries, providing essential healthcare services and treatments to marginalized communities. Her commitment to improving global health outcomes exemplifies the profound impact of targeted philanthropy and compassionate care.

Supporting Social Entrepreneurship: A young entrepreneur named Thomas launched a socially conscious business that donates a percentage of profits to environmental conservation projects. By aligning financial success with environmental stewardship, he demonstrate how business ventures can contribute to both economic growth and sustainable development.

Legacy of Generosity: Reflect on the legacy of Chris, a philanthropist who established a foundation to address systemic issues such as homelessness and education inequality. His visionary leadership and substantial contributions continue to catalyze social change and empower future generations to create a more just and equitable society.

Personal Transformation: Witness the story of Lucy who experienced a life-altering encounter with generosity when receiving unexpected financial assistance during a personal crisis. Inspired by this act of kindness, she committed to paying it forward, initiating a ripple effect of generosity and compassion in their community.

These stories underscore the profound influence of stewardship and generosity in shaping communities, advancing causes, and transforming lives.

Fostering a mindset of service and generosity is foundational to integrating biblical principles of stewardship into our financial lives. Here are some ways to do it.

By adopting a mindset of generosity, individuals not only bless others but also experience personal fulfillment and spiritual enrichment. Proverbs 11:24-25 reminds us, "One person gives freely, yet gains even more; another withholds unduly, but comes to poverty. A generous person will prosper; whoever refreshes others will be refreshed."

Seek opportunities to serve others within your community, workplace, or local organizations. Whether volunteering time, skills, or financial resources, active participation in service initiatives cultivates empathy, compassion, and a deeper understanding of human needs.

Gratitude fuels generosity by acknowledging blessings and acknowledging the impact of others' generosity on our lives. Recognize the privilege of financial stability and commit to sharing resources with those less fortunate. Gratitude fosters humility and a sense of responsibility toward stewarding wealth for the greater good.

Incorporate charitable giving into your financial plan as a priority rather than an afterthought. Set aside a specific percentage of income for donations to causes aligned with your values and passions. Implementing a structured approach ensures consistency and maximizes the impact of your contributions.

Influence friends, family, and colleagues through your actions. Inspire a culture of generosity within your social circles and empower others to make a difference through their financial resources and talents.

Incorporating biblical principles into daily habits is pivotal for those seeking to align their financial decisions with values of stewardship and generosity. Practical application begins with cultivating mindfulness and intentionality in how we manage our resources. Start each day with a moment of reflection, acknowledging gratitude for the blessings in your life. This practice not only centers your mindset on abundance but also fosters a spirit of thankfulness that underpins generous actions.

Next, integrate regular financial planning sessions into your routine. Set aside time each month to review your budget, track expenses, and assess progress toward your financial goals. This disciplined approach ensures that your spending aligns with your values and priorities, including provisions for charitable giving and supporting causes that resonate with you.

Another essential habit is to prioritize savings and investments that reflect long-term stewardship. Allocate a portion of your income towards savings accounts, retirement plans, or investment portfolios that uphold ethical standards and align with biblical principles. Seek opportunities to diversify your investments while considering impact investing options that support sustainable development and community empowerment.

Furthermore, engage in ongoing education and reflection on biblical teachings related to wealth and stewardship. Regularly study scriptures and attend discussions or seminars that explore the intersection of faith and finance. By deepening your understanding of biblical principles, you equip yourself to make informed financial decisions that honor God and benefit others.

Practicing discernment in spending habits is also crucial. Evaluate purchases based on necessity, quality, and ethical considerations.

Choose to support businesses and products that uphold integrity and contribute positively to society, reflecting your commitment to ethical stewardship in everyday transactions.

Lastly, nurture a supportive community of like-minded individuals who share your values of generosity and stewardship. Surround yourself with mentors, peers, or accountability partners who encourage and challenge you to live out your faith through practical actions. Together, you can inspire one another to embody biblical principles in financial management and amplify your collective impact on the world.

Crafting a personal mission statement serves as a guiding compass for people navigating their financial journey with purpose and clarity. Much like a business defines its mission to steer decisions and actions, your personal mission statement articulates your values, aspirations, and commitment to stewardship and generosity.

Begin by reflecting on your core beliefs and values that shape your financial decisions. Consider how biblical principles of stewardship, integrity, and compassion influence your perspective on wealth and its purpose in your life. Your mission statement should encapsulate these values, serving as a constant reminder of what matters most to you amidst the complexities of financial management.

Outline specific goals and objectives that align with your mission statement. Define short-term and long-term milestones that reflect your commitment to financial stewardship, such as achieving debt freedom, building savings, or increasing charitable giving. These goals should be measurable and actionable, guiding your daily decisions and financial planning efforts.

Let's explore some inspiring case studies that demonstrate successful implementation of financial priorities aligned with faith. These stories illustrate how individuals have integrated biblical principles of stewardship, generosity, and purpose into their financial practices, inspiring others to follow suit in their own journey towards financial well-being and impact.

Consider the story of Sarah and James, a young couple dedicated to living out their faith through their finances. Sarah, a healthcare professional, and James, an engineer, decided early in their marriage to prioritize giving by allocating a significant portion of their income to charitable organizations and missions. They embraced a budgeting strategy that allowed them to not only meet their living expenses and save for future goals but also support causes dear to their hearts. By adhering to a disciplined financial plan, they were able to achieve their dream of funding a clean water project in a developing country, impacting countless lives with access to safe drinking water.

Another example is John, a successful entrepreneur who founded a tech startup guided by principles of ethical investing and community impact. From the inception of his company, John made intentional decisions to ensure that business practices aligned with biblical values of fairness, integrity, and compassion. He implemented profit-sharing programs for employees, supported local charities through corporate donations, and dedicated a percentage of company profits to sustainable initiatives that benefited marginalized communities. John's commitment to ethical entrepreneurship not only fostered a positive work culture but also attracted investors and clients who shared his values, resulting in sustainable growth and profitability for his business.

Lastly, consider Maria, a professional in the finance industry, who found fulfillment by integrating generosity into her personal financial plan. Despite living in a competitive and financially demanding environment, Maria made giving a cornerstone of her financial strategy. She volunteered her time mentoring young adults in financial literacy, donated a portion of her bonuses to educational scholarships, and actively supported local nonprofits addressing social justice issues. Maria's deliberate choices not only aligned with her Christian values but also brought purpose and fulfillment to her career and personal life, demonstrating that impactful giving is achievable at any stage of one's financial journey.

By prioritizing generosity, stewardship, and ethical practices, Sarah and James, John, and Maria have not only achieved financial stability and success but also made a lasting impact on others. Their stories serve as inspiration for those seeking to align their financial priorities with faith, fostering a legacy of purpose-driven stewardship and generosity in today's world.

As you continue to prioritize aligning your financial decisions with faith-based principles, it's crucial to cultivate a supportive environment and seek encouragement along the way. Building a strong foundation of stewardship and generosity requires ongoing commitment and growth, which can be nurtured through various avenues.

Firstly, consider joining or forming a community of like-minded individuals who share your values and aspirations.

Engaging with peers who prioritize faith-based financial stewardship can provide valuable insights, accountability, and encouragement. Whether through local church groups, online forums, or professional networks, surrounding yourself with supportive relationships strengthens your resolve and inspires continued growth in your financial journey.

Secondly, seek out mentors or advisors who align with your values and can offer guidance from a faith-based perspective. These mentors can provide wisdom gleaned from their own experiences, helping you navigate challenges, make informed financial decisions, and stay focused on your long-term goals. Their mentorship can offer invaluable perspective and encouragement as you strive to integrate faith into your financial practices.

Additionally, prioritize ongoing education and personal development in areas of financial stewardship and generosity. Attend workshops, seminars, or read books that explore biblical principles of money management and charitable giving. Continual learning equips you with new strategies, deepens your understanding of stewardship, and empowers you to make informed decisions that reflect your faith and values.

Furthermore, maintain regular self-assessment and reflection on your financial journey. Evaluate your progress in aligning your financial priorities with faith-based principles, celebrate achievements, and identify areas for growth. This introspection fosters a sense of purpose and direction, ensuring your actions remain intentional and aligned with your values.

Lastly, embrace a spirit of gratitude and resilience in your financial stewardship.

Recognize the blessings in your life and the opportunities to positively impact others through your financial resources. Despite challenges or setbacks, maintaining a resilient mindset grounded in faith allows you to persevere and continue striving toward your goals with confidence and determination.

Remember that growth is a continual process.

Chapter 2

The Financial Blueprint: Budgeting for Success

The 70-10-10-10 Principle

Understanding the 70-10-10-10 budgeting rule can transform how you manage your finances and help you achieve both financial stability and growth. This rule is a straightforward guideline for allocating your income in a balanced way, ensuring that all aspects of your financial life are taken into account.

The principle breaks down your income into four main categories: spending, investing, saving, and giving. Here's how it works:

70% for Spending

The largest portion, 70%, is allocated to spending. This covers all your necessary living expenses, such as housing, utilities, groceries, transportation, and other day-to-day costs. The idea is to live comfortably within this limit, ensuring that you are not overspending and staying within your means. By capping your spending at 70% of your income, you avoid the trap of living paycheck to paycheck and create room for other important financial activities.

10% for Investing

The next 10% of your income is dedicated to investing. This is about building wealth for the future. Investments can include stocks, bonds, mutual funds, real estate, or any other assets that have the potential to grow over time. Investing is essential because it helps your money work for you, generating returns that can significantly increase your wealth over the long term.

10% for Saving

Another 10% is earmarked for saving. This is your safety net, your "security blanket" for unexpected expenses or emergencies. It's crucial to have liquid funds readily available to cover unforeseen circumstances, such as medical emergencies, car repairs, or sudden job loss. The goal is to build up savings that can cover at least three to six months' worth of expenses. Once you have reached this emergency fund target, you can then redirect this 10% towards other financial goals, such as additional investments or larger purchases.

10% for Giving

The final 10% is for giving. This could be donations to charitable organizations, tithing to your church, or helping out friends and family in need. Giving is not only a way to contribute to the well-being of others but also enriches your own life. It fosters a sense of purpose and fulfillment, reminding you of the importance of generosity and community.

By following the 70-10-10-10 rule, you create a balanced financial strategy that promotes spending within your means, investing for growth, saving for emergencies, and giving back to the community. This holistic approach ensures that all aspects of your financial life are nurtured, leading to long-term stability and prosperity.

The 70-10-10-10 budgeting rule, while simple in its structure, has deep roots in the history of financial management and personal finance. Understanding its origins and how it has been adopted over time provides valuable insight into its effectiveness and enduring relevance.

The concept of dividing income into specific categories is not new. Ancient civilizations, including the Mesopotamians and Egyptians, practiced forms of budgeting to manage resources efficiently. They allocated portions of their harvests and resources for immediate use, future planting, and communal sharing. These early practices laid the groundwork for structured financial planning.

In more recent history, the idea of budgeting became more formalized with the rise of personal finance literature in the 20th century. Influential figures like George S. Clason, author of "The Richest Man in Babylon," emphasized principles of saving, investing, and prudent spending. Clason's parables, set in ancient Babylon, highlighted the timeless wisdom of allocating a portion of one's income for different purposes. His advice to "save at least 10% of what you earn" resonates closely with the principles behind the 70-10-10-10 rule.

The 70-10-10-10 rule itself emerged as a modern adaptation of these enduring principles, aiming to simplify and update them for contemporary use. Financial advisors and personal finance experts recognized the need for a straightforward, easy-to-remember framework that could help individuals manage their finances more effectively. By breaking down income into clear, manageable portions, this rule addresses the common challenges of overspending and under-saving that many people face today.

The 70% allocated for spending reflects a realistic approach to living expenses, ensuring that essential needs are met without excessive extravagance. The 10% set aside for investing encourages the growth of wealth through long-term financial instruments, building on the age-old advice to make your money work for you.

Saving 10% provides a crucial safety net, echoing the wisdom of ancient and modern financial teachings about the importance of preparing for emergencies. Finally, the 10% for giving embodies the principle of generosity, which has been a cornerstone of many cultures and religions throughout history.

As the 70-10-10-10 rule gained popularity, it became a staple recommendation in personal finance workshops, books, and online resources. Its simplicity and adaptability make it accessible to a wide range of people, from young adults just starting their financial journey to seasoned professionals looking to refine their money management strategies.

By understanding the historical context and origins of the 70-10-10-10 budgeting rule, we can appreciate its time-tested wisdom and practical application. This principle not only helps manage finances effectively but also promotes a balanced, fulfilling approach to money that aligns with both ancient practices and modern financial insights.

The 70-10-10-10 rule has been a transformative budgeting strategy for many individuals across various financial situations. Let's explore some real-life scenarios where this rule has been successfully applied to illustrate its practical benefits.

Consider the story of Sarah, a recent college graduate who landed her first full-time job. With a modest starting salary, Sarah was determined to manage her finances wisely. She adopted the 70-10-10-10 rule, allocating 70% of her income to cover her living expenses, including rent, utilities, groceries, and transportation. This structure helped Sarah avoid overspending and maintain a balanced lifestyle.

She dedicated 10% of her income to a savings account, building an emergency fund for unexpected expenses. Another 10% went into a beginner's investment portfolio, focusing on low-risk index funds. The final 10% was earmarked for charitable donations, allowing Sarah to support causes she cared about deeply. Over time, Sarah saw her savings grow, her investments start to yield returns, and felt fulfilled by her contributions to charity.

Another example is John and Maria, a couple in their mid-30s with two young children. They had accumulated some debt over the years and were looking to get their finances back on track. Implementing the 70-10-10-10 rule was a game-changer for them. They allocated 70% of their combined income to necessary expenses, ensuring they lived within their means while paying down debt. They split the remaining income into 10% for investing, focusing on a diversified portfolio for long-term growth, 10% for savings to build a robust emergency fund, and 10% for giving, which included both charitable donations and support for family members in need. This disciplined approach not only helped them reduce their debt significantly but also set them on a path towards financial security and growth.

Lisa, a single mother running her own small business, is another success story. Her income varied month to month, making budgeting a challenge. By adhering to the 70-10-10-10 rule, Lisa was able to stabilize her finances. In months with higher income, she adhered to the rule strictly, and in leaner months, she adjusted the percentages slightly while still maintaining the overall structure. This consistency allowed her to manage her expenses effectively, save for her daughter's education, invest in her business, and continue her tradition of donating to local charities. The 70-10-10-10 rule provided a flexible yet reliable framework that adapted to her fluctuating income.

These scenarios illustrate that the 70-10-10-10 rule is not a one-size-fits-all solution but a versatile strategy that can be tailored to different financial circumstances. By providing a clear, balanced approach to budgeting, it helps individuals and families make informed decisions about spending, saving, investing, and giving. This rule encourages financial discipline and long-term planning, fostering a sense of security and fulfillment.

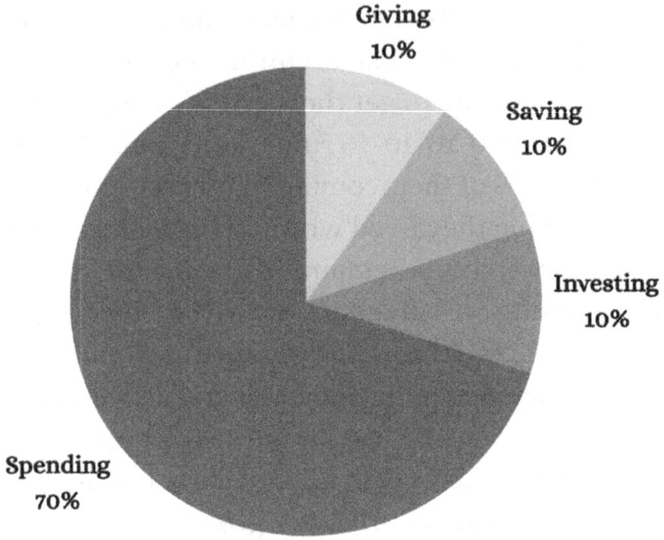

To see how this rule works with a specific income, let's take a monthly income of $4000 and apply the 70-10-10-10 rule. The bar chart below shows how the $4000 income is divided:

- **$2800 for spending**: This amount is used for all your monthly expenses.
- **$400 for investing**: This portion is invested in various financial instruments to grow your wealth.
- **$400 for saving**: This amount goes into your savings or emergency fund.
- **$400 for giving**: This part is allocated for charitable contributions or donations.

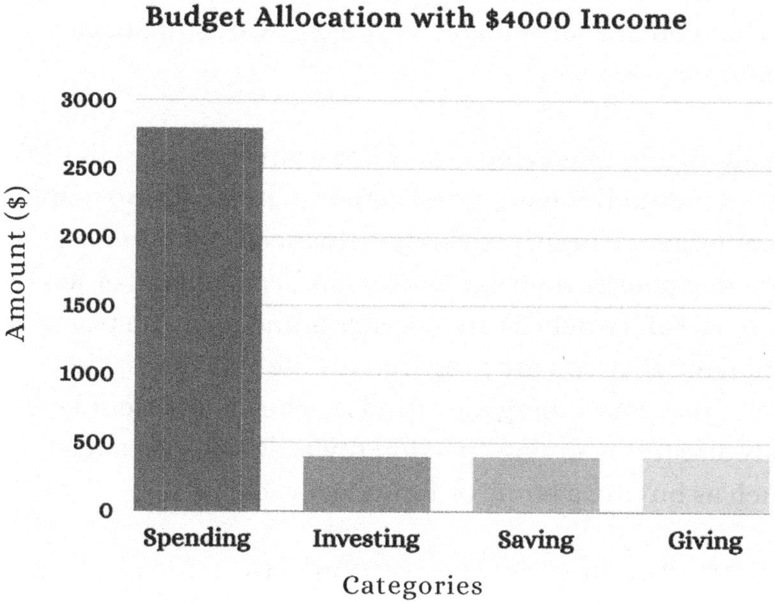

This method is designed to provide a clear, structured approach to managing your finances, making it easier to achieve your financial goals while maintaining a healthy balance in your life.

First, the 70-10-10-10 method ensures that your essential needs and discretionary expenses are adequately covered. By allocating 70% of your income to spending, you can comfortably manage your daily living costs, such as housing, food, transportation, utilities, and entertainment. This allocation helps prevent the common pitfall of overspending, ensuring that you live within your means while still enjoying a reasonable quality of life.

Next, dedicating 10% of your income to investing is a key component of this budgeting rule. Investing is crucial for building long-term wealth and achieving financial independence. Whether you choose to invest in stocks, bonds, mutual funds, or real estate, this consistent contribution helps you grow your assets over time.

The discipline of regularly investing a portion of your income ensures that you are continually working towards financial growth and security.

The 10% allocation for saving is another significant benefit of the 70-10-10-10 method. Having a dedicated savings portion helps you build an emergency fund, providing a financial cushion for unexpected expenses such as medical bills, car repairs, or job loss. This financial safety net can reduce stress and give you peace of mind, knowing that you are prepared for life's uncertainties. Moreover, once your emergency fund reaches a sufficient level, you can redirect this savings portion towards other financial goals, such as buying a home or funding a vacation.

Additionally, allocating 10% of your income to giving fosters a sense of purpose and community involvement. Whether you contribute to charities, support your church, or help those in need, giving back can be immensely rewarding. It not only benefits others but also instills a sense of gratitude and fulfillment in your own life. This practice of generosity aligns with many people's values and can enhance your overall sense of well-being and connectedness.

This structure helps you avoid the trap of living paycheck to paycheck, supports long-term financial planning, and ensures that you are making progress towards your financial goals.

Adjusting the rule based on financial circumstances

Adjusting the 70-10-10-10 rule based on your financial circumstances is not only practical but also essential for maintaining financial flexibility and achieving long-term success.

Everyone's financial situation is unique, and adapting this budgeting method to fit your needs can help you manage your money more effectively as your income and expenses change over time.

For those just starting their financial journey, it might be more realistic to begin with a variant like the 85-5-5-5 rule. This approach allocates 85% of your income to spending, 5% to investing, 5% to saving, and 5% to giving. This allows you to cover immediate expenses while still forming the habit of setting aside money for future growth and charitable contributions. As your financial situation stabilizes, you can gradually adjust the percentages to better align with your goals.

Starting out

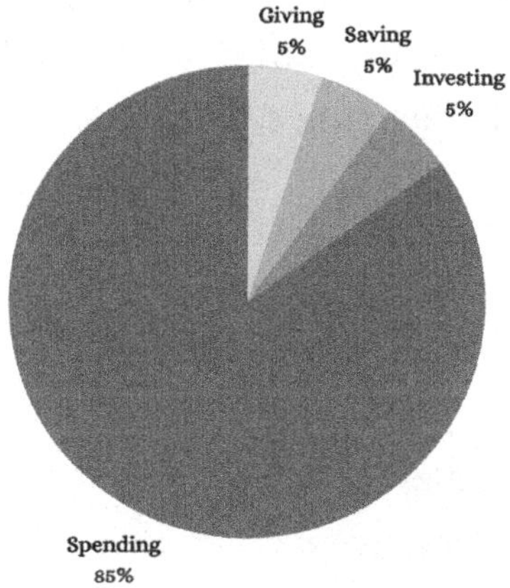

As your income increases or your expenses decrease, transitioning to the 70-10-10-10 rule becomes more feasible. This balanced approach provides a solid foundation for managing your finances, ensuring that you are living within your means while steadily building wealth and supporting charitable causes. The discipline of regularly investing, saving, and giving fosters financial health and a sense of purpose, contributing to overall well-being.

Intermediate Stage

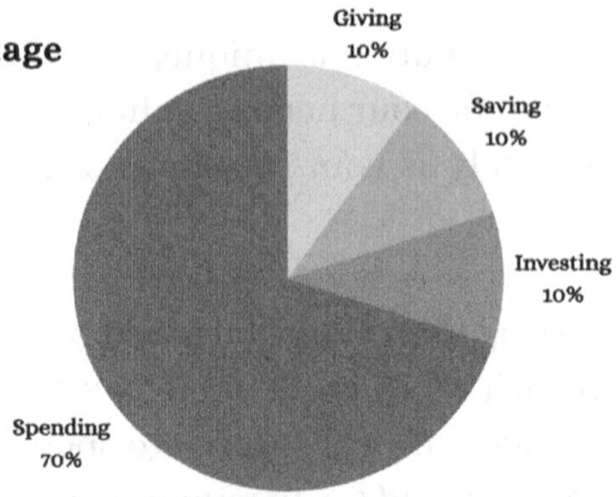

For individuals experiencing significant income growth or those who have achieved a stable financial footing, further adjustments can be made to maximize financial growth. A variant such as the 50-30-10-10 rule allocates only 50% of income to spending, allowing for 30% to be directed towards investing, and maintaining 10% for saving and 10% for giving. This approach emphasizes aggressive wealth-building through increased investments while still ensuring savings and philanthropic efforts are sustained.

Advanced Stage

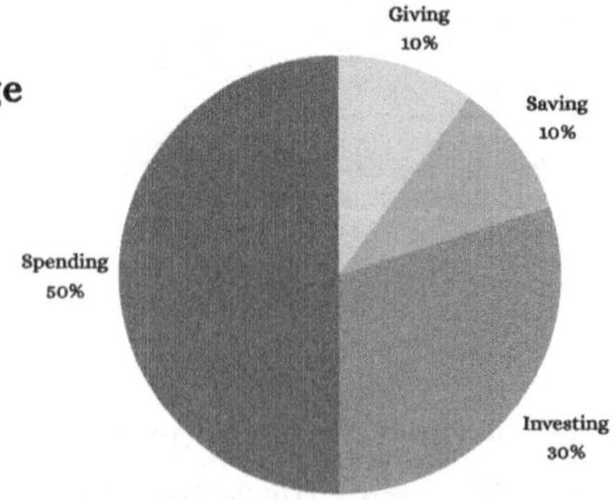

Another important aspect to consider is the purpose of the savings allocation. Initially, the 10% savings can be used to build an emergency fund, providing a financial safety net for unexpected expenses. Once this fund reaches a sufficient level—typically covering three to twelve months of living expenses—you can redirect the savings portion towards other financial goals.

For example, you could transition from a 70-10-10-10 distribution to a 70-20-0-10 allocation, where the additional 10% previously set aside for savings now boosts your investments.

It's also essential to recognize that personal circumstances, such as changes in employment, family growth, or major life events, may necessitate further adjustments to your budget. Flexibility is key; periodically reviewing and modifying your budgeting allocations ensures that you remain aligned with your financial goals and can adapt to life's inevitable changes.

Creating a Personal Budget

This is a crucial step in managing your finances effectively. A well-structured budget helps you track your income and expenses, ensuring you allocate funds appropriately according to the 70-10-10-10 rule. Here's how to set up your budget:

Start by listing your total monthly income at the top of your budget. This includes all sources of income such as your salary, bonuses, and any side income. Once you have your total income, you can begin to allocate it into four main categories: Spending, Investing, Saving, and Giving.

Monthly Income: $______

Category	Budget Amount	Actual Amount
Income		
Salary	$_____	$_____
Bonuses/ Side Income	$_____	$_____
Total Income	$_____	$_____

Spending (70%): This category covers all your essential and discretionary expenses. Essentials include rent or mortgage, utilities, groceries, transportation, and healthcare. Discretionary spending covers non-essential items such as entertainment, dining out, and hobbies. By allocating 70% of your income here, you ensure you have enough to cover your living expenses while also enjoying some leisure activities.

Category	Budget Amount	Actual Amount
Essentials		
Rent/Mortgage	$____	$____
Utilities	$____	$____
Groceries	$____	$____
Transportation	$____	$____
Healthcare	$____	$____
Discretionary		
Entertainment	$____	$____
Dining Out	$____	$____
Hobbies	$____	$____
Others	$____	$____
Debt Pay Down		
Credit Card 1	$____	$____
Credit Card 2	$____	$____

Auto Loan	$____	$____
Total Spending	$____	$____

Investing (10%): Allocate 10% of your income to investments. This can include stocks, bonds, retirement accounts, and other investment opportunities. Diversifying your investments is key to building a robust financial portfolio and securing your financial future.

Category	Budget Amount	Actual Amount
Stocks	$____	$____
Bonds	$____	$____
Retirement Accounts	$____	$____
Others	$____	$____
Total Investing	$____	$____

Saving (10%): This category is for building your savings. Start by creating an emergency fund to cover unexpected expenses, aiming for 3 to 12 months' worth of income. Once your emergency fund is established, you can allocate more towards other savings goals like a down payment for a house or a vacation.

Category	Budget Amount	Actual Amount
Emergency Fund	$____	$____
Short-term Goals	$____	$____
Long-term Goals	$____	$____
Total Saving	$____	$____

Giving (10%): Dedicate 10% of your income to charitable causes, donations, or tithing. Giving back is a vital aspect of financial stewardship and helps support communities and causes that matter to you.

Category	**Budget Amount**	**Actual Amount**
Charities	$____	$____
Donations	$____	$____
Tithing	$____	$____
Others	$____	$____
Total Giving	$____	$____

Remember, it's important to rack your actual spending against the budgeted amounts throughout the month to stay on top of your finances. You should also review and adjust your budget regularly to ensure it aligns with your financial goals and changing circumstances.

Tracking income and expenses

Tracking your income and expenses is crucial to effective financial management. It helps you understand where your money is going and ensures you stay within your budget. Here's how to monitor your financial activities effectively.

Start by keeping a detailed record of your income. This includes your regular salary, bonuses, freelance earnings, and any other sources of income.

Use a spreadsheet, a budgeting app, or even a simple notebook to log every dollar that comes in. Make it a habit to record your income as soon as you receive it to ensure accuracy.

Next, track your expenses meticulously. Categorize your spending into essential and discretionary expenses. Essential expenses are necessary for your day-to-day living, such as rent, utilities, groceries, and transportation. Discretionary expenses, on the other hand, are for non-essential items like dining out, entertainment, and hobbies. By categorizing your expenses, you can easily see where your money is going and identify areas where you might be overspending.

To get started, save all your receipts and bills. At the end of each day, log these expenses in your tracking system. Many budgeting apps can link to your bank accounts and credit cards, automatically categorizing your transactions. This automation makes tracking easier and more accurate. However, manually reviewing and categorizing your expenses periodically is a good practice to ensure nothing is missed or incorrectly categorized.

Review your spending weekly or bi-weekly. This helps you stay aware of your financial habits and make timely adjustments if you're veering off course. Compare your actual spending against your budgeted amounts in each category. If you find you're overspending in one area, look for ways to cut back or reallocate funds from another category.

Monitoring your financial activities isn't just about keeping track of where your money goes. It's also about understanding your spending patterns and making informed decisions. For instance, if you notice you're consistently spending more on dining out than you've budgeted, you can decide to cook more at home or set a stricter limit on restaurant visits.

Additionally, tracking your income and expenses helps you prepare for unexpected costs and emergencies. By being aware of your financial situation, you can adjust your budget to save more or spend less as needed. This proactive approach ensures you're always in control of your finances.

Remember, the goal of tracking is not to restrict yourself but to give you a clear picture of your financial health. It empowers you to make informed choices, avoid debt, and achieve your financial goals. Regularly monitoring your income and expenses builds discipline and fosters a mindset of financial responsibility, setting you on the path to long-term financial stability.

In today's digital age, managing your finances has never been easier with the plethora of tools and apps available. These digital resources can help you create and maintain a budget, track your spending, and even save money.
Here are some of the best tools and apps for budgeting.

First, let's talk about budgeting apps. Apps like **YNAB (You Need A Budget)**, and **EveryDollar** are excellent for helping you keep track of your income and expenses. These apps offer a comprehensive overview of your finances, allowing you to connect your bank accounts, credit cards, and bills in one place. YNAB is particularly useful for those who need a structured approach to budgeting, helping you give every dollar a job and stay on top of your finances. EveryDollar, created by financial guru Dave Ramsey, follows a zero-based budgeting method, ensuring you allocate every dollar to a specific purpose.

In addition to budgeting apps, there are various tools to assist with investment and savings. **Acorns** and **Robinhood** are popular for beginners looking to dip their toes into investing.

Acorns automatically invests your spare change from everyday purchases, while Robinhood offers commission-free trading, making it easy to start building an investment portfolio.

When it comes to saving money, choosing the right bank can make a significant difference. Traditional banks often offer low interest rates on savings accounts, but online banks typically provide higher returns. **Ally Bank**, for instance, is well-known for its high-yield savings accounts with competitive interest rates and no monthly maintenance fees. **Discover Bank** also offers attractive rates on savings accounts, along with cash-back rewards on debit card purchases. **Marcus by Goldman Sachs** is another excellent option, providing high interest rates and flexible transfer options.

Personal Capital is another robust app, particularly for those interested in both budgeting and investing. This app offers detailed insights into your spending patterns while also providing tools for managing your investment portfolio. With features like retirement planning and net worth tracking, Personal Capital is ideal for users with more complex financial needs who want a comprehensive view of their finances.

For those who prefer simplicity, **PocketGuard** is a straightforward app that helps you keep tabs on how much spendable money you have. After accounting for bills, goals, and necessities, PocketGuard shows you what's left to spend, helping you avoid overspending. Its user-friendly interface and basic functionality make it a great choice for budgeting beginners.

Additionally, **Goodbudget** operates on the envelope budgeting method, where you allocate portions of your income to different spending categories or "envelopes." This app is particularly useful for those who prefer a visual approach to budgeting and like to plan their finances in advance.

Goodbudget's system helps enforce discipline by making you stick to your predefined spending limits.

Lastly, **EveryDollar** is a zero-based budgeting app that requires you to assign every dollar of your income to specific categories until you reach zero. Created by financial guru Dave Ramsey, EveryDollar is designed to help you make the most of your money and achieve financial peace. The app offers both a free version and a paid version with additional features like bank connectivity. Using these tools can significantly ease the process of budgeting, making it less daunting and more manageable. They provide structure, visibility, and automation, helping you stay on track with your financial goals.

Incorporating tithing into your budget is an important consideration, especially for those who prioritize giving as part of their financial practice. The concept of tithing, giving 10% of your income, is rooted in biblical teachings, as seen in Malachi 3:10: *"Bring the whole tithe into the storehouse, that there may be food in my house. Test me in this," says the Lord Almighty, "and see if I will not throw open the floodgates of heaven and pour out so much blessing that there will not be room enough to store it."*

If you allocate 10% of your income to tithing, you need to adjust the remaining budget accordingly. Here's how you can divide and allocate the other funds. Spending (60%), Investing (10%), Saving (10%) and Giving (10%): This amount, dedicated to tithing, honors the biblical principle of giving back to God. It not only fulfills a spiritual obligation but also cultivates a generous heart and trust in God's provision.

Budgeting can come with its own set of challenges. Overcoming these common obstacles requires a mix of practical strategies and a mindset geared towards flexibility and discipline.

One common challenge is inconsistent income, which many freelancers, entrepreneurs, and commission-based workers face. When income varies from month to month, it can be tough to stick to a fixed budget. The solution is to create a baseline budget based on your lowest monthly income and then allocate any extra income towards savings, investments, or paying off debt. This approach ensures that your essential expenses are always covered, and surplus funds can enhance your financial stability.

Unexpected expenses are another hurdle. They can disrupt even the most meticulously planned budgets. To tackle this, build an emergency fund with three to six months' worth of living expenses. This fund acts as a financial buffer, allowing you to handle surprises without derailing your budget. Regularly contributing to this fund, even in small amounts, can provide significant peace of mind.

Many people struggle with **overspending**, especially in discretionary categories like dining out or entertainment. A practical solution is to use the envelope system, where you allocate a specific amount of cash for each spending category. Once the cash is gone, you can't spend any more in that category. This physical limitation helps curb impulsive spending. Additionally, tracking your expenses meticulously with budgeting apps can reveal patterns and highlight areas where you can cut back.

Lack of motivation can cause budgeting efforts to fizzle out over time. To stay motivated, set clear, achievable financial goals and regularly remind yourself of the benefits of budgeting, such as reduced stress and increased savings. Celebrate small victories along the way, whether it's paying off a debt or reaching a savings milestone. This positive reinforcement keeps you focused and driven.

Communicating and cooperating with family members can also pose a challenge. If budgeting affects everyone in the household, it's crucial to get buy-in from all members. Hold regular family meetings to discuss financial goals, review progress, and adjust the budget as needed. This collaborative approach ensures everyone understands the importance of budgeting and works together towards common goals.

Lastly, **complexity and time management** can deter people from maintaining a budget. Simplify your budgeting process by using tools and apps that automate tracking and provide insights. Schedule a regular time, perhaps weekly or bi-weekly, to review and adjust your budget. Keeping the process straightforward and routine helps integrate budgeting into your daily life seamlessly.

While budgeting can be challenging, understanding and addressing these common issues can significantly enhance your financial health.

Allocating Income for Spending

First, let's distinguish between **essentials** and **discretionary** spending. Essential expenses are those necessary for basic living, such as housing, utilities, groceries, transportation, insurance, and healthcare. These are non-negotiable costs that must be met to maintain your standard of living. Discretionary spending, on the other hand, includes non-essential expenses such as dining out, entertainment, vacations, and luxury items. While these are enjoyable and can enhance your quality of life, they are not necessary for your basic needs.

Implementing **strategies for mindful spending** is a powerful way to control discretionary expenses. Mindful spending involves being aware of your spending habits and making intentional choices about where your money goes.

One effective strategy is to create a spending plan that aligns with your values and priorities. For example, if travel is important to you, allocate a portion of your discretionary budget specifically for that purpose, but ensure it doesn't detract from your essential expenses.

Another strategy is to practice delayed gratification; before making a non-essential purchase, wait for a set period (e.g., 24 hours) to see if you still feel it is necessary. This pause can help reduce impulse buys and promote more thoughtful spending.

Setting spending limits and goals is another key aspect of managing your finances. Start by analyzing your monthly income and categorizing your expenses into essentials and discretionary items. Determine a reasonable limit for each category, ensuring that your total spending does not exceed your income. Setting clear financial goals, such as saving for a down payment on a house or paying off debt, can also guide your spending decisions. Having specific targets helps maintain focus and motivation, and tracking your progress can provide a sense of accomplishment and encourage further financial discipline.

Finally, here are some tips for **reducing unnecessary expenses**. One effective approach is to create and stick to a grocery list, which helps avoid impulse purchases and reduces food waste. Canceling unused subscriptions and memberships can also save money without impacting your lifestyle significantly. Consider adopting energy-saving practices at home, such as using energy-efficient appliances and being mindful of electricity usage, which can lower utility bills. Additionally, embracing a minimalist mindset can help you focus on what truly adds value to your life, reducing the desire for unnecessary purchases.

Types of Investments Suitable for Beginners

1. **Savings Accounts and Certificates of Deposit (CDs)**: These are among the safest investment options. While they offer lower returns compared to other investments, they provide stability and security, making them ideal for beginners. Savings accounts offer liquidity, meaning you can access your money anytime, whereas CDs require you to lock in your funds for a specified period in exchange for a slightly higher interest rate.

2. **Bonds**: Bonds are essentially loans you give to governments or corporations, which they pay back with interest. They are less volatile than stocks and provide regular income through interest payments. Government bonds, especially U.S. Treasury bonds, are considered very safe.

3. **Mutual Funds and Exchange-Traded Funds (ETFs)**: These funds pool money from many investors to purchase a diversified portfolio of stocks, bonds, or other securities. Mutual funds are actively managed by professionals, while ETFs typically track a specific index and can be traded like stocks. Both options offer diversification and professional management, making them suitable for beginners.

4. **Stock Market Index Funds**: These funds track a specific index, such as the S&P 500, which includes a wide range of large-cap U.S. companies. They offer diversification within the stock market and are a low-cost way to invest in a broad swath of the market.

5. **Robo-Advisors**: Robo-advisors use algorithms to manage your investments based on your risk tolerance and financial goals. They are a convenient, low-cost option for beginners who want professional management without the high fees of traditional financial advisors.

Importance of Diversification

Diversification is a fundamental principle in investing, aimed at spreading your investments across various asset classes to reduce risk. Here's why it's crucial:

1. **Risk Management**: By diversifying, you minimize the impact of a poor-performing investment on your overall portfolio. If one investment loses value, others may gain or remain stable, balancing out potential losses.

2. **Smoother Returns**: Diversification helps in achieving more stable and predictable returns. While no investment is entirely risk-free, a diversified portfolio is less likely to experience extreme volatility.

3. **Capitalizing on Different Market Conditions**: Different asset classes perform well under different economic conditions. For instance, while stocks may do well during economic growth, bonds may perform better during downturns. Diversifying allows you to benefit from various market conditions.

4. **Long-Term Growth**: A diversified portfolio is more likely to grow steadily over the long term. By including a mix of assets, you can capture the growth potential of different sectors and industries, enhancing overall portfolio performance.

Putting It All Together

As a beginner, start with safe and straightforward investment options like savings accounts, bonds, mutual funds, and ETFs. Consider using robo-advisors for automated, low-cost management. Always keep diversification in mind, spreading your investments across different asset classes to manage risk and smooth out returns.

Remember, the goal is to build a robust, resilient portfolio that can weather market fluctuations and grow steadily over time.

Strategies for Becoming Debt-Free

Budgeting can be challenging, especially when dealing with debt. However, by employing effective debt repayment strategies and visualizing your debt through spreadsheets, you can gain control over your finances. Here, we discuss different debt repayment methods and provide a visual tool to help you manage your debts effectively.

One of the most common challenges in budgeting is managing and paying off debt. High-interest debts, such as credit card balances, can quickly accumulate, making it difficult to allocate funds for other financial goals. However, with the right strategies, you can tackle your debt and move towards financial freedom.

Debt Repayment Strategies:

Debt Avalanche Method: This method focuses on paying off debts with the highest interest rates first. By doing so, you reduce the overall interest paid over time. Here's how it works:

- List all your debts, including the balance and interest rate for each.
- Allocate any extra funds towards the debt with the highest interest rate while making minimum payments on the others.
- Once the highest-interest debt is paid off, move to the next highest and repeat the process.

Debt Snowball Method: This approach prioritizes paying off the smallest debts first to build momentum and motivation. The steps are:

- List all your debts from smallest to largest balance.
- Focus extra payments on the smallest debt while making minimum payments on the others.
- After paying off the smallest debt, move to the next smallest and continue the process.

Debt Consolidation: Combining multiple debts into a single loan with a lower interest rate can simplify payments and potentially save on interest. Consider transferring high-interest credit card balances to a card with a 0% introductory rate or taking out a personal loan to consolidate debt.

Once the smallest debt is cleared, move on to the next smallest. This method provides quick wins that can keep you motivated and give you the psychological momentum needed to tackle larger debts. While it might not save you as much in interest compared to the avalanche method, the emotional rewards can be invaluable.

Balance Transfer: Transferring high-interest credit card debt to a card with a lower interest rate can reduce the amount of interest you pay, allowing more of your payment to go towards the principal balance.

To effectively manage and visualize your debt, create a spreadsheet that lists each credit card, its balance, and the interest rate. This tool helps you track your progress and decide which repayment strategy works best for you.

Credit Card	Balance	Interest Rate	Minimum Payment	Extra Payment	New Balance
Card A	$2,000	18%	$50	$150	$1,850
Card B	$1,500	20%	$45	$45	$1,455
Card C	$3,000	15%	$75	$75	$2,925

In this example, applying the **Debt Avalanche Method**, extra funds are allocated to **Card B** with the highest interest rate. Using the **Debt Snowball Method**, extra funds would be directed to **Card B** with the smallest balance. This table helps you stay organized and focused on your debt repayment goals.

Additional Payments Directly to the Principal

One of the most effective ways to manage debt is to make additional payments directly toward the principal of your loan. When you pay extra toward the principal, you reduce the overall balance faster. This has a twofold benefit: it shortens the loan term and decreases the amount of interest you will pay over the life of the loan. For example, if you have a mortgage, making just one extra payment each year can take several years off the term of your loan and save you thousands in interest.

The key here is to ensure that any additional payments are explicitly directed toward the principal. Some lenders apply extra payments to future interest or the next scheduled payment unless specified otherwise. By reducing the principal faster, each subsequent interest calculation is based on a lower amount, further speeding up your journey to becoming debt-free. This strategy is particularly powerful with high-interest loans, such as credit card debt or personal loans, where the interest savings can be substantial.

Maintaining Good Credit

Maintaining good credit is a cornerstone of financial health and stability. It involves consistently making timely payments and managing your credit responsibly. Here's why it's so important:

- **Timely Payments**: Consistently making on-time payments is crucial. Late payments can negatively impact your credit score, making it more challenging and expensive to obtain loans in the future.

Lenders view timely payments as a sign of reliability and financial responsibility. To ensure you never miss a payment, consider setting up automatic payments or reminders.

- **Responsible Credit Management**: Beyond just making payments on time, responsible credit management includes keeping your credit card balances low relative to your credit limit. This is known as your credit utilization ratio, and it has a significant impact on your credit score. Aim to use no more than 30% of your available credit at any given time. Additionally, avoid opening too many new credit accounts in a short period, as this can signal financial instability to lenders.

Maintaining good credit opens doors to better interest rates on loans and credit cards, saving you money over time. It also enhances your ability to qualify for mortgages, car loans, and even certain jobs or rental agreements, as many employers and landlords consider creditworthiness in their decision-making processes.

By implementing these strategies, you can take control of your finances, reduce your debt faster, and move closer to achieving financial freedom. Remember, the key to success is consistency and making informed choices that align with your financial goals.

Chapter 3

Building a Solid Financial Foundation

Creating a financial inventory is a critical first step in assessing your current financial situation and building a solid financial foundation. This process involves taking a comprehensive snapshot of your finances to understand where you stand and to identify areas for improvement. Think of it as creating a detailed map of your financial landscape, which will guide you in making informed decisions and setting realistic goals.

To begin, gather all relevant financial documents. This includes bank statements, credit card statements, investment accounts, loan documents, insurance policies, and any other financial records. Having these documents at hand ensures that you have accurate and up-to-date information.

Start by listing your assets. Assets are anything you own that has value. This can include cash in your bank accounts, investments (such as stocks, bonds, and retirement accounts), real estate, vehicles, and valuable personal property (like jewelry or collectibles). Documenting your assets helps you understand your net worth and what resources you have available.

Next, list your liabilities. Liabilities are any debts or financial obligations you owe. Common liabilities include mortgages, car loans, student loans, credit card balances, and other personal loans. By listing your liabilities, you get a clear picture of your financial commitments and can prioritize debt repayment strategies.

To create a clear and organized financial inventory, use a spreadsheet or financial management software. Here's an example of how to structure your financial inventory:

Category	Details	Value
Assets		
Bank Accounts	Checking and Savings Accounts	$_______
Investments	Stocks, Bonds, Retirement Accounts	$_______
Real Estate	Primary Residence, Investment Properties	$_______
Vehicles	Cars, Motorcycles	$_______
Personal Property	Jewelry, Art, Collectibles	$_______
Total Assets		$_______
Liabilities		
Mortgage	Home Loans	$_______
Car Loans	Auto Loans	$_______
Student Loans	Education Loans	$_______
Credit Card Debt	Outstanding Balances	$_______
Personal Loans	Other Loans	$_______
Total Liabilities		$_______
Net Worth	Total Assets - Total Liabilities	$_______

After listing all assets and liabilities, calculate your net worth by subtracting the total liabilities from the total assets. This figure represents your financial health and is a crucial metric for tracking progress over time.

Creating a financial inventory also involves reviewing your income and expenses. Document your sources of income, such as your salary, freelance work, rental income, and any other streams. Additionally, track your monthly expenses, including fixed costs (like rent or mortgage, utilities, and insurance) and variable costs (like groceries, entertainment, and dining out).

Assessing your net worth is a vital step in understanding your financial health, and there are several tools available to make this process easier and more accurate. One of the most accessible tools is a net worth calculator, which you can find on many financial websites. These calculators allow you to input your assets and liabilities, automatically computing your net worth.

Personal finance software, such as **Quicken** or **YNAB (You Need A Budget)**, offers more comprehensive solutions. These tools not only help track your net worth but also provide features for budgeting, tracking expenses, and setting financial goals. They integrate with your bank accounts and investment portfolios, giving you real-time updates on your financial status.

Mobile apps are also excellent for net worth tracking. They categorize your transactions and provide insights into your spending habits, and also offer a detailed view of your investments and their performance. These apps sync with your financial accounts, ensuring your net worth calculations are always up-to-date.

Spreadsheets, such as those available in Microsoft Excel or Google Sheets, are a customizable option for those who prefer a hands-on approach. You can create a personalized template to regularly update and track your assets and liabilities, offering a clear and organized method for monitoring your net worth over time.

Understanding your income and expenditure patterns is crucial for building a solid financial foundation. By gaining clarity on how money flows in and out of your accounts, you can make informed decisions, set realistic goals, and avoid financial pitfalls.

Firstly, take a comprehensive look at your income. This includes your salary, bonuses, freelance work, rental income, and any other sources of money. It's essential to track not just your primary income but also any secondary or irregular sources. A detailed understanding of your total income helps in planning effectively, ensuring that your financial strategies are grounded in reality.

Next, examine your expenditure patterns. Categorize your spending into essentials and discretionary expenses. Essentials include rent or mortgage payments, utilities, groceries, insurance, and transportation. Discretionary spending covers dining out, entertainment, vacations, and hobbies. By distinguishing between these two categories, you can identify areas where you might be overspending and opportunities to save.

Start by tracking every expense for a month or two. This can be done using budgeting apps like YNAB (You Need A Budget), or even a simple spreadsheet. Recording every purchase, no matter how small, provides a clear picture of your spending habits. You might be surprised at how much the little expenses add up over time.

After tracking your expenses, review and analyze the data. Look for patterns and trends. Are there particular times of the month when you tend to spend more? Are there specific categories where your spending is consistently high? Identifying these patterns can help you make adjustments and set realistic budgets for each category.

One effective strategy for managing expenditures is the 70/10/10/10 rule: 70% of your income goes towards essentials, 10% towards discretionary spending, 10% towards savings, and 10% towards debt repayment. This ensures you cover necessary expenses while also allocating funds for leisure, savings, and debt reduction. For those seeking further financial optimization, transitioning to a 50/25/15/10 rule can be beneficial, with 50% for essentials, 25% for investments, 15% for savings, and 10% for giving. This approach promotes financial stability, growth, and philanthropy, encouraging a well-rounded approach to personal finance.

Another critical aspect of understanding expenditure patterns is to plan for irregular expenses. These can include annual insurance premiums, holiday gifts, or car repairs. By setting aside a small amount each month for these irregular costs, you avoid the financial strain when they arise.

Understanding your income and expenditure patterns also involves assessing the impact of lifestyle changes. For instance, a new job, a move to a different city, or a significant life event like marriage or having a child can drastically alter your financial landscape.

Identifying your financial strengths and weaknesses is a crucial process that involves a thorough analysis of your financial habits.

Start by assessing your financial strengths. These are the areas where you are performing well and can build upon. For instance, a consistent savings habit is a significant strength. If you regularly save a portion of your income, you have a solid foundation for financial security. Another strength might be having a diversified investment portfolio, which indicates that you are not relying on a single source of growth and are spreading your risk. Additionally, strong financial strengths include having little or no debt, excellent credit scores, and a well-maintained emergency fund.

To identify these strengths, review your financial statements, credit reports, and investment accounts. Look for patterns of positive financial behavior, such as regular contributions to retirement accounts, disciplined spending, and timely bill payments. Acknowledging these strengths boosts your confidence and provides a basis for further financial planning.

Next, turn your attention to identifying financial weaknesses. These are areas where you may be struggling or could improve. Common weaknesses include high levels of debt, inconsistent savings, poor credit scores, and lack of a budget. For example, if you often find yourself living paycheck to paycheck, this indicates a need for better budgeting and saving strategies. Another weakness could be relying too heavily on credit cards and accumulating high-interest debt, which can be a significant financial burden.

To pinpoint these weaknesses, scrutinize your spending habits and debt levels. Analyze your monthly expenses and identify any patterns of overspending or unnecessary expenditures. Check your credit report for any signs of poor credit management, such as missed payments or high credit utilization. Recognizing these weaknesses is the first step toward addressing them.

Once you have identified your financial strengths and weaknesses, create a plan to leverage your strengths and mitigate your weaknesses. For instance, if one of your strengths is a regular saving habit, consider increasing your savings rate or investing in higher-yield accounts. If a weakness is high debt, prioritize debt repayment strategies such as the avalanche or snowball methods, which target high-interest debts first or focus on paying off smaller balances quickly, respectively.

Another approach is to seek professional financial advice. Financial planners can provide tailored strategies to enhance your strengths and address your weaknesses, ensuring a comprehensive approach to financial health.

Case studies of initial financial assessments offer valuable insights into how individuals can evaluate their financial situations and develop effective strategies for improvement. By examining real-life scenarios, we can understand the importance of a thorough financial assessment and how it can lead to better financial decisions and outcomes.

Consider the case of Sarah, a 30-year-old marketing professional. Sarah had a stable income but struggled with managing her finances. Her initial financial assessment revealed that she had substantial credit card debt, no emergency fund, and little savings for retirement. She spent a significant portion of her income on discretionary expenses such as dining out and shopping. Her credit score was also lower than she had hoped, primarily due to missed payments.

Through her assessment, Sarah identified her financial strengths and weaknesses. Her strengths included a steady income and the potential to save more.

Her weaknesses were her high debt levels, lack of savings, and poor credit management. With this information, Sarah developed a plan to improve her financial health. She created a budget to reduce unnecessary spending, prioritized debt repayment using the avalanche method, and set up automatic transfers to build her emergency fund. Within a year, Sarah reduced her debt significantly, improved her credit score, and started contributing regularly to her retirement savings.

Another case is that of John and Lisa, a married couple in their early 40s with two children. They had a combined income that was adequate to cover their expenses, but they often felt financially strained. Their initial financial assessment showed that they were living paycheck to paycheck, with minimal savings and a mortgage that consumed a large portion of their income. Additionally, they had several outstanding loans, including a car loan and student loans, with varying interest rates.

By conducting a detailed financial assessment, John and Lisa discovered that their primary financial strengths were their stable jobs and the potential for income growth. Their weaknesses included high monthly expenses, fragmented debt management, and lack of a comprehensive savings plan. They decided to consolidate their high-interest loans into a single loan with a lower interest rate, freeing up cash flow. They also restructured their budget to reduce discretionary spending and set aside a portion of their income for an emergency fund and retirement savings. Over time, this approach helped them achieve greater financial stability and peace of mind.

Lastly, consider Michael, a recent college graduate who had just started his first job. Michael's initial financial assessment highlighted his minimal debt but also his lack of a savings plan and understanding of investments.

He had a tendency to spend impulsively and had not yet started building his credit history. Recognizing these factors, Michael sought advice on budgeting and investing. He began by setting up a simple budget, allocating a portion of his income to savings and investments. He also opened a credit card account and used it responsibly to build his credit score.

Through these case studies, we see the transformative impact of an initial financial assessment. By identifying strengths and weaknesses, individuals can create targeted plans to improve their financial health. These examples demonstrate that regardless of one's financial starting point, a thorough assessment is a crucial first step toward achieving financial stability and long-term success.

Setting financial goals is a fundamental step in building a solid financial foundation. However, not all goals are created equal. To ensure your financial aspirations are achievable and meaningful, it's essential to frame them using the SMART criteria. SMART goals are Specific, Measurable, Achievable, Relevant, and Time-bound. This structured approach helps you create clear, actionable objectives that lead to real financial progress.

First, let's discuss the "**Specific**" aspect of SMART goals. A goal should be clear and precise, leaving no room for ambiguity. Instead of saying, "I want to save money," a specific goal would be, "I want to save $5,000 for a vacation to Europe." This clarity provides a defined target, making it easier to focus your efforts and stay motivated.

Next, "**Measurable**" goals enable you to track your progress. By quantifying your goal, you can assess how close you are to achieving it and make necessary adjustments along the way.

For instance, if your goal is to save $5,000, you can break it down into smaller milestones, such as saving $1,250 every three months. This way, you can regularly monitor your progress and celebrate small victories, which keeps you motivated.

The "**Achievable**" component ensures that your goals are realistic and attainable. While it's great to aim high, setting an unrealistic goal can lead to frustration and discouragement. Consider your current financial situation, income, expenses, and any potential obstacles. If saving $5,000 seems too ambitious within your current circumstances, adjust the amount or extend the timeline. The key is to set a goal that challenges you but remains within the realm of possibility.

"**Relevant**" goals align with your broader financial objectives and personal values. They should reflect what is truly important to you. If traveling is a priority, then saving for a vacation is relevant. However, if your primary concern is paying off debt, then focusing on debt repayment should take precedence. Relevance ensures that your goals are meaningful and contribute to your overall financial well-being.

Finally, "**Time-bound**" goals have a clear deadline, creating a sense of urgency and prompting you to take action. A goal without a deadline can lead to procrastination. By setting a specific timeframe, such as "I want to save $5,000 in 12 months," you establish a concrete timeline that motivates you to start immediately and stay on track.

In summary, setting SMART financial goals transforms vague aspirations into clear, actionable plans. By being Specific, Measurable, Achievable, Relevant, and Time-bound, you create a roadmap that guides you toward financial success.

Short-Term Goals

Short-term goals typically span a timeframe of a few months to a couple of years. These goals are more immediate and often serve as stepping stones toward larger, long-term objectives. Here are some examples:

- **Creating an Emergency Fund**: One of the most crucial short-term goals is establishing an emergency fund. Aim to save at least three to six months' worth of living expenses. For instance, if your monthly expenses are $2,000, your goal could be to save between $6,000 and $12,000 within the next 12 months.

- **Paying Off Credit Card Debt**: If you have high-interest credit card debt, prioritize paying it off. Set a goal to reduce or eliminate this debt within a specific timeframe. For example, if you owe $3,000 on a credit card with a 20% interest rate, you might aim to pay off this debt within 12 to 18 months by making consistent monthly payments above the minimum amount.

- **Saving for a Vacation**: Planning a vacation can be a motivating short-term goal. Suppose you want to take a $2,000 trip in a year. This would mean saving about $167 per month. Automate these savings to ensure you reach your target without stress.

- **Building a Down Payment Fund**: If buying a home is on your horizon, start saving for a down payment. Even if you plan to purchase a home in a few years, beginning with a short-term goal of saving $10,000 over the next 24 months can set you on the right track.

Long-Term Goals

Long-term goals typically span several years to decades and require sustained effort and planning. These goals often have a significant impact on your overall financial well-being. Here are some examples:

- **Retirement Savings**: Saving for retirement is a paramount long-term goal. Determine how much you'll need to retire comfortably and set yearly savings targets. For instance, aiming to save $1 million by retirement might involve consistently contributing to your 401(k) or IRA and taking advantage of employer matching and tax benefits.

- **Buying a Home**: If homeownership is a long-term goal, calculate how much you'll need for a down payment and other associated costs. Suppose you aim to buy a $300,000 home in five years. You might set a goal to save $60,000 for a 20% down payment, which would require saving $1,000 per month.

- **Funding Children's Education**: College education costs can be daunting, but starting early can make a significant difference. Estimate the future costs of tuition and set up a 529 plan or other education savings accounts. For example, saving $200 a month for 18 years can grow substantially with compounded interest.

- **Investment Portfolio Growth**: Another long-term goal could be growing your investment portfolio. Setting a goal to achieve a specific portfolio value, such as $500,000 within 20 years, can guide your investment strategies and savings plans.

By setting both short-term and long-term SMART financial goals, you create a clear roadmap to financial stability and success.

Setting financial goals is more than just a numbers game; it's about aligning your financial strategies with your personal values and priorities, particularly those rooted in your faith. This alignment ensures that your financial goals are not only achievable but also meaningful and fulfilling. Here's how to make sure your financial goals reflect your Christian values.

Identify Your Core Values

Begin by identifying your core values, which as Christians, often include faith, family, service, stewardship, and generosity. Reflect on these principles that guide your life decisions and give you a sense of purpose. Take some time to pray and meditate on what truly matters to you and how God is leading you to live out these values. Write down your top five values to keep them at the forefront of your goal-setting process.

Prioritize Your Goals Based on Values

Prioritize your financial goals accordingly. For example, if family is a top value, you might prioritize saving for your children's education or building a comfortable home. If stewardship and service are important, investing in quality health insurance to ensure you can serve others effectively might take precedence. By aligning your goals with your values, you ensure that your financial decisions support your overall life satisfaction and reflect God's plan for your life.

Create a Values-Based Budget

A values-based budget helps you allocate your resources in a way that reflects your priorities and honors God. Start by listing your income and expenses, and then categorize your spending according to your values.

For instance, if generosity is important to you, make sure your budget includes a designated amount for tithing and charitable donations. This approach not only keeps you financially on track but also reinforces your commitment to living a life that pleases God.

Set Meaningful Milestones

To stay motivated, set meaningful milestones that celebrate your progress. These milestones should resonate with your values and provide a sense of accomplishment. For instance, if stewardship and service are important to you, reaching a savings milestone for a mission trip can be a powerful motivator. Celebrate these achievements in ways that reinforce your values and bring joy to your journey.

Reevaluate and Adjust Regularly

Life is dynamic, and so are your values and priorities. Regularly reevaluate your financial goals to ensure they still align with what matters most to you and your walk with Christ. Major life events, such as marriage, the birth of a child, career changes, or retirement, can shift your priorities. Be flexible and willing to adjust your goals and strategies as needed to stay aligned with your evolving values and God's plan for your life.

Communicate with Stakeholders

If you share financial responsibilities with a partner or family, open communication is crucial. Discuss your values and goals together to ensure everyone is on the same page. This collaborative approach helps prevent conflicts and ensures that your collective financial decisions support shared Christian values and priorities.

Aligning your financial goals with your personal values and priorities creates a harmonious and fulfilling approach to financial planning. It transforms your financial journey from a series of impersonal tasks into a meaningful pursuit that enhances your overall quality of life and glorifies God. By staying true to your values, you ensure that every step you take brings you closer to not just financial success, but also personal fulfillment and a deeper relationship with Christ.

Here's a step-by-step approach to creating SMART goals that align with your values and priorities.

Step 1: Be Specific
Start by defining your goal with clarity and precision. A specific goal answers the questions: What do you want to accomplish? Why is this goal important? Who is involved? Where will it take place? For example, instead of saying, "I want to save money," specify, "I want to save $5,000 for an emergency fund."

Step 2: Make It Measurable
A measurable goal includes criteria to track your progress and determine when you've achieved it. This involves quantifying your goal. For example, "I want to save $5,000 for an emergency fund by saving $500 each month." This gives you a concrete figure to aim for and allows you to monitor your monthly savings.

Step 3: Ensure It's Achievable
Your goal should be realistic and attainable, considering your current resources and constraints. Assess your financial situation to determine if your goal is within reach. For instance, if saving $500 a month isn't feasible, adjust the amount or extend the timeline. The aim is to set a goal that challenges you but remains possible.

Step 4: Keep It Relevant

Your goal should align with your broader life values and long-term objectives. Ask yourself if this goal is worthwhile and if it matches your other efforts and needs. For example, if financial security is a core value, saving for an emergency fund is highly relevant. Ensure your goal fits into your overall financial plan and supports your key priorities.

Step 5: Set a Time-Bound Framework

Every goal needs a target date to focus your efforts and create a sense of urgency. This time frame helps you stay motivated and accountable. For example, "I want to save $5,000 for an emergency fund within 10 months." Setting a deadline prompts you to take regular, actionable steps toward your goal.

Example of a SMART Goal

Putting it all together, a well-formulated SMART goal might look like this: "I want to save $5,000 for an emergency fund by saving $500 each month over the next 10 months. This will provide financial security and peace of mind."

For more complex or long-term objectives, break them down into smaller, manageable sub-goals. For example, if your goal is to save for a down payment on a house, you might start with a smaller target like saving $10,000 in the first year, then adjusting your monthly savings plan as your income and expenses change.

Life circumstances and priorities can change, so it's essential to review your goals regularly. Assess your progress and make adjustments as needed to stay on track. This ongoing evaluation ensures that your goals remain relevant and achievable.

Tracking and measuring progress is essential for achieving your financial goals. It ensures you stay on course, make necessary adjustments, and celebrate your successes along the way. Here's how you can effectively monitor your financial journey.

The first step in tracking progress is establishing a reliable system. This can be as simple or sophisticated as you prefer. Some people use spreadsheets to log their financial activities, while others might prefer financial software or apps that offer automated tracking and real-time updates. Choose a system that fits your lifestyle and makes it easy for you to regularly input and review data.

Consistency is key when tracking progress. Set aside time each month to review your financial goals and update your tracking system. Compare your current status to your targets, noting any discrepancies. This regular check-in helps you stay aware of your progress and quickly identify areas that need adjustment. For instance, if your goal is to save $500 each month but you only managed $400 one month, understanding why can help you make necessary changes.

Break your long-term goals into smaller milestones and track your progress against these markers. Milestones make your journey more manageable and provide frequent opportunities for celebration, which can be motivating. For example, if your goal is to save $10,000 over two years, set milestones for every $2,500 saved. Each milestone reached reaffirms that you're on the right path and provides a sense of accomplishment.

Flexibility is crucial. Life is unpredictable, and your financial situation can change.

Regularly review your progress and be prepared to adjust your goals and strategies as needed. If an unexpected expense arises, it might temporarily slow your progress. Rather than getting discouraged, reassess your plan and modify it to accommodate the change. This could mean extending your timeline or finding ways to cut expenses elsewhere.

Visual aids can be very effective in tracking progress. Charts, graphs, and other visual tools can make it easier to see your progress at a glance. For instance, a simple bar graph showing your savings growth over time can provide a clear visual representation of how close you are to your goal. These tools can also make the process more engaging and satisfying.

Consider sharing your goals with a trusted friend, family member, or financial advisor who can act as an accountability partner. Regularly discussing your progress with someone else can provide additional motivation and help you stay committed to your objectives. This person can offer encouragement, advice, and a fresh perspective on your progress.

Don't forget to celebrate your successes, no matter how small. Recognizing your accomplishments along the way keeps you motivated and reinforces positive financial behaviors. Whether it's treating yourself to a small reward or simply taking a moment to acknowledge your progress, celebrating milestones is an important part of the journey.

While tracking day-to-day progress is important, it's also crucial to keep an eye on the big picture. Regularly revisit your long-term goals and remind yourself why you set them. Keeping your ultimate objectives in mind helps maintain motivation and ensures that short-term setbacks don't derail your overall progress.

Breaking Down Goals into Actionable Steps

Creating actionable plans for financial success involves breaking down your goals into manageable steps. This process transforms lofty ambitions into concrete tasks that you can tackle one by one. Here's how to do it effectively.

Begin by clearly defining your financial goals. Whether it's saving for a house, paying off debt, or building an emergency fund, specificity is key. A well-defined goal, such as "Save $20,000 for a home down payment in two years," provides a clear target to aim for.

Next, break your goal into smaller, achievable milestones. Milestones create a roadmap that guides you step-by-step toward your ultimate objective. For example, if your goal is to save $20,000 in two years, divide this into monthly savings targets: $20,000 divided by 24 months equals approximately $834 per month. This smaller target is more manageable and allows you to track progress more frequently.

For each milestone, identify specific actions you need to take. These actions should be clear and actionable. For instance, to save $834 each month, you might:

1. **Automate Savings**: Set up an automatic transfer of $834 from your checking account to your savings account each month.
2. **Cut Expenses**: Identify and reduce discretionary spending by $200 per month.
3. **Increase Income**: Find additional sources of income, such as freelance work, to add an extra $100 to your savings.

By detailing these actions, you create a practical plan that outlines exactly what you need to do.

Assign deadlines to each action to ensure timely progress. For example, set a deadline to set up automatic transfers by the end of the week. Prioritize tasks based on their importance and impact. If reducing expenses has the most immediate benefit, tackle that first. Deadlines and prioritization help maintain momentum and keep you focused.

Developing a solid financial plan requires the right tools and resources. Leveraging these can make the process more efficient, accurate, and manageable. Here's a guide to some of the most effective tools and resources available to help you create and execute your financial plan. These are over and above the budgeting software and apps I had discussed earlier.

Educational Resources

Educating yourself is key to effective financial planning. Websites like Investopedia, The Balance, and NerdWallet offer a wealth of articles, tutorials, and guides on a wide range of financial topics. Additionally, consider reading books by reputable financial experts. Titles like "The Total Money Makeover" by Dave Ramsey, "Your Money or Your Life" by Vicki Robin and Joe Dominguez, and "Rich Dad Poor Dad" by Robert Kiyosaki provide valuable insights and practical advice.

Financial Advisors

Sometimes, personalized guidance from a financial advisor can be invaluable. Advisors can help tailor a financial plan to your specific circumstances, provide investment advice, and offer strategies to achieve your financial goals. Look for certified professionals, such as Certified Financial Planners (CFPs), who adhere to a strict code of ethics and have the necessary expertise to guide you.

Community Resources and Workshops
Many communities offer financial planning workshops and resources through local banks, credit unions, and nonprofit organizations. These workshops can provide practical advice, hands-on assistance, and opportunities to ask questions and get personalized feedback. Additionally, community centers and libraries often host free or low-cost financial education events.

Accountability Partners
Having someone to keep you accountable can significantly enhance your financial planning efforts. This could be a trusted friend, family member, or even a financial coach. Regular check-ins with an accountability partner can provide motivation, encouragement, and a fresh perspective on your progress and challenges.

Online Forums and Support Groups
Joining online forums and support groups can also be beneficial. Platforms like Reddit's *r/personalfinance*, *Bogleheads,* and various Facebook groups offer communities of like-minded individuals who share tips, advice, and experiences. Engaging with these communities can provide support, answer questions, and offer diverse perspectives on financial planning strategies.

Emergency Fund
Establishing an emergency fund is a crucial step in building a solid financial foundation. This fund acts as a financial safety net, protecting you from unexpected expenses and financial setbacks.

Here's why having an emergency fund is vital for your financial stability and peace of mind:

Financial Security and Stability: Life is full of surprises, and not all of them are pleasant.

Unforeseen events such as medical emergencies, car repairs, job loss, or urgent home maintenance can occur at any time. An emergency fund provides a cushion to absorb these shocks, preventing you from falling into debt or depleting your long-term savings. It ensures that you have the financial resources to handle crises without derailing your financial progress.

Avoiding High-Interest Debt: Without an emergency fund, unexpected expenses can lead you to rely on credit cards or high-interest loans to cover costs. This can quickly lead to a cycle of debt that's difficult to escape. By having a dedicated emergency fund, you can pay for unexpected expenses outright, avoiding the financial strain and stress of accruing interest on borrowed money.

Peace of Mind: Knowing you have a financial buffer in place provides immense peace of mind. It reduces anxiety about potential financial disruptions and allows you to focus on other aspects of your life with confidence. This sense of security is invaluable, as it contributes to your overall well-being and reduces stress.

Protection of Long-Term Savings: An emergency fund protects your long-term savings and investments. Without this fund, you might be forced to dip into retirement accounts or other savings to cover unexpected costs. This can jeopardize your long-term financial goals, as early withdrawals from retirement accounts often come with penalties and tax implications. An emergency fund ensures that your long-term savings remain intact and continue to grow.

Increased Financial Flexibility: Having an emergency fund gives you greater financial flexibility. It allows you to make decisions without the immediate pressure of financial constraints.

For instance, if you face a sudden job loss, an emergency fund gives you the breathing room to find a job that fits your career goals rather than settling for the first available option out of necessity.

Improved Budgeting and Planning: Establishing and maintaining an emergency fund encourages disciplined budgeting and financial planning. It forces you to prioritize savings and manage your expenses effectively. This habit of regular saving and careful planning lays a strong foundation for overall financial health and helps you build resilience against future financial challenges.

Achieving Financial Independence: An emergency fund is a critical step toward financial independence. It provides the foundation upon which you can build other financial goals, such as homeownership, retirement, or starting a business. By ensuring that you can handle unexpected expenses, an emergency fund allows you to pursue your financial dreams with confidence and stability.

Determining the right amount to save for emergencies is a crucial step in your financial planning. As a general rule, financial experts recommend setting aside three to six months' worth of living expenses in your emergency fund. This range provides a solid buffer to cover unexpected costs like medical bills, car repairs, or temporary loss of income.

To calculate this, start by adding up your essential monthly expenses, including rent or mortgage, utilities, groceries, transportation, insurance, and minimum debt payments. Multiply this total by three to six to determine your target emergency fund amount. For instance, if your monthly expenses are $3,000, your emergency fund should be between $9,000 and $18,000.

However, the exact amount you need can vary based on personal circumstances. If you have a stable job with a secure income, three months' worth of expenses might suffice. On the other hand, if your income is variable, or if you have dependents or high medical expenses, aiming for six months or more is advisable.

Building this fund may take time, but the peace of mind and financial security it provides are well worth the effort. Start small, contribute regularly, and gradually work towards your goal.

Building an Opportunity Fund for Investments

In addition to an emergency fund, building an opportunity fund for investments is a strategic step toward achieving long-term financial goals. Unlike an emergency fund, which is designed to cover unexpected expenses, an opportunity fund is earmarked for seizing financial opportunities that can accelerate wealth-building.

Building an Opportunity Fund begins after you have fully funded your Emergency Fund. When using the 70/10/10/10 method, you allocate 10% of your income to savings. Once your Emergency Fund is complete, continue to use this 10% savings allocation to build your Opportunity Fund. This fund is separate from your 10% allocation for investments, providing a dedicated pool of resources for potential opportunities.

To keep things simple, you can add this additional savings to your 10% Investments bucket. By doing so, you create a flexible financial buffer that allows you to take advantage of opportunities without disrupting your regular investment strategy. This approach ensures that you are prepared for both emergencies and opportunities, enhancing your overall financial stability and growth potential.

Purpose and Benefits

An opportunity fund serves as a reservoir of capital ready to capitalize on promising investment opportunities. These opportunities might include purchasing stocks during market downturns, investing in real estate when prices are favorable, funding a business venture, or taking advantage of other financial opportunities that arise.

Building Your Opportunity Fund

Start by assessing your current financial situation and identifying disposable income that can be allocated toward your opportunity fund. Consider automating contributions to ensure consistent savings. Allocate a portion of windfalls, such as bonuses or tax refunds, toward your fund to accelerate its growth.

Risk Management

While an opportunity fund is designed for investments, it's important to manage risk wisely. Diversify your investments to mitigate potential losses and maximize growth opportunities. Consider a mix of asset classes such as stocks, bonds, real estate, and alternative investments based on your risk tolerance and investment horizon.

Liquid and Accessible

Unlike retirement accounts with early withdrawal penalties, an opportunity fund should be relatively liquid and accessible. Choose investment vehicles that offer flexibility and liquidity, allowing you to seize opportunities quickly when they arise.
Regular Review and Adjustment

Regularly review your opportunity fund's performance and adjust your strategy as needed. Monitor market conditions, economic trends, and changes in your financial goals to optimize returns and manage risk effectively.

Periodic rebalancing ensures your fund remains aligned with your long-term objectives.

Professional Guidance
Consider consulting with a financial advisor to develop a tailored investment strategy for your opportunity fund. A professional can provide insights, expertise, and personalized recommendations based on your financial situation and goals. They can also help navigate market volatility and optimize investment opportunities.

Regular Financial Reviews

Regular financial reviews are essential for maintaining and improving your financial health. Just as you schedule regular check-ups with a doctor to monitor your physical well-being, conducting financial check-ups allows you to assess your financial status, track progress toward goals, and make informed decisions.

Here's why these reviews are crucial:

Assessing Financial Health: Regular reviews provide a snapshot of your overall financial health. They help you evaluate your income, expenses, savings, investments, debts, and net worth. By analyzing these components, you gain clarity on where you stand financially and identify areas that need improvement.

Monitoring Progress Toward Goals: Financial goals evolve over time. Regular reviews allow you to measure your progress toward these goals. Whether you're saving for a down payment, planning for retirement, or paying off debt, monitoring your milestones helps you stay on track and adjust your strategies as needed. Identifying Opportunities and Risks: Market conditions, economic changes, and personal circumstances can impact your financial situation.

Regular reviews enable you to identify opportunities for growth, such as investment opportunities during market downturns, as well as risks that may threaten your financial stability.

Making Informed Decisions: Informed decision-making is crucial for financial success. Through regular reviews, you gather the necessary data to make informed choices about budgeting, saving, investing, debt management, and other financial activities. This proactive approach minimizes surprises and maximizes opportunities.

Establishing a review schedule ensures that you consistently monitor and manage your finances. The frequency of your financial reviews may vary based on individual circumstances and goals. Here's a recommended framework for creating a review schedule:

Monthly Reviews: Monthly reviews are ideal for tracking income and expenses, analyzing spending patterns, and adjusting your budget accordingly. Review bank statements, credit card statements, and bills to ensure accuracy and identify any discrepancies or unnecessary expenditures.

Quarterly Reviews: Quarterly reviews allow for a deeper analysis of your financial progress. Evaluate savings contributions, debt reduction strategies, and investment performance. Review changes in net worth and update your financial goals if necessary. Use this time to rebalance your investment portfolio and ensure it aligns with your risk tolerance and objectives.

Annual Reviews: Annual reviews serve as comprehensive assessments of your overall financial health. Review tax returns, retirement accounts, insurance policies, and estate planning documents.

Evaluate long-term financial goals and milestones achieved over the past year. Consider meeting with a financial advisor or tax professional to optimize strategies and minimize tax liabilities.

Utilizing tools and resources enhances the effectiveness of your financial reviews. Here are valuable tools to consider integrating into your check-up process:

- Financial Planning Software
- Budgeting Apps
- Investment Tracking Tools
- Financial Advisor Consultation
- Credit Monitoring Services: Services like Credit Karma or AnnualCreditReport.com allow you to monitor your credit score and report for any changes or inaccuracies. Maintaining good credit is essential for qualifying for loans, mortgages, and favorable interest rates.
- Retirement Calculators: Online retirement calculators, often provided by financial institutions or retirement planning websites, help you estimate retirement savings needs, project income sources, and plan contributions to retirement accounts like IRAs and 401(k)s.

Chapter 4
Introduction to Investment Vehicles

Understanding Exchange-Traded Funds (ETFs) and Index Funds
Investing in the financial markets can be both exciting and intimidating, especially for young professionals eager to build wealth and secure their financial future. Among the many investment vehicles available, Exchange-Traded Funds (ETFs) and Index Funds stand out for their simplicity, efficiency, and potential for long-term growth. To navigate these options effectively, it's crucial to understand their basics, differences, and benefits.

Definition and Basics of ETFs and Index Funds

Exchange-Traded Funds (ETFs) are investment funds that trade on stock exchanges, similar to individual stocks. They are designed to track the performance of a specific index, sector, commodity, or other assets. For instance, an ETF might follow the S&P 500, a group of technology stocks, or a basket of commodities. ETFs hold a diversified portfolio of assets and are valued for their flexibility and ease of trading.

Index Funds, on the other hand, are a type of mutual fund that aims to replicate the performance of a specific index, such as the S&P 500 or the Dow Jones Industrial Average. They offer a passive investment strategy, meaning they are not actively managed by a portfolio manager seeking to outperform the market. Instead, they mirror the index they track, providing broad market exposure and typically lower fees.

Comparison Between ETFs and Mutual Funds

While ETFs and Index Funds share similarities, particularly in their passive investment approach, there are key differences to consider. ETFs are traded on stock exchanges throughout the day, allowing investors to buy and sell shares at market prices. This intraday trading capability offers greater flexibility and the potential to take advantage of price fluctuations.

Mutual funds, including Index Funds, are priced once at the end of the trading day based on their net asset value (NAV). Investors can buy and sell mutual fund shares directly from the fund company at this daily price. While mutual funds do not offer the same intraday trading flexibility as ETFs, they can be advantageous for investors looking to avoid the complexities of trading.

Another difference lies in the fee structure. ETFs generally have lower expense ratios compared to actively managed mutual funds, making them cost-effective. However, investors may incur trading commissions when buying or selling ETFs, depending on their brokerage. Mutual funds may have higher management fees but often include features like automatic reinvestment of dividends and capital gains.

How to Buy and Sell ETFs

Buying and selling ETFs is straightforward. Investors can purchase ETFs through a brokerage account, similar to buying shares of individual stocks. The process involves selecting the desired ETF, placing an order, and specifying the number of shares to buy or sell. Orders can be placed during market hours, and transactions are executed at the current market price.

It's important to be aware of different order types, such as market orders and limit orders. A market order executes the trade immediately at the best available price, while a limit order allows you to specify the maximum or minimum price at which you are willing to buy or sell. Understanding these order types can help you manage your trades more effectively.

Investing in ETFs and Index Funds offers numerous benefits that make them attractive to both novice and experienced investors. One of the most significant advantages is diversification. By investing in a single ETF or Index Fund, you gain exposure to a broad range of securities, reducing the risk associated with individual stock picking. This built-in diversification is particularly beneficial for young investors who may not have the capital to invest in a variety of individual stocks.

Cost efficiency is another major benefit. Due to their passive management strategy, ETFs and Index Funds typically have lower expense ratios compared to actively managed funds. Lower costs mean more of your investment returns stay in your pocket, compounding over time to help grow your wealth.

ETFs and Index Funds also offer transparency. Because they track specific indexes, investors can easily see the underlying holdings and understand what they are investing in. This transparency provides peace of mind and allows for more informed investment decisions.

To illustrate the potential of ETF investments, let's look at a few real-world examples. Consider the SPDR S&P 500 ETF (SPY), one of the most popular ETFs tracking the S&P 500 index. Since its inception in 1993, SPY has provided investors with a simple and cost-effective way to gain broad exposure to the U.S. stock market.

Over the years, SPY has delivered substantial returns, mirroring the performance of the S&P 500 and allowing investors to benefit from the long-term growth of the U.S. economy.

Another example is the Vanguard Total Stock Market ETF (VTI), which offers exposure to the entire U.S. stock market, including small, mid, and large-cap stocks. VTI's diversified portfolio has made it a favorite among investors seeking broad market exposure with minimal fees. Over the years, investors in VTI have enjoyed steady growth, illustrating the long-term benefits of holding diversified ETFs.

The iShares MSCI Emerging Markets ETF (EEM) provides another interesting case study. EEM offers exposure to stocks in emerging markets, such as China, India, and Brazil. While emerging markets can be more volatile than developed markets, they also offer higher growth potential. Investors in EEM have benefited from the economic expansion and growth in these regions, making it a valuable addition to a diversified portfolio.

Exchange-Traded Funds (ETFs) and Index Funds have become popular investment vehicles for their simplicity, cost-efficiency, and potential for diversification. Understanding the benefits and risks associated with these investment options is crucial for young professionals and individuals seeking to build wealth and achieve long-term financial goals.

Diversification and Low Fees Benefits

One of the most compelling benefits of investing in ETFs and Index Funds is the diversification they offer. Diversification is the practice of spreading your investments across a wide range of assets to reduce risk.

When you invest in an ETF or Index Fund, you gain exposure to a broad spectrum of securities within a specific index or market segment. For example, by investing in an ETF that tracks the S&P 500, you are effectively investing in 500 of the largest publicly traded companies in the U.S. This diversification minimizes the impact of any single company's poor performance on your overall portfolio.

Another significant advantage is the low fees associated with these investment vehicles. Because ETFs and Index Funds follow a passive investment strategy, they do not require active management. This results in lower expense ratios compared to actively managed funds, where fund managers buy and sell securities to try and outperform the market. Lower fees mean more of your investment returns are reinvested, allowing your wealth to grow more efficiently over time. This cost-effectiveness is particularly beneficial for young investors who are just starting their investment journey and may have limited capital.

Despite their many advantages, ETFs and Index Funds are not without risks. Market volatility is one of the primary risks investors face. Since these funds track specific indexes or sectors, their performance is directly tied to the performance of the underlying assets. In times of market turbulence, the value of ETFs and Index Funds can fluctuate significantly. This volatility can be unsettling, especially for new investors who may not have experienced market downturns before.

Tracking error is another potential risk. Tracking error occurs when an ETF or Index Fund does not perfectly replicate the performance of its benchmark index. While most funds aim to closely follow their respective indexes, discrepancies can arise due to factors such as management fees, trading costs, and changes in the index's composition.

Although tracking errors are generally small, they can impact the overall returns of the fund.

Balancing ETFs with Other Investment Types

To mitigate risks and enhance portfolio stability, it's essential to balance ETFs and Index Funds with other investment types. Diversification across asset classes, such as bonds, real estate, and commodities, can provide a cushion against market volatility. Bonds, for example, tend to be less volatile than stocks and can offer a steady income stream. Real estate investments can provide a hedge against inflation and add another layer of diversification to your portfolio.

Consider your risk tolerance and investment goals when balancing your portfolio. Younger investors with a longer time horizon might allocate a larger portion of their portfolio to stocks, including ETFs and Index Funds, to capitalize on potential growth. Conversely, those closer to retirement might prioritize stability and income, favoring bonds and other less volatile assets.

One of the most compelling reasons to invest in Index Funds is their long-term growth potential. Historically, broad market indexes like the S&P 500 have delivered substantial returns over extended periods. By investing in Index Funds, you can benefit from the overall growth of the market without needing to pick individual stocks. This passive approach is particularly effective for investors with a long-term perspective, as it allows you to ride out short-term market fluctuations and capitalize on the market's upward trajectory.

Moreover, the compounding effect plays a significant role in the growth potential of Index Funds. Reinvesting dividends and capital gains can lead to exponential growth over time.

Practical Tips for Choosing ETFs and Index Funds

Selecting the right ETFs and Index Funds requires careful consideration and research. Here are some practical tips to guide you in making informed investment decisions:

Understand Your Investment Goals: Clearly define your financial objectives, whether they are short-term, such as saving for a down payment on a house, or long-term, like retirement planning. Your goals will influence the types of funds you choose and your overall investment strategy.

Assess the Fund's Expense Ratio: Look for funds with low expense ratios, as lower fees can significantly impact your returns over time. Compare expense ratios across similar funds to ensure you are getting the best value for your investment.

Review the Fund's Holdings: Examine the underlying assets of the ETF or Index Fund. Ensure that the fund's holdings align with your investment goals and risk tolerance. Diversification within the fund is crucial for minimizing risk.

Consider the Fund's Performance: While past performance is not indicative of future results, it can provide insight into the fund's stability and management effectiveness. Look for funds with a consistent track record of performance that aligns with your expectations.

Evaluate the Fund's Liquidity: Ensure that the ETF or Index Fund you choose has sufficient trading volume and liquidity. Highly liquid funds are easier to buy and sell, reducing the risk of significant price fluctuations during transactions.

Stay Informed: Keep abreast of market trends and economic developments that could impact your investments. Regularly review your portfolio and make adjustments as needed to stay aligned with your financial goals.

Understanding the various investment vehicles available is essential for building a robust and diversified portfolio. This section explores mutual funds, bonds, and other investment options, providing insights into their differences, benefits, and potential drawbacks.

Overview of Mutual Funds, Bonds, and Other Vehicles

Mutual funds are pooled investment vehicles that collect money from multiple investors to buy a diversified portfolio of stocks, bonds, or other securities. Managed by professional portfolio managers, mutual funds aim to achieve specific investment objectives. Investors in mutual funds own shares that represent a portion of the holdings of the fund.

Bonds are fixed-income securities that represent a loan made by an investor to a borrower, typically a corporation or government. Bonds pay periodic interest and return the principal at maturity. They are considered lower-risk investments compared to stocks and provide a steady income stream.

Other investment vehicles include real estate investment trusts (REITs), commodities, and alternative investments such as hedge funds and private equity. REITs allow investors to invest in real estate without owning physical properties, while commodities include assets like gold, oil, and agricultural products. Alternative investments often involve higher risk and are typically suited for more experienced investors.

Differences Between Various Investment Types

The key differences between these investment types lie in their risk profiles, return potential, and liquidity. Mutual funds offer diversification and professional management, making them accessible to a broad range of investors. They can be actively or passively managed, with the former aiming to outperform a benchmark and the latter replicating an index.

Bonds, on the other hand, are less volatile and provide predictable income. They are ideal for risk-averse investors or those nearing retirement who prioritize capital preservation. However, bonds generally offer lower returns compared to equities.

REITs and commodities add another layer of diversification. REITs offer exposure to real estate, providing potential for income and capital appreciation, while commodities can act as a hedge against inflation. Alternative investments, though riskier and less liquid, can deliver substantial returns and are often used to enhance portfolio performance.

Pros and Cons of Mutual Funds

Mutual funds come with distinct advantages. They provide instant diversification, reducing the impact of any single security's poor performance. Professional management ensures that experienced fund managers make informed investment decisions on behalf of investors. Additionally, mutual funds offer liquidity, allowing investors to buy and sell shares easily.

However, mutual funds also have drawbacks. Management fees and expense ratios can eat into returns, particularly for actively managed funds.

Investors have no control over the individual securities within the fund, and there can be tax implications due to frequent trading within the fund.

Role of Fixed Income Investments in a Portfolio

Fixed income investments, such as bonds, play a crucial role in a diversified portfolio. They provide stability and income, acting as a counterbalance to the volatility of equities. In times of market turbulence, bonds tend to hold their value better than stocks, making them a safe haven for investors.

For young professionals, including bonds in their portfolio can provide a stable income stream and reduce overall portfolio risk. As one approaches retirement, increasing the allocation to bonds can help preserve capital and ensure a steady income during retirement years.

Case Studies of Diversified Investment Strategies

Consider the case of Maria, a young professional in her late twenties. Maria has just started investing and wants to build a diversified portfolio to achieve long-term financial goals. She allocates 60% of her portfolio to equity mutual funds to capture growth, 20% to bonds for stability, 10% to REITs for real estate exposure, and 10% to commodities as a hedge against inflation. This diversified approach helps Maria spread risk and enhance her portfolio's resilience.

Another example is John, a middle-aged investor nearing retirement. John seeks to preserve his capital while generating income. He allocates 40% of his portfolio to bonds, 30% to equity mutual funds, 20% to high-dividend stocks, and 10% to REITs. This strategy provides a balance between income generation and growth potential, aligning with John's retirement goals.

Diversification across different asset classes is essential for managing risk and optimizing returns. By understanding the unique characteristics of mutual funds, bonds, and other investment vehicles, investors can tailor their portfolios to meet their individual financial objectives.

Tools for Investment Research and Selection

Investing wisely requires thorough research and an understanding of various tools and resources. As you venture into the world of investments, knowing where to find reliable information and how to interpret it is crucial. This section covers key resources for researching investments, understanding investment ratings and reports, using financial news and analysis platforms, practical examples of investment research, and building a balanced portfolio based on research.

Key Resources for Researching Investments

To make informed investment decisions, you need access to high-quality, reliable information. Several resources can aid your research, starting with financial websites like Yahoo Finance, Bloomberg, and MarketWatch. These platforms offer up-to-date market news, stock quotes, and comprehensive financial data. Websites like Morningstar and Seeking Alpha provide in-depth analysis and ratings on stocks, mutual funds, and ETFs, helping you gauge the performance and potential of various investments.

Government websites such as the U.S. Securities and Exchange Commission (SEC) offer access to public companies' financial filings, including annual reports (10-K) and quarterly reports (10-Q). These documents provide detailed insights into a company's financial health, business operations, and risk factors.

Understanding Investment Ratings and Reports

Investment ratings and reports are essential tools for evaluating potential investments. Agencies like Moody's, Standard & Poor's (S&P), and Fitch provide credit ratings for bonds, indicating the issuer's creditworthiness. Ratings range from high-grade (AAA) to speculative (junk) bonds, helping you assess the risk level associated with each bond.

For mutual funds and ETFs, services like Morningstar provide star ratings based on past performance, risk, and fees. A five-star rating indicates a fund has historically performed well compared to similar funds, while lower ratings suggest poorer performance. These ratings, however, are not guarantees of future performance but serve as a useful starting point for your research.

Using Financial News and Analysis Platforms

Staying updated with financial news is crucial for making timely investment decisions. Platforms like CNBC, Reuters, and The Wall Street Journal offer comprehensive coverage of financial markets, economic indicators, and global events that may impact investments. Subscribing to newsletters or setting up news alerts can ensure you stay informed about significant market movements and trends.

Analysis platforms such as Zacks Investment Research and The Motley Fool provide expert commentary, stock picks, and in-depth analysis, helping you understand the implications of market news on your portfolio. These platforms often feature articles, podcasts, and videos, catering to various learning preferences.

Practical Examples of Investment Research

Consider the case of Sarah, a young professional interested in investing in tech stocks. She starts by visiting Yahoo Finance to gather basic information on major tech companies like Apple, Microsoft, and Google. Sarah reviews their financial statements, recent news articles, and analyst reports to understand their business models, revenue trends, and growth prospects.

Next, Sarah visits Morningstar to check the star ratings of tech-focused mutual funds and ETFs. She reads through fund reports to assess their performance history, expense ratios, and top holdings. By comparing these funds, Sarah narrows down her choices to those with consistent returns and lower fees.

Sarah also uses the SEC's EDGAR database to download Apple's latest 10-K report. She carefully reads through the management discussion and analysis (MD&A) section to gain insights into the company's future strategies and potential risks. Additionally, she watches interviews with tech analysts on CNBC to hear their perspectives on the tech industry's outlook.

By utilizing these resources, Sarah builds a comprehensive understanding of her investment options, allowing her to make informed decisions that align with her financial goals.

Building a Balanced Portfolio Based on Research

Building a balanced portfolio requires diversifying across various asset classes to spread risk and optimize returns. Start by determining your risk tolerance, investment horizon, and financial goals. For instance, a young professional with a high risk tolerance and a long investment horizon may allocate a significant portion of their portfolio to equities, while maintaining some exposure to bonds and alternative investments for stability.

Based on your research, select a mix of individual stocks, mutual funds, and ETFs that align with your investment strategy. Ensure that your portfolio includes a variety of sectors, such as technology, healthcare, finance, and consumer goods, to mitigate the impact of sector-specific downturns.

Regularly review and adjust your portfolio to maintain its balance and adapt to changing market conditions. This might involve rebalancing by selling overperforming assets and buying underperforming ones, ensuring that your portfolio remains aligned with your risk tolerance and financial objectives.

For example, if you find that your tech stock allocation has grown significantly due to market gains, you might sell a portion and reinvest in other sectors or asset classes to maintain diversification.

Practical Steps to Start Investing

To begin your investment journey, you'll be allocating 10% of your earned income and side hustle profits to your investments. This percentage will grow to 20% after you've saved an emergency fund of 3-6 months of expenses. At that point, you'll reallocate the 10% from the savings bucket to the investments bucket.

Setting Up a Brokerage Account

When setting up a brokerage account, you have various options. Alongside popular platforms like Charles Schwab, Fidelity, and Robinhood, you can consider alternatives such as Webull. Once you've chosen your brokerage, link it to a dedicated investment savings account where you will automatically deposit a portion of your paycheck. This setup ensures easy transfers between your investment savings account and your brokerage, streamlining your investment process.

When selecting a brokerage, consider factors like trading fees, account minimums, available investment options, and the quality of research tools and customer service.

To open an account, you'll need to provide personal information, including your Social Security number, employment details, and financial information. This process usually takes just a few minutes online. Once your account is set up, you can fund it by transferring money from your bank account, and you'll be ready to start investing.

Initial Investment Strategies for Beginners

When you're new to investing, it's wise to start with strategies that are straightforward and low-risk. One popular approach is dollar-cost averaging, which involves investing a fixed amount of money at regular intervals, regardless of market conditions. This method helps mitigate the impact of market volatility by spreading your investments over time, allowing you to buy more shares when prices are low and fewer shares when prices are high.

Another effective strategy for beginners is investing in broad-based index funds or ETFs. These funds track major market indices, such as the S&P 500, and provide exposure to a wide range of companies, offering diversification and reducing the risk associated with individual stocks. As you gain confidence and experience, you can gradually expand your portfolio to include other types of investments.

Importance of Regular Contributions

Regular contributions are key to growing your investment portfolio. For instance, if you start with $200 and invest an additional $200 each month, achieving a 7% annual return, your investment will grow to $105,600.83 in 20 years, $247,040.80 in 30 years, and $531,287.24 in 40 years.

Aim for a minimum average annual return of 7%, with a goal of 10% or more. Consistent investing, even in small amounts, leverages the power of compound interest, which is essential for long-term wealth building.

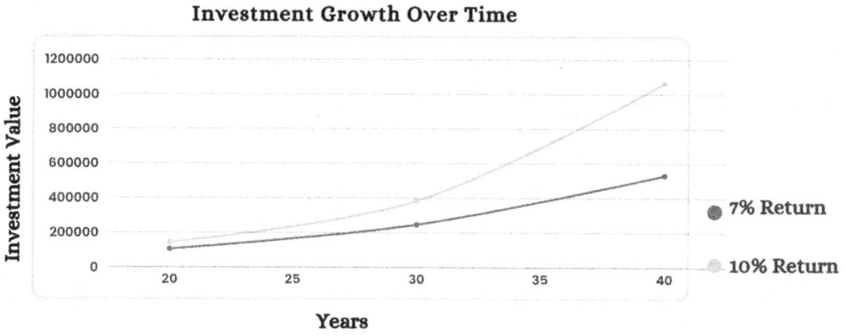

Monitoring and Rebalancing the Portfolio

Once your investments are in place, it's crucial to monitor their performance regularly. Keep track of your portfolio's value, the performance of individual investments, and any changes in the market or economic conditions that might affect your holdings. Most brokerage platforms provide tools and reports to help you stay informed about your portfolio's performance.

Periodically, you'll need to rebalance your portfolio to maintain your desired asset allocation. Rebalancing involves adjusting your investments to ensure that your portfolio remains aligned with your risk tolerance and financial goals. For instance, if one asset class performs exceptionally well and grows to represent a larger portion of your portfolio than intended, you might sell some of those assets and reinvest the proceeds in underperforming or target asset classes. This practice helps manage risk and maintain diversification.

Case Studies of Beginner Investors

Before we dive into the case studies, let's revise the importance of diversification. Diversifying your investments helps to manage risk by spreading your money across different asset classes.

Consider shifting your investment to a different ETF or asset class if you believe it will better align with your financial goals. For example, ETFs like SPY and VOO offer broad market exposure and are popular choices among investors.

In the case of James, a 25-year-old professional who decided to start investing to build his wealth over time. James opened a brokerage account with Fidelity, attracted by their robust research tools and commission-free trading options.

He funded his account with $1,000 and set up a recurring transfer of $200 per month.

James chose to begin with dollar-cost averaging, investing his initial deposit and subsequent contributions into a low-cost S&P 500 index fund. Over the next year, he consistently invested each month, taking advantage of both market dips and rises. This disciplined approach helped James build a diversified portfolio without needing to time the market.

As James became more comfortable with investing, he started exploring other options, such as individual stocks and sector-specific ETFs. He also made it a habit to review his portfolio quarterly, using Fidelity's tools to analyze performance and make necessary adjustments.

Another example is Maria, a 30-year-old who wanted to save for her children's college education. Maria opened a brokerage account with Vanguard, known for its low-cost index funds. She set up an automatic monthly contribution of $300 and invested in a mix of total stock market and bond index funds to balance growth and stability.

Maria diligently monitored her portfolio and rebalanced annually. When the stock market experienced a downturn, she stayed the course, understanding that her investments were for the long-term. Over the years, Maria's consistent contributions and strategic rebalancing helped her accumulate significant savings for her children's future education expenses.

These case studies illustrate that with the right approach and mindset, anyone can start investing and build a solid financial future.

Chapter 5

INVESTING IN STOCKS FOR GROWTH

Investing in the stock market is one of the most effective ways to build wealth over time. To get started, it's essential to understand the fundamentals, how stocks are bought and sold, the key factors influencing stock prices, the different types of stocks, and practical examples and case studies that illustrate these concepts.

Stock Market Fundamentals

The stock market is a marketplace where shares of publicly traded companies are bought and sold. These shares represent ownership in a company, and owning stock means you own a piece of that company. Companies issue stock to raise capital for growth and expansion, and investors buy stock to earn a return on their investment through price appreciation and dividends.

The stock market operates through exchanges, such as the New York Stock Exchange (NYSE) and the NASDAQ, where stocks are listed and traded. These exchanges provide a platform for buyers and sellers to transact, ensuring transparency and liquidity in the market. The stock market is regulated by government bodies, such as the Securities and Exchange Commission (SEC) in the United States, to maintain fair and efficient markets.

How Stocks Are Bought and Sold

Buying and selling stocks is facilitated through brokerage accounts, which serve as intermediaries between investors and the stock market.

To buy stocks, you need to open a brokerage account with a firm like Charles Schwab, Fidelity, or Robinhood. Once your account is funded, you can place buy or sell orders for stocks through the brokerage's trading platform.

When you place an order, you can choose between a market order or a limit order. A market order executes immediately at the current market price, while a limit order sets a specific price at which you are willing to buy or sell. If the stock reaches your limit price, the order is executed.

Several factors influence stock prices, and understanding these can help you make informed investment decisions. Company performance is a primary driver, including earnings reports, revenue growth, and profit margins. Positive financial performance typically leads to higher stock prices, while poor performance can cause prices to fall.

Market sentiment, or how investors feel about a stock or the market in general, also plays a significant role. News events, economic indicators, and geopolitical developments can impact investor sentiment and cause stock prices to fluctuate. For instance, positive news about a company's new product launch can boost its stock price, while negative news about regulatory issues can lead to a decline.

Additionally, macroeconomic factors such as interest rates, inflation, and economic growth influence stock prices. Lower interest rates often make stocks more attractive as borrowing costs decrease, leading to higher corporate profits. Conversely, high inflation can erode purchasing power and negatively affect stock prices.

Types of Stocks: Growth, Value, and Dividend

Stocks can be categorized into different types, each with unique characteristics and investment potential. Growth stocks represent companies expected to grow rapidly in terms of revenue and earnings. These companies often reinvest profits into expansion rather than paying dividends. Investors are drawn to growth stocks for their potential for significant capital appreciation. Tech companies like Amazon and Tesla are prime examples of growth stocks.

Value stocks, on the other hand, are shares of companies that appear undervalued based on fundamental analysis. These stocks often trade at lower price-to-earnings (P/E) ratios and offer attractive investment opportunities for those seeking to buy stocks at a discount. Value investing focuses on finding companies with solid fundamentals that the market has overlooked. An example of a value stock is JPMorgan Chase.

Dividend stocks are shares of companies that regularly distribute a portion of their earnings to shareholders in the form of dividends. These stocks are attractive to investors seeking steady income and are often found in well-established, financially stable companies. Utilities and consumer staples are sectors known for dividend-paying stocks, such as Coca-Cola and Procter & Gamble.

Practical Examples and Case Studies

To illustrate these concepts, consider the case of Sarah, a young professional who decided to invest in the stock market to build her wealth. Sarah opened a brokerage account with Fidelity and started by researching different types of stocks. She decided to invest in a mix of growth, value, and dividend stocks to diversify her portfolio.

Sarah allocated a portion of her funds to Amazon, recognizing its potential for significant growth. She also invested in JPMorgan Chase, seeing it as a value stock with strong fundamentals and growth potential. To balance her portfolio with steady income, Sarah included shares of Procter & Gamble, a reliable dividend-paying stock.

Over the next few years, Sarah diligently monitored her investments and the factors influencing stock prices. When Amazon's stock price surged due to its successful expansion into new markets, Sarah saw substantial capital gains. JPMorgan Chase's stock appreciated as the financial sector recovered from a downturn, validating her value investing strategy. Meanwhile, the consistent dividends from Procter & Gamble provided a steady stream of income, adding stability to her portfolio.

Another example is John, who started investing with a focus on dividend stocks for long-term income. John invested in a diversified set of dividend-paying stocks across various sectors, including utilities, consumer staples, and telecommunications. Over the years, John reinvested his dividends, allowing his investment to grow through the power of compounding. This strategy provided John with a reliable income stream, enhancing his financial security and peace of mind.

Selecting quality stocks is a crucial step in building a successful investment portfolio. To make informed decisions, investors often employ both fundamental and technical analysis. These methodologies provide insights into a stock's intrinsic value and market behavior, guiding investors toward potential high-quality picks.

Introduction to Fundamental Analysis

Fundamental analysis is the foundation of stock evaluation. It involves examining a company's financial health, business model, industry position, and growth prospects. By analyzing these aspects, investors can determine the intrinsic value of a stock and compare it to its current market price. This helps in identifying undervalued stocks with strong potential for appreciation.

Key Financial Metrics to Consider

When conducting fundamental analysis, several key financial metrics are essential. Revenue and earnings are primary indicators of a company's profitability and growth. Revenue shows the total income generated from sales, while earnings represent the net profit after expenses. Consistent growth in both metrics often signals a healthy, expanding business.

The price-to-earnings (P/E) ratio is another critical metric. It compares a company's current share price to its earnings per share (EPS). A lower P/E ratio might indicate that the stock is undervalued, while a higher P/E ratio could suggest overvaluation. However, context matters, and comparing P/E ratios within the same industry is more meaningful.

The debt-to-equity (D/E) ratio assesses a company's financial leverage by comparing its total debt to shareholders' equity. A lower D/E ratio generally indicates a more financially stable company, as it relies less on borrowed funds. Conversely, a high D/E ratio might signal potential financial risk.

Return on equity (ROE) measures a company's profitability relative to shareholders' equity. It indicates how effectively a company uses investors' funds to generate profits.

Higher ROE values are typically favorable, suggesting efficient management and strong financial performance.

While fundamental analysis focuses on a company's intrinsic value, technical analysis examines market behavior through historical price and volume data. This approach helps investors identify trends, patterns, and potential entry and exit points for trades. Technical analysis relies on various tools and indicators, such as moving averages, relative strength index (RSI), and support and resistance levels.

Moving averages smooth out price fluctuations over a specified period, providing a clearer view of the overall trend. The 50-day and 200-day moving averages are commonly used to identify long-term trends. When a stock's price crosses above its moving average, it may signal a potential buy opportunity, while a cross below could indicate a sell signal.

RSI measures the speed and change of price movements, oscillating between 0 and 100. Values above 70 suggest that a stock may be overbought, while values below 30 indicate it might be oversold. By using RSI, investors can gauge the strength of a stock's recent price performance and anticipate potential reversals.

Support and resistance levels represent price points where a stock tends to find buying or selling pressure, respectively. Support levels act as a floor, preventing the stock from falling further, while resistance levels act as a ceiling, capping price increases. Identifying these levels helps investors make informed decisions about when to enter or exit a trade.

Strategies for Stock Selection and Evaluation

Combining fundamental and technical analysis enhances stock selection strategies. One effective approach is the growth investing strategy, which focuses on companies with strong revenue and earnings growth potential. Growth investors seek out innovative companies in expanding industries, such as technology or healthcare, expecting their stocks to outperform the market over time.

Value investing, another popular strategy, involves identifying undervalued stocks with strong fundamentals. Value investors look for companies trading below their intrinsic value, believing that the market will eventually recognize their true worth. This approach often requires patience, as it may take time for the stock's price to reflect its underlying value.

Income investing is geared toward generating regular income through dividends. Investors in this category prioritize stocks of companies with a history of consistent dividend payments. These stocks, often found in sectors like utilities and consumer staples, provide a steady income stream, making them attractive to conservative investors seeking stability.

Another strategy is momentum investing, which capitalizes on the continuation of existing trends. Momentum investors look for stocks showing strong upward or downward price movements, assuming these trends will persist. This strategy requires careful monitoring of market conditions and timely decision-making to capture gains and avoid losses.

Case Studies of Successful Stock Picks

Consider the case of Apple Inc. (AAPL), a company that has consistently demonstrated strong growth and innovation.

Investors who recognized Apple's potential in the early 2000s and held onto their shares saw substantial returns. By analyzing Apple's robust revenue growth, expanding product line, and increasing market share, investors could identify it as a promising growth stock.

Another example is Johnson & Johnson (JNJ), a company known for its stability and dividend payments. Value investors appreciated J&J's strong fundamentals, including a low debt-to-equity ratio and consistent profitability. By investing in J&J, they benefited from both capital appreciation and regular dividend income.

For momentum investing, Tesla Inc. (TSLA) provides a compelling case study. Investors who noticed the upward price momentum driven by Tesla's innovative electric vehicles and strong market demand capitalized on significant gains. Monitoring technical indicators like moving averages and RSI helped investors time their entry and exit points effectively.

Importance of Diversification in Stock Investing

Diversification is a fundamental principle in stock investing that significantly enhances the stability and potential of your investment portfolio. The concept of diversification revolves around spreading your investments across a variety of assets to minimize risk. Imagine you have all your money invested in a single stock. If that company performs poorly or faces an unforeseen crisis, your entire investment could suffer. By diversifying, you reduce the impact of a single stock's poor performance on your overall portfolio.

Diversification works because different assets respond differently to market conditions.

When some investments underperform, others may perform well, balancing out the overall performance of your portfolio. This strategy doesn't guarantee against loss but can significantly mitigate risk. For young adults and professionals starting their investment journey, understanding and applying diversification can protect against significant losses and provide more stable returns over time.

Building a Diversified Stock Portfolio

This involves selecting a mix of investments that align with your financial goals, risk tolerance, and investment horizon. The first step is to understand the different types of stocks and sectors available. You can diversify by investing in various industries such as technology, healthcare, finance, and consumer goods. Each sector responds differently to economic changes, which helps spread risk.

For instance, during an economic downturn, consumer goods and healthcare sectors might perform better than technology or finance. By holding stocks across multiple sectors, you can cushion your portfolio against sector-specific downturns. Additionally, consider diversifying by company size, including a mix of large-cap, mid-cap, and small-cap stocks. Large-cap stocks are generally more stable, while small-cap stocks offer higher growth potential but come with increased risk.

Geographical diversification is another critical aspect. Investing in both domestic and international stocks exposes you to global markets, reducing the risk associated with any single country's economic performance. Emerging markets might provide higher growth opportunities, whereas developed markets offer stability.

Exchange-traded funds (ETFs) and mutual funds are excellent tools for diversification, especially for new investors.

These funds pool money from many investors to purchase a broad range of stocks, offering immediate diversification. For example, an S&P 500 ETF includes stocks from the 500 largest companies in the U.S., providing exposure to a diverse set of industries and companies.

Managing Risk Through Diversification

Risk management is a key reason for diversifying your portfolio. By spreading your investments across various assets, you can reduce the volatility and potential losses. Diversification helps manage both unsystematic risk (specific to individual companies or industries) and systematic risk (related to overall market conditions).

Consider the concept of correlation, which measures how investments move in relation to each other. Ideally, you want a portfolio with assets that have low or negative correlation. This means that when one investment performs poorly, another might perform well, balancing the overall performance of your portfolio.

For example, if you hold stocks in both energy companies and technology firms, a decline in oil prices might hurt the energy sector but could benefit tech companies that rely on energy inputs, thus balancing your portfolio. Diversification doesn't eliminate risk entirely, but it reduces the impact of specific risks and helps achieve more consistent returns over time.

Tools for Portfolio Tracking and Management

Tracking and managing a diversified portfolio requires effective tools that provide insights into your investments and help you make informed decisions. Many online platforms and apps offer comprehensive portfolio management features. These tools allow you to monitor performance, analyze asset allocation, and assess risk.

For instance, tools like **Empower** or **Morningstar** offer portfolio tracking services that give you a detailed view of your investments. They provide performance metrics, asset allocation breakdowns, and risk assessments, helping you ensure your portfolio remains diversified and aligned with your goals.

Robo-advisors like **Betterment** and **Wealthfront** offer automated portfolio management services. They use algorithms to create and manage a diversified portfolio based on your risk tolerance and financial goals. These platforms regularly rebalance your portfolio to maintain optimal asset allocation, ensuring you stay on track with your investment strategy.

Regularly reviewing your portfolio is crucial. Set a schedule to assess your investments, rebalance your portfolio, and make adjustments as needed. Rebalancing involves buying and selling assets to maintain your desired asset allocation. For example, if one sector outperforms and its proportion in your portfolio grows, rebalancing involves selling some of those assets and buying others to restore balance.

Case Studies of Diversified Portfolios

Examining real-world examples can illustrate the benefits of diversification. Consider an investor who, in the early 2000s, allocated their entire portfolio to technology stocks during the dot-com boom. When the bubble burst, they experienced significant losses. In contrast, an investor with a diversified portfolio that included technology, healthcare, and consumer goods stocks likely saw a more balanced performance and lower overall losses. Another example is the 2008 financial crisis. Investors heavily weighted in financial stocks faced substantial losses.

However, those with diversified portfolios that included bonds, international stocks, and other asset classes fared better, as these assets helped offset losses in the financial sector.

An interesting case is Warren Buffett's approach to diversification. While he famously advocates for concentrated investments in high-quality companies, Berkshire Hathaway's portfolio is still diversified across various industries such as insurance, energy, and consumer goods. This balance allows Berkshire to manage risk while pursuing growth opportunities.

These examples underscore the importance of diversification in managing risk and achieving long-term investment success. By spreading investments across different asset classes, sectors, and geographies, investors can protect against significant losses and increase the potential for stable, long-term returns.

Long-term investment strategies are essential for building substantial wealth over time. By committing to a long-term approach, you can take advantage of various benefits that short-term investing might not offer. Let's explore the advantages of long-term investing, the power of compounding returns, strategies for weathering market volatility, case studies of long-term success, and practical tips for maintaining your investment journey.

Investing for the long term provides numerous advantages that can significantly enhance your financial well-being. One of the primary benefits is the potential for higher returns. Historically, the stock market has shown an upward trajectory over extended periods, despite short-term fluctuations.

By staying invested for the long haul, you position yourself to benefit from this overall growth.

Another key benefit is the reduction of transaction costs and taxes. Frequent buying and selling of investments can lead to substantial costs in the form of brokerage fees and taxes on short-term capital gains. Long-term investing minimizes these expenses, allowing more of your money to work for you.

Moreover, long-term investing fosters a disciplined and patient mindset. It encourages you to focus on your financial goals and resist the temptation to react to short-term market movements. This disciplined approach can help you avoid emotional decision-making, which often leads to poor investment choices.

Compounding is the process where the returns on your investments generate their own returns. It is a powerful mechanism that can significantly enhance your wealth over time. The earlier you start investing, the more time your money has to compound, leading to exponential growth.

Consider this example: If you invest $1,000 at an annual return of 8%, without adding any additional money over that period of time, it will grow to $2,159 in ten years, $4,661 in twenty years, and $10,937 in thirty years. The longer you remain invested, the more pronounced the compounding effect becomes.

Compounding also underscores the importance of reinvesting dividends and interest. By reinvesting these earnings, you allow them to generate additional returns, further boosting the growth of your investment portfolio.

Strategies for Holding Investments Through Volatility

Market volatility is an inherent part of investing. While it can be unsettling, especially for new investors, adopting strategies to manage and embrace volatility can enhance your long-term investment success.

One effective strategy is to maintain a diversified portfolio. Diversification spreads your investments across different asset classes, industries, and geographic regions, reducing the impact of poor performance in any single area. This balance helps stabilize your portfolio during turbulent market conditions.

Another strategy is to stay focused on your long-term goals and ignore short-term noise. Market fluctuations are often driven by temporary factors that do not affect the long-term prospects of your investments. By keeping your eye on the big picture, you can avoid making impulsive decisions based on short-term volatility.

Additionally, consider implementing a dollar-cost averaging approach. This strategy involves investing a fixed amount of money at regular intervals, regardless of market conditions. Dollar-cost averaging reduces the risk of investing a large sum at an inopportune time and takes advantage of market dips by purchasing more shares when prices are lower.

Examining real-world examples can illustrate the power of long-term investing. Consider the case of Warren Buffett, one of the most successful investors of all time. Buffett has consistently advocated for long-term investing, and his investment philosophy has yielded tremendous returns over the decades. His company, Berkshire Hathaway, has delivered substantial value to shareholders through disciplined, long-term investments in high-quality companies.

Another notable example is the S&P 500 index. Historically, the S&P 500 has delivered an average annual return of about 10% since its inception. Investors who held an S&P 500 index fund for multiple decades have enjoyed significant wealth accumulation, despite experiencing various market downturns along the way.

A third case study involves individuals who invested in tech giants like Apple or Amazon in their early days. Those who maintained their investments through periods of volatility and uncertainty have seen their holdings grow exponentially as these companies evolved into industry leaders.

Practical Tips for Staying the Course

Staying committed to a long-term investment strategy requires discipline, patience, and a proactive mindset. Here are some practical tips to help you stay the course:

First, establish clear and realistic financial goals. Having a defined purpose for your investments can provide motivation and keep you focused during periods of market turbulence. Whether you're saving for retirement, a home, or your child's education, clear goals can guide your investment decisions.

Second, create a well-thought-out investment plan and stick to it. Your plan should outline your asset allocation, risk tolerance, and investment horizon. Regularly review and adjust your plan as your financial situation and goals evolve, but avoid making changes based on short-term market movements.

Third, educate yourself about investing. The more you understand the principles of long-term investing and the behavior of financial markets, the better equipped you will be to make informed decisions and resist emotional reactions to market volatility.

Fourth, seek support from a financial advisor or a mentor. Professional guidance can provide valuable insights and help you navigate complex financial situations. An advisor can also offer an objective perspective, helping you stay on track with your long-term strategy.

Finally, cultivate a patient and resilient mindset. Investing is a marathon, not a sprint. There will be ups and downs along the way, but maintaining a long-term perspective can help you weather short-term challenges and achieve your financial goals.

Stock investing can be a powerful tool for building wealth, but it also comes with pitfalls that can derail your financial goals if not navigated carefully. Understanding these common mistakes and how to avoid them is crucial for any investor, especially young adults and professionals who are starting their investment journey. This section will explore the typical errors investors make, the impact of emotional investing and market timing, the importance of thorough research and patience, lessons from historical market trends, and practical tips to steer clear of these mistakes.

Common Pitfalls and Mistakes in Stock Investing

One of the most common mistakes in stock investing is chasing after hot stocks. Investors often get swept up by hype and invest heavily in trending stocks without doing proper research. This approach can be dangerous because these stocks are often overvalued and subject to significant volatility. Another mistake is failing to diversify. Putting all your money into a single stock or sector exposes you to higher risk. If that stock or sector performs poorly, your entire portfolio can suffer substantial losses.

Another pitfall is overtrading. Some investors frequently buy and sell stocks, trying to capitalize on short-term price movements.

This behavior not only racks up transaction fees but also leads to suboptimal decision-making based on short-term market noise rather than long-term value. Overtrading is often fueled by the misconception that active trading leads to higher returns, which is rarely the case for individual investors.

Failing to have a clear investment plan is another mistake. Without a well-defined strategy, investors can make impulsive decisions that deviate from their financial goals. An investment plan should outline your risk tolerance, investment horizon, and diversification strategy to guide your decisions and keep you on track.

Emotional Investing and Market Timing

This is a major hurdle for many investors. Fear and greed are powerful emotions that can drive irrational investment decisions. During market downturns, fear can lead to panic selling, causing investors to lock in losses instead of riding out the volatility. Conversely, greed can lead to overconfidence and excessive risk-taking, particularly during bull markets when investors may chase high-flying stocks without regard for fundamentals.

Market timing, the attempt to predict market movements and buy or sell stocks accordingly, is another risky behavior. Even seasoned investors find it challenging to consistently time the market correctly. Attempting to do so can result in missing out on significant gains during market recoveries. Instead of trying to time the market, a more effective strategy is to stay invested through market cycles and focus on long-term growth.

Importance of Research and Patience

Thorough research is the cornerstone of successful investing.

Investing without adequate knowledge about the companies or sectors you're investing in can lead to poor decisions and significant losses. Before buying a stock, it's essential to understand the company's business model, financial health, competitive position, and growth prospects. Reading annual reports, following industry news, and analyzing financial statements can provide valuable insights.

Patience is equally important. The stock market is inherently volatile, and short-term fluctuations are normal. Long-term investing requires the ability to withstand these ups and downs without panicking. Historical data shows that markets tend to recover over time, and staying invested through downturns can lead to substantial gains in the long run. Patience allows your investments to benefit from the power of compounding and the general upward trajectory of the stock market.

Lessons from Historical Market Trends

Historical market trends offer valuable lessons for investors. One key lesson is the importance of staying invested during market downturns. For example, during the 2008 financial crisis, many investors who sold their stocks at the market's lowest points missed out on the subsequent recovery and growth. Those who remained invested saw their portfolios recover and grow significantly in the years following the crisis.

Another lesson is the cyclicality of markets. Bull and bear markets are natural phases of the market cycle. Understanding this cyclicality can help investors maintain perspective during periods of volatility. Historically, bear markets have been followed by bull markets, and the overall long-term trend of the stock market has been upward.

Additionally, historical trends highlight the benefits of diversification. During the dot-com bubble of the late 1990s, many investors were heavily invested in technology stocks. When the bubble burst, diversified portfolios that included other sectors were better able to weather the storm. Diversification reduces the impact of poor performance in any single investment or sector, contributing to more stable and consistent returns.

To avoid common investing mistakes, it's crucial to adopt a disciplined and informed approach. Here are some practical tips to help you stay on the right path:

- Establish a clear investment plan. Define your financial goals, risk tolerance, and investment horizon. This plan will serve as a roadmap, guiding your investment decisions and helping you stay focused on your long-term objectives.

- Prioritize diversification. Spread your investments across different asset classes, sectors, and geographic regions. This approach reduces the risk associated with any single investment and enhances the stability of your portfolio.

- Commit to thorough research. Before investing in any stock, take the time to understand the company's fundamentals, industry position, and growth potential. Use reliable sources of information and stay informed about market trends and economic developments.

- Avoid emotional investing. Recognize that fear and greed can lead to irrational decisions. Stick to your investment plan and avoid making impulsive moves based on short-term market fluctuations. Remember that market volatility is normal and often temporary.

- Adopt a long-term perspective. Focus on the long-term growth potential of your investments rather than trying to time the market. Historical data shows that staying invested through market cycles yields better results than attempting to predict short-term movements.

- Utilize tools and resources for portfolio management. There are numerous online platforms and financial apps that can help you track your investments, analyze performance, and make informed decisions. These tools provide valuable insights and can simplify the process of managing your portfolio.

- Consider seeking advice from a financial advisor. Professional guidance can provide an objective perspective and help you navigate complex financial situations. An advisor can also assist in developing a comprehensive investment plan tailored to your specific goals and circumstances.

Chapter 6
EXPLORING OPTIONS TRADING STRATEGIES

Introduction to Options Contracts and Terminology

Understanding options contracts and their associated terminology is crucial for anyone looking to delve into options trading. This introduction will cover the definition of options contracts, key terms such as call options, put options, and strike prices, how options contracts work, and will include basic examples and illustrations, as well as case studies to provide a comprehensive overview.

An options contract is a financial derivative that gives the holder the right, but not the obligation, to buy or sell an underlying asset at a specified price within a specific time frame. The underlying asset could be a stock, an index, or even a commodity. Options are versatile financial instruments used for hedging, speculation, and income generation. They are a fundamental part of many investment strategies due to their ability to manage risk and enhance returns.

Before diving into how options contracts work, it's essential to understand some key terms.

Call Options: A call option gives the holder the right to buy the underlying asset at the strike price before or on the expiration date. Investors purchase call options when they anticipate the price of the underlying asset will rise.

Call Options

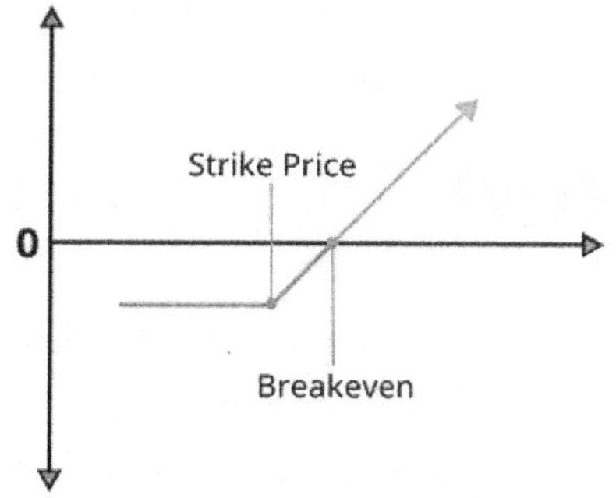

Call Option (Buy)

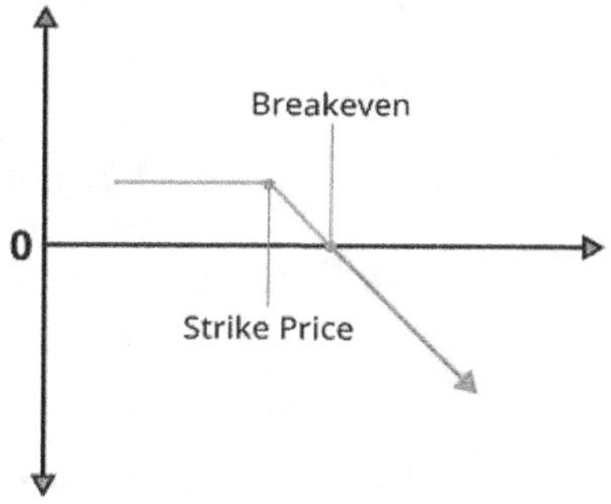

Call Option (Sell)

Put Options: A put option gives the holder the right to sell the underlying asset at the strike price before or on the expiration date. Investors buy put options when they expect the price of the underlying asset to fall.

Put Options

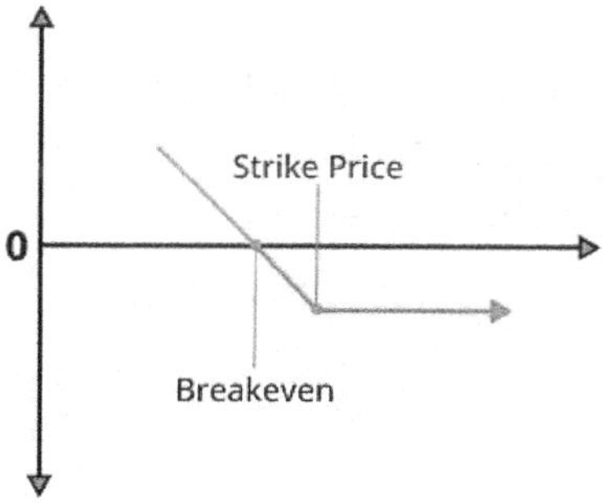

Put Option (Buy)

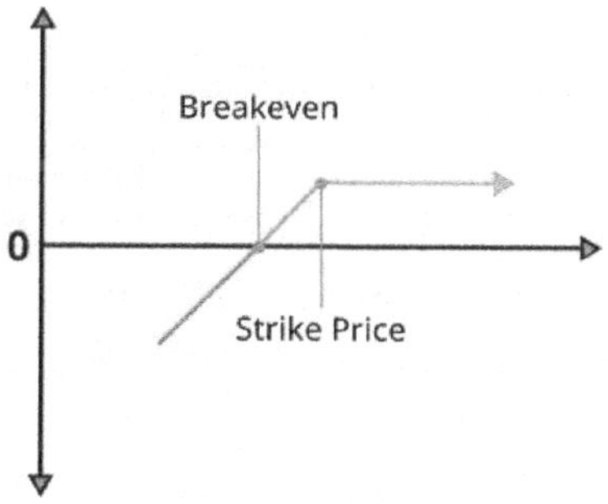

Put Option (Sell)

Strike Price: The strike price, also known as the exercise price, is the predetermined price at which the underlying asset can be bought (call option) or sold (put option) by the option holder. The strike price is a critical factor in determining the option's value and profitability.

How Options Contracts Work

Options contracts operate based on the rights they confer to the holder and the obligations they impose on the writer (seller). When you buy an options contract, you pay a premium for the right to exercise the option. This premium is the cost of the contract and varies based on several factors, including the underlying asset's price, the strike price, the time until expiration, and market volatility.

For a call option, if the underlying asset's price exceeds the strike price, the option is "in the money," and the holder can buy the asset at the strike price and potentially sell it at the higher market price for a profit. Conversely, if the asset's price is below the strike price, the option is "out of the money," and the holder would likely let the option expire worthless.

For a put option, if the underlying asset's price falls below the strike price, the option is "in the money," and the holder can sell the asset at the higher strike price, even if the market price is lower. If the asset's price is above the strike price, the option is "out of the money," and the holder would probably let it expire.

To illustrate, let’s consider a few basic examples.

Call Option Example:

Imagine you buy a call option for Company ABC's stock, with a strike price of $50 and an expiration date one month from now. You pay a premium of $2 per share for this option.

If, at expiration, ABC's stock is trading at $60, you can exercise your option to buy at $50, then sell at the market price of $60, making a profit of $8 per share (market price - strike price - premium). If the stock is below $50, you let the option expire and only lose the premium paid.

Put Option Example:
Suppose you purchase a put option for Company XYZ's stock, with a strike price of $40 and an expiration date two months from now, paying a premium of $1.50 per share. If XYZ's stock falls to $30 by expiration, you can sell your shares at the strike price of $40, realizing a profit of $8.50 per share (strike price - market price - premium). If the stock price is above $40, you let the option expire, losing only the premium paid.

These examples demonstrate how options can be used to capitalize on market movements while limiting potential losses to the premium paid.

It's important to note that options are traded in sets of 100 shares. This means that to sell a call option on shares you own (Covered Calls), you need to have 100 of those shares per option contract sold. The same applies to buying straight call or put options, and covered puts—each contract represents 100 shares.

Case Studies of Options Trading Scenarios
Examining real-world case studies can further illustrate the practical applications of options trading.

Hedging with Options:
Consider an investor holding a significant position in a tech stock, concerned about potential short-term volatility.

To protect against a decline, the investor purchases put options. If the stock price drops, the put options gain value, offsetting the losses in the stock position. This strategy, known as protective puts, is a common hedging technique.

Speculating with Options:
A trader believes that a pharmaceutical company's stock will surge following the release of a new drug. The trader buys call options with a strike price close to the current stock price. If the stock price rises as anticipated, the trader can exercise the calls for a substantial profit, far exceeding the initial premium paid. This strategy demonstrates the leverage options provide for speculation.

Income Generation with Options:
An investor owns shares of a stable utility company and wants to generate additional income. The investor sells covered call options, agreeing to sell the shares at a higher strike price if exercised. The premiums collected from selling these calls provide additional income, and if the options expire worthless, the investor retains both the shares and the premium. This strategy, known as covered call writing, is widely used for income generation.

These case studies highlight the versatility of options in various trading scenarios, from risk management to speculative opportunities and income generation.

Exploring Covered Calls and Covered Puts
Understanding covered calls and covered puts is essential for any investor looking to enhance their portfolio's performance.

These strategies are relatively simple and provide a way to generate income or hedge against potential losses.

In this section, we'll explore what covered calls and covered puts are, when to use them, their risk and reward profiles, and provide case studies to illustrate their practical applications.

A covered call is an options strategy where an investor holds a long position in a stock and sells call options on the same stock. This strategy is "covered" because the investor owns the underlying shares that can be delivered if the call options are exercised. By selling the call options, the investor collects a premium, which provides some income and can offset potential declines in the stock's value.

Covered calls are most effective in a neutral to slightly bullish market where the investor expects the stock to rise modestly or remain flat. The strategy is used to generate additional income from the premium received for selling the call options. This can be particularly attractive for investors looking to enhance their returns on stocks they already own. Additionally, covered calls can be a way to set a target selling price for the stock. If the stock price rises above the strike price, the call options may be exercised, and the investor sells the stock at the agreed-upon price, realizing a profit.

Let us develop a comprehensive understanding of the covered call payoff concept with the help of the graph and explanation provided on the next page:

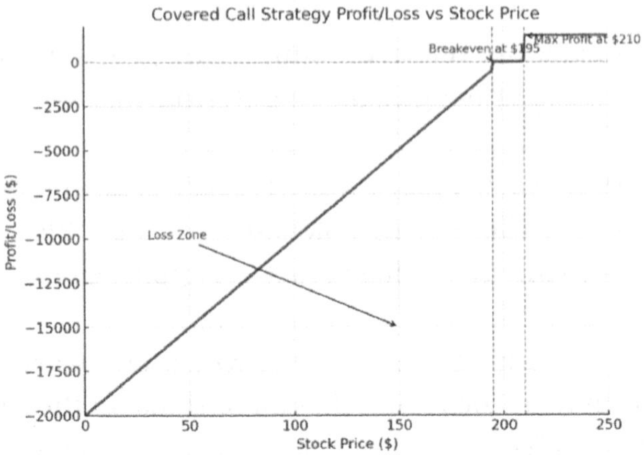

Imagine David buys Stock A at $200 and simultaneously sells a call option with a $210 strike price for $5. This action effectively reduces the cost of the initial investment by $5 per share, meaning the breakeven point and cost basis for the long stock position now sit at $195.

If the stock's price drops below this breakeven point, the downside risk becomes significant, potentially extending all the way to $0, less the adjusted cost basis. However, if the call option ends up being in the money (ITM), David's profit potential will be capped at the strike price of the option plus the total premium earned from selling that option.

When assigned, David will be obligated to sell his shares of Stock A at the short strike price, effectively closing his long stock position. If Stock A closes above $210 at expiration, David will realize a profit of $1,500 per contract, as the stock would have appreciated by $10 per share ($1,000), plus the $500 premium from selling the covered call option. Conversely, if the stock closes below the short call at expiration, the option will expire worthless, and David will retain the premium received.

It's important to note that selling a covered call limits the potential profit but does not eliminate the downside risk.

Covered Puts and Their Applications
A covered put strategy involves selling put options while simultaneously holding a short position in the underlying stock. This strategy is "covered" because the short position offsets the obligation to buy the stock if the put options are exercised. Covered puts are typically used in a neutral to slightly bearish market, where the investor expects the stock to fall or remain flat. The graph shows that breakeven occurs at a price of $90, with a maximum profit of $2,500. This is calculated as follows:

$$[\$5 \times 500 \text{ shares}] = \$2,500$$

Losses will begin if the price exceeds $90. This strategy is viable if the investor believes ABC's price won't fall below $80 before the option expires. If the price drops below $80, shorting the stock could yield higher profits, while rising prices could lead to significant losses.

In this strategy, the investor collects a premium from selling the put options. If the stock price falls below the strike price, the investor may be obligated to buy the stock at the strike price. However, because they already hold a short position, they can cover the purchase with the shares from the short sale.

Example: The following is an illustration of a covered put transaction. Let's suppose a trader does the following transaction:

- Sells 500 shares of ABC for $85
- Sells 5 ABC 80 puts @ 5

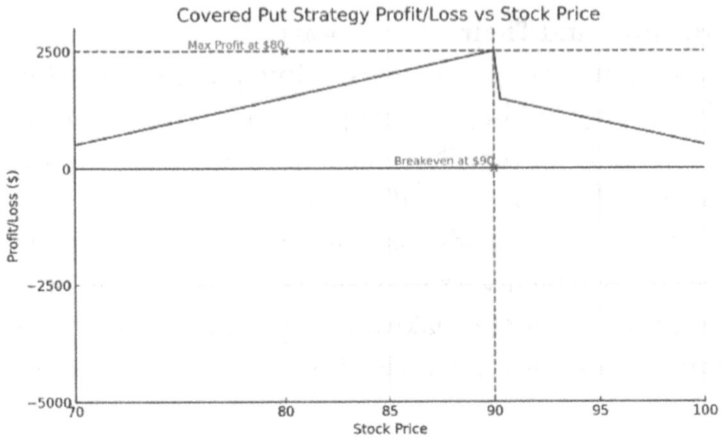

Risk and Reward Analysis of Covered Strategies

Covered Calls:

Rewards: The primary reward is the premium received from selling the call options. This income can enhance overall returns, especially in a sideways market. If the stock price rises to the strike price, the investor can sell the stock at a profit.

Risks: The main risk is the stock price rising significantly above the strike price, meaning the investor misses out on potential gains beyond the strike price. Additionally, if the stock price falls, the premium received may not fully offset the loss in the stock's value.

Covered Puts:

Rewards: The premium received from selling the put options provides immediate income. If the stock price falls, the short position gains value, offsetting the obligation to buy the stock if the put options are exercised.

Risks: The primary risk is the stock price rising significantly, resulting in potential losses on the short position that may not be fully covered by the premium received from the put options.

Case Studies of Covered Options Strategies

Case Study 1: Covered Call:
An investor owns 100 shares of Company XYZ, currently trading at $50 per share. The investor sells a call option with a strike price of $55, expiring in one month, and receives a premium of $2 per share. If XYZ's stock remains at $50 or rises to $55, the investor keeps the premium, enhancing their returns. If the stock rises above $55, the investor sells the shares at the strike price, realizing a profit of $5 per share plus the $2 premium. If the stock falls, the $2 premium provides a cushion against losses.

Case Study 2: Covered Put:
An investor is short 100 shares of Company ABC, currently trading at $40 per share. The investor sells a put option with a strike price of $35, expiring in one month, and receives a premium of $1.50 per share. If ABC's stock remains at $40 or falls to $35, the investor keeps the premium. If the stock falls below $35, the investor buys the shares at the strike price, covering their short position and potentially profiting from the decline. If the stock rises, the loss on the short position is partially offset by the premium received.

In conclusion, covered calls and covered puts are versatile strategies that can enhance income and manage risk. By understanding when and how to use these strategies, investors can better navigate various market conditions and improve their overall portfolio performance. Through careful planning and execution, these strategies offer practical ways to achieve financial and wealth-building goals.

Advanced Options Strategies

Exploring advanced options strategies can provide investors with more sophisticated tools to manage risk, enhance returns, and navigate different market conditions.

This section will introduce spreads and straddles, discuss the benefits and risks of these advanced strategies, provide practical examples and illustrations, explain how to implement them, and present case studies of successful advanced options trades.

Introduction to Spreads and Straddles
Advanced options strategies, such as spreads and straddles, involve multiple options contracts to achieve specific financial goals.

Spreads: A spread involves simultaneously buying and selling options of the same class (either call or put) on the same underlying asset but with different strike prices or expiration dates. Common types of spreads include vertical spreads, horizontal spreads (also known as calendar spreads), and diagonal spreads. Each type has its unique characteristics and is used to capitalize on different market conditions.

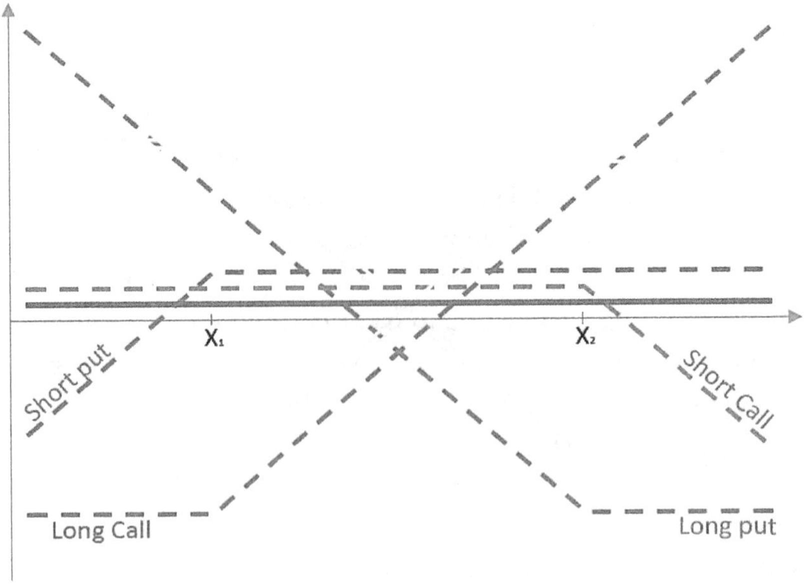

Straddles: A straddle involves buying a call option and a put option on the same underlying asset with the same strike price and expiration date. This strategy is used when an investor expects significant volatility in the asset's price but is unsure of the direction.

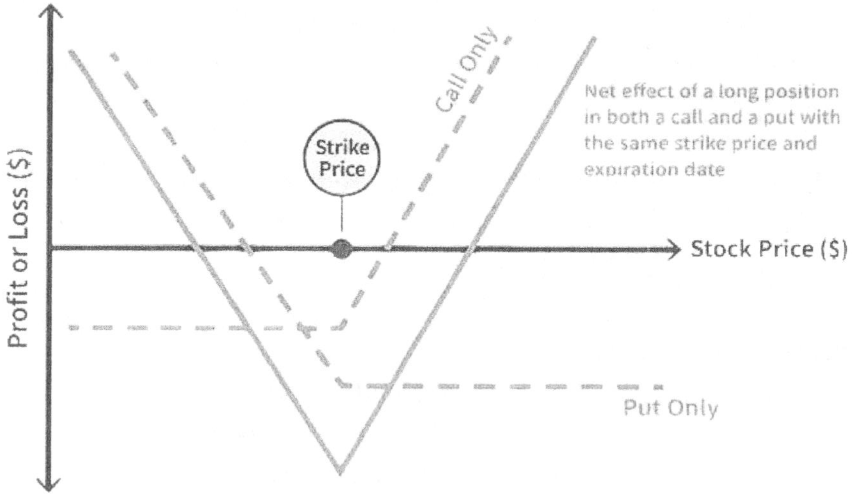

Benefits:

- ***Risk Management***: Advanced strategies like spreads can limit potential losses while still providing upside potential. By simultaneously buying and selling options, investors can create a defined risk-reward profile.
- ***Profit from Volatility***: Strategies like straddles allow investors to profit from significant price movements, regardless of the direction, making them suitable for volatile markets.
- **Flexibility**: Advanced options strategies offer flexibility to tailor positions according to specific market views and risk tolerance.

Risks:

- ***Complexity***: Advanced strategies can be more complex than basic options trades, requiring a deeper understanding of options pricing and market dynamics.
- ***Transaction Costs***: Implementing these strategies often involves multiple trades, leading to higher transaction costs that can eat into profits.
- ***Limited Profit Potential***: Some strategies, like vertical spreads, have limited profit potential because gains on one leg of the spread may be offset by losses on the other.

Vertical Spread Example:
A bull call spread involves buying a call option with a lower strike price and selling a call option with a higher strike price on the same underlying asset and expiration date. For instance, an investor might buy a call option on Stock XYZ with a strike price of $50 and sell a call option with a strike price of $60. This strategy profits if XYZ's stock price rises but has limited downside risk and upside potential.

Straddle Example:
An investor expecting significant volatility in Company ABC's stock might buy a straddle by purchasing both a call and a put option with a strike price of $100, expiring in one month. If ABC's stock moves significantly in either direction, the gains from one option could offset the losses from the other, potentially leading to a profit.

Implementing advanced options strategies requires a step-by-step approach:

- **Identify Market Outlook**: Determine your expectations for the underlying asset's price movement and volatility.
- **Select the Appropriate Strategy**: Choose a strategy that aligns with your market outlook and risk tolerance.
- **Determine Strike Prices and Expiration Dates**: Based on the strategy, select the strike prices and expiration dates for the options contracts.
- **Execute Trades**: Place the necessary trades to establish the position. Ensure that you understand the potential outcomes and have a plan for managing the position.
- **Monitor and Adjust**: Regularly monitor the position and make adjustments as needed based on market conditions and changes in your outlook.

Case Studies of Successful Advanced Options Trades

Bull Call Spread:
An investor expects a moderate rise in Stock DEF over the next three months. They buy a call option with a strike price of $100 for $5 and sell a call option with a strike price of $110 for $2. The net cost is $3. If DEF rises to $110 or above, the spread's maximum profit is $7 ($10 spread - $3 cost). If DEF stays below $100, the loss is limited to the $3 premium paid.

Straddle:
An investor anticipates significant earnings announcement volatility for Company GHI. They buy a call and a put option, both with a strike price of $50, each costing $4. If GHI's stock moves significantly, the gains from one option could offset the cost of both options, leading to a profit. For instance, if the stock price rises to $60, the call option gains $6 ($10 gain - $4 cost), while the put option expires worthless, resulting in a net profit of $2.

This net profit equates to $2 per share, or $200 per contract.

Navigating the world of options trading requires the right tools and resources to make informed decisions and execute strategies effectively. This section will introduce key platforms and tools for options trading, discuss how to analyze options data and charts, provide practical tips for using trading platforms, offer case studies of successful options trading tools, and highlight resources for continuous learning and improvement.

Key Platforms and Tools for Options Trading
To trade options efficiently, it's essential to have access to robust trading platforms that offer comprehensive tools and resources. Some of the most popular platforms for options trading include:

Thinkorswim by TD Ameritrade: Known for its advanced charting capabilities and extensive options analysis tools, Thinkorswim is favored by many options traders. It provides real-time data, customizable charts, and an options-specific layout that simplifies complex trades.

E*TRADE: E*TRADE offers a user-friendly platform with a variety of tools for options trading, including options screeners, strategy builders, and real-time data. Its mobile app is also highly rated, making it convenient for trading on the go.

Interactive Brokers: This platform is renowned for its low-cost trading and powerful tools. It caters to both professional traders and retail investors, providing access to a wide range of options markets and sophisticated trading tools.

Robinhood: For beginners, Robinhood offers a straightforward, commission-free platform with an easy-to-use interface.

While it lacks some of the advanced tools of other platforms, it is a good starting point for those new to options trading.

Analyzing Options Data and Charts

Successful options trading relies on analyzing data and charts to make informed decisions. Key data points include:

Implied Volatility (IV): This measures the market's expectation of future volatility and impacts options pricing. High IV typically increases options premiums.

Delta, Gamma, Theta, and Vega: These are the "Greeks" that describe how options prices change with respect to various factors. Delta measures price sensitivity to the underlying asset, Gamma measures the rate of change of Delta, Theta measures time decay, and Vega measures sensitivity to volatility.

Options Chains: An options chain is a listing of all available options contracts for a particular security, organized by expiration date and strike price. Reviewing an options chain helps traders identify the best contracts to trade based on their strategies.

Candlestick Charts: Candlestick charts are used to visualize stock price movements and can help investors 'time' market movements. Each 'candlestick' represents one trading day, showing the stock's opening, closing, high, and low prices. Many beginner investors use this method to identify patterns that predict price direction.

Practical Tips for Using Trading Platforms

When using trading platforms, consider the following practical tips to enhance your trading experience:

Customization: Customize the platform's layout to suit your trading style. Arrange windows and tools so that the most critical information is easily accessible.

Utilize Demo Accounts: Many platforms offer demo or paper trading accounts. Use these to practice strategies without risking real money.

Set Alerts and Notifications: Set alerts for key price levels, IV changes, or specific market conditions. This helps you stay informed and react quickly to market movements.

Leverage Educational Resources: Most platforms offer extensive educational resources, including webinars, tutorials, and articles. Regularly engage with these materials to improve your trading skills.

Case Studies of Options Trading Tools

Case Study 1: **Thinkorswim's Analyze Tab**:

An options trader uses Thinkorswim's Analyze tab to simulate potential trades and evaluate their potential outcomes. By inputting various strategies, the trader can visualize profit and loss scenarios, helping them to understand the impact of different market conditions on their trades. For instance, by analyzing a vertical spread, the trader can see how changes in the underlying asset's price, volatility, and time decay will affect their position. This detailed analysis enables the trader to make more informed decisions and manage risks effectively.

Case Study 2: **Interactive Brokers' OptionTrader Tool**:
A professional trader utilizes Interactive Brokers' OptionTrader tool, which offers a comprehensive view of the options market. This tool provides access to real-time data, options chains, and advanced analytics. By using the strategy builder, the trader can construct complex strategies, such as iron condors and butterfly spreads, and evaluate their potential performance.

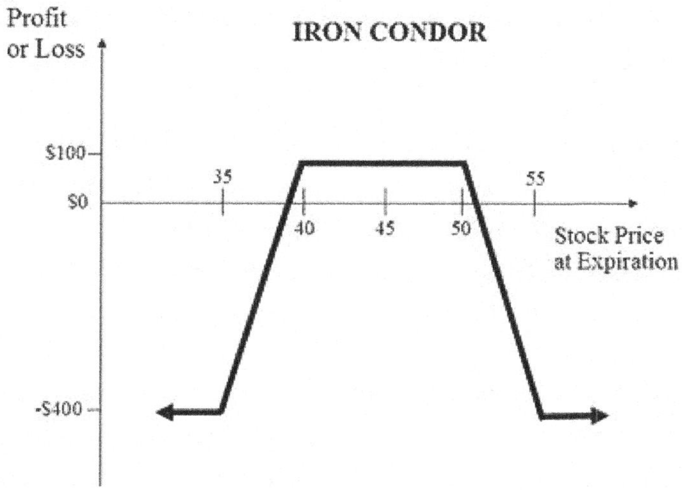

The Iron condor profit profile consists of limited profit and limited risk (the potential risk is usually greater than the potential profit). If the stock remains in the middle of the profit range, the seller will be profitable. If the stock breaches one side, the trader will lose.

The real-time risk analysis feature allows the trader to monitor their positions and make adjustments as needed, ensuring they stay within their risk tolerance.

Resources for Continuous Learning and Improvement
Continuous learning is crucial for success in options trading. Numerous resources are available to help traders stay updated on market trends, enhance their skills, and refine their strategies:

Online Courses and Webinars: Platforms like Coursera, Udemy, and Investopedia offer comprehensive courses on options trading. Additionally, many brokerage firms provide free webinars hosted by experienced traders and financial analysts.

Books: Several books provide in-depth knowledge about options trading. Notable titles include "Options as a Strategic Investment" by Lawrence G. McMillan and "The Options Playbook" by Brian Overby. These books cover various strategies, risk management techniques, and market insights.

Trading Communities and Forums: Engaging with other traders through online communities and forums like Reddit's r/options, Elite Trader, and Trade2Win can provide valuable insights and support. These platforms allow traders to share experiences, discuss strategies, and stay informed about market developments.

Financial News and Analysis: Staying updated with financial news is essential. Websites like Bloomberg, CNBC, and Seeking Alpha provide real-time news, expert analysis, and market commentary. Subscribing to newsletters and following market analysts on social media can also keep you informed about the latest trends and developments.

Brokerage Firm Resources: Many brokerage firms offer a wealth of educational resources, including articles, video tutorials, and interactive tools. Utilizing these resources can help you understand the platform's features and improve your trading skills.

Managing risk is crucial in options trading, given the complexity and volatility associated with the market. Effective risk management helps protect your investments and ensures long-term success.

This section will discuss the importance of risk management in options trading, strategies for mitigating risk, using stop-loss orders and position sizing, provide practical examples of risk management, and present case studies of effective risk management.

Importance of Risk Management in Options Trading
Options trading can be highly rewarding, but it also comes with significant risks. Without proper risk management, traders can face substantial losses that can wipe out their capital. Risk management is essential to safeguard investments and maintain financial stability. It involves identifying potential risks, assessing their impact, and implementing strategies to minimize their effects. By prioritizing risk management, traders can navigate the options market with greater confidence and resilience.

Several strategies can help mitigate risk in options trading:

Diversification: Spreading investments across different assets and strategies reduces the impact of any single loss. Diversification can involve trading options on various underlying assets, such as stocks, indices, and commodities.

Hedging: This involves using options to protect against potential losses in other investments. For example, buying put options on a stock you own can limit losses if the stock price declines.

Defining Risk Limits: Setting predefined risk limits for each trade ensures that losses are kept within acceptable boundaries. This includes establishing maximum loss thresholds and sticking to them.

Position Sizing: Proper position sizing involves determining the appropriate amount of capital to allocate to each trade based on your risk tolerance and account size. This helps prevent overexposure to any single trade.

Using Stop-Loss Orders: Implementing stop-loss orders automatically closes a position when it reaches a certain price level, limiting potential losses.

Stop-loss orders and position sizing are fundamental components of effective risk management:

Stop-Loss Orders: A stop-loss order is an instruction to sell an option or underlying asset if it reaches a specified price. For instance, if you buy a call option on a stock at $50, you might set a stop-loss order at $45. If the stock price falls to $45, the stop-loss order will trigger, selling the option and limiting your loss.

Position Sizing: Position sizing involves calculating the appropriate amount of capital to risk on each trade. A common approach is the 2% rule, where you risk no more than 2% of your total account balance on any single trade. For example, if you have a $10,000 account, you would risk no more than $200 per trade. This ensures that even a series of losing trades will not significantly deplete your capital.

Practical Examples of Risk Management

Example 1: Hedging with Options
Suppose you own 100 shares of XYZ stock, currently trading at $100 per share. You are concerned about a potential decline in the stock price. To hedge against this risk, you purchase a put option with a strike price of $95, expiring in three months.

If the stock price falls below $95, the put option will increase in value, offsetting the loss on your stock holdings.

Example 2: Implementing a Stop-Loss Order
You buy a call option on ABC stock for $5. To limit potential losses, you set a stop-loss order at $3. If the option's price falls to $3, the stop-loss order will trigger, selling the option and limiting your loss to $2 per option contract.

Case Studies of Effective Risk Management

Managing Risk with Covered Calls
An investor owns 500 shares of a technology company and wants to generate additional income while managing risk. They sell covered calls with a strike price above the current market price. If the stock price rises above the strike price, the options are exercised, and the investor sells the shares at the strike price, capturing the premium from the options.

If the stock price does not reach the strike price, the investor keeps the premium and the shares, reducing overall risk.

Using Spreads to Limit Risk
A trader believes that a particular stock will not move significantly in the short term. They implement an iron condor strategy by selling an out-of-the-money call spread and an out-of-the-money put spread.

This strategy profits from low volatility and has defined risk and reward parameters. By carefully selecting the strike prices and expirations, the trader limits their potential loss while maintaining a favorable risk-reward ratio.

Chapter 7

Understanding Bonds and Fixed Income Investments

Bonds are a cornerstone of fixed income investments, offering stability and reliable income for investors. Understanding the various types of bonds and how they function is essential for building a diversified investment portfolio. This section will provide an overview of government, corporate, and municipal bonds, highlight the differences between these bond types, explain how bonds generate income, offer practical examples of bond investments, and present case studies of bond portfolios.

Government Bonds:
Government bonds are issued by national governments to finance public spending and projects. They are considered one of the safest investments because they are backed by the government's credit. Examples include U.S. Treasury bonds, UK Gilts, and Japanese Government Bonds (JGBs). These bonds come in various maturities, ranging from short-term Treasury bills to long-term Treasury bonds. Interest payments, known as coupon payments, are typically made semi-annually.

Corporate Bonds:
Corporate bonds are issued by companies to raise capital for business operations, expansion, or other expenditures. These bonds tend to offer higher yields than government bonds due to the increased risk associated with the issuing corporation's creditworthiness. Corporate bonds can be investment-grade, issued by financially stable companies, or high-yield (junk) bonds, issued by companies with lower credit ratings. The higher yield on junk bonds compensates for the greater risk.

Municipal Bonds:
Municipal bonds, or "munis," are issued by state and local governments or their agencies to fund public projects such as schools, highways, and hospitals. One key feature of municipal bonds is that the interest income is often exempt from federal income taxes and, in some cases, state and local taxes as well. This tax advantage makes munis particularly attractive to investors in higher tax brackets.

The primary differences between these bond types lie in their issuers, risk levels, yields, and tax treatments:

- **Issuers**: Government bonds are issued by national governments, corporate bonds by private or public companies, and municipal bonds by local government entities.
- **Risk Levels**: Government bonds generally carry the lowest risk, followed by investment-grade corporate bonds, municipal bonds, and high-yield corporate bonds.
- **Yields**: Due to their low risk, government bonds offer the lowest yields. Corporate bonds provide higher yields, with high-yield bonds offering the highest. Municipal bonds' yields can be competitive, especially considering their tax-exempt status.
- **Tax Treatments**: Interest from government and corporate bonds is subject to federal and state taxes, whereas municipal bond interest is often exempt from federal and sometimes state and local taxes.

How Bonds Generate Income
Bonds generate income primarily through their coupon payments, which are regular interest payments made to bondholders. The coupon rate, expressed as a percentage of the bond's face value, determines the amount of interest received. For example, a bond with a face value of $1,000 and a 5% coupon rate pays $50 annually.

Additionally, bonds can generate income through capital gains if they are sold for more than their purchase price. However, bonds are generally less volatile than stocks, and capital gains are not the primary income source for bond investors.

Practical Examples of Bond Investments

Example 1: U.S. Treasury Bonds:
An investor seeking safety and stable income might invest in U.S. Treasury bonds. These bonds offer a low-risk investment with regular interest payments. For instance, a 10-year Treasury bond purchased at face value with a 2% coupon rate would pay $20 annually per $1,000 invested.

Example 2: Investment-Grade Corporate Bonds:
A more yield-oriented investor might purchase investment-grade corporate bonds from a well-known company like Apple or Microsoft. If Apple issues a 5-year bond with a 3% coupon rate, the investor would receive $30 annually per $1,000 invested, in addition to the bond's principal upon maturity.

Example 3: Municipal Bonds:
An investor in a high tax bracket might choose municipal bonds from their home state. Suppose a local government issues a 15-year municipal bond with a 4% coupon rate, and the interest income is tax-exempt. In this case, the investor receives $40 annually per $1,000 invested, with the added benefit of tax savings.

Case Studies of Bond Portfolios
Conservative Portfolio with Government Bonds:
Jane, a retiree, prioritizes capital preservation and steady income. She allocates 70% of her portfolio to U.S. Treasury bonds, 20% to investment-grade corporate bonds, and 10% to municipal bonds.

This diversified bond portfolio provides stability, with government bonds offering security, corporate bonds enhancing yield, and municipal bonds providing tax-free income.

Balanced Portfolio with Corporate and Municipal Bonds:
John, a mid-career professional, seeks a balance between risk and return. He invests 50% of his bond allocation in investment-grade corporate bonds and 50% in municipal bonds. This strategy allows him to benefit from higher yields while taking advantage of the tax-exempt status of municipal bonds. Over time, John's portfolio generates a stable income stream, with a moderate risk profile.

Aggressive Portfolio with High-Yield Bonds:
Emily, a young professional with a higher risk tolerance, includes high-yield corporate bonds in her portfolio. She allocates 40% to investment-grade corporate bonds, 30% to municipal bonds, and 30% to high-yield bonds. While this strategy involves more risk, the higher yields from high-yield bonds enhance her income potential. Emily monitors her portfolio closely to manage risk and adjusts her allocations as needed.

Investing in bonds can be a key component of a well-rounded portfolio, providing stability and predictable income. However, like all investments, bonds come with risks that need to be understood and managed. This section will explore the various risk factors in bond investing, including interest rate risk, credit risk, and duration risk. We will also discuss how to evaluate bond yields and returns, the importance of diversifying bond investments, practical tips for mitigating bond risks, and case studies of effective bond risk management.

Risk Factors in Bond Investing: Interest Rate, Credit, and Duration Risk

Interest Rate Risk:
Interest rate risk is the risk that changes in market interest rates will affect the value of a bond. When interest rates rise, the price of existing bonds typically falls because new bonds are issued with higher yields, making older bonds less attractive. Conversely, when interest rates fall, the price of existing bonds usually rises. Long-term bonds are more sensitive to interest rate changes than short-term bonds because their fixed interest payments extend further into the future.

Credit Risk:
Also known as default risk, is the risk that the bond issuer will be unable to make interest payments or repay the principal at maturity. Government bonds, especially those from stable countries, generally have low credit risk. However, corporate bonds, particularly high-yield (junk) bonds, carry higher credit risk. Credit ratings provided by agencies like Moody's, S&P, and Fitch can help investors assess the creditworthiness of bond issuers.

Duration Risk:
This measures a bond's sensitivity to changes in interest rates, incorporating both the bond's time to maturity and the timing of its interest payments. Bonds with longer durations are more affected by interest rate changes. Duration is a crucial concept because it helps investors understand the potential volatility of a bond's price in response to interest rate movements.

Evaluating Bond Yields and Returns

Current Yield:
The current yield is calculated by dividing the bond's annual interest payment by its current market price. It provides a snapshot of the bond's income-generating potential but does not account for potential capital gains or losses.

Yield to Maturity (YTM):
YTM is a more comprehensive measure of a bond's return. It considers the bond's current market price, coupon interest payments, and the amount received at maturity. YTM assumes that all interest payments are reinvested at the same rate, providing a more accurate picture of the bond's total return if held to maturity.

Yield to Call (YTC):
For callable bonds, YTC measures the yield assuming the bond is called, or repaid early, by the issuer. This yield is relevant for bonds with call provisions, which allow issuers to repay the bond before its maturity date, usually when interest rates decline.

Diversifying Bond Investments

Diversification is crucial in bond investing to manage risk and optimize returns. Here are some strategies:

Across Sectors:
Investing in government, corporate, and municipal bonds can help spread risk across different sectors. Government bonds provide stability, corporate bonds offer higher yields, and municipal bonds can provide tax advantages.

Across Credit Ratings:
Combining investment-grade bonds with a smaller allocation to high-yield bonds can balance risk and return. Investment-grade bonds provide safety, while high-yield bonds offer higher income potential.

Across Maturities:
A laddered bond portfolio, with bonds maturing at different times, can reduce interest rate risk. This strategy ensures that some bonds are maturing regularly, allowing reinvestment in different interest rate environments.

Practical Tips for Mitigating Bond Risks

Monitor Interest Rate Trends:
Stay informed about economic conditions and central bank policies that influence interest rates. Adjust your bond portfolio accordingly, perhaps by shortening durations when interest rates are expected to rise.

Assess Creditworthiness:
Use credit ratings and financial analysis to evaluate the credit risk of bond issuers. Diversify across issuers and sectors to mitigate the impact of potential defaults.

Use Duration to Manage Risk:
Align the duration of your bond portfolio with your investment horizon and risk tolerance. For example, if you anticipate needing funds in the near term, focus on short-duration bonds to reduce interest rate risk.

Consider Bond Funds and ETFs:
Bond funds and exchange-traded funds (ETFs) can provide instant diversification and professional management. These funds often hold a wide range of bonds, spreading risk and offering more liquidity than individual bonds.

Reinvest Interest Payments:
Reinvesting interest payments can help compound returns over time. Use these payments to purchase additional bonds or other investments, depending on your strategy and market conditions.

Case Studies of Bond Risk Management

Managing Interest Rate Risk:
Tom, a conservative investor, was concerned about rising interest rates. He shifted his portfolio to shorter-duration bonds, which are less sensitive to interest rate changes. Additionally, he included floating-rate bonds, whose interest payments adjust with market rates, further mitigating interest rate risk. As rates rose, Tom's portfolio experienced less volatility than if he had held longer-duration bonds.

Diversifying Credit Risk:
Lisa, an income-focused investor, diversified her bond holdings across different credit ratings. She allocated 60% to investment-grade corporate bonds and 40% to high-yield bonds. When one of the high-yield bond issuers faced financial difficulties, the impact on her overall portfolio was cushioned by the stability of her investment-grade bonds. Her diversified approach balanced higher income potential with manageable risk.

Laddering to Manage Duration Risk:
Mike, planning for retirement, created a bond ladder with maturities ranging from 1 to 10 years.

Each year, one set of bonds matured, providing liquidity and the opportunity to reinvest in current market conditions. This laddering strategy minimized the impact of interest rate changes on his portfolio and provided regular cash flow to meet his financial needs.

Role of Bonds in a Diversified Portfolio

In the journey towards building a robust financial foundation, diversification plays a critical role. Bonds are a cornerstone of a diversified investment portfolio, providing stability, income, and a hedge against market volatility. This section delves into the importance of bonds for portfolio stability, strategies for balancing bonds with stocks and other assets, practical examples of diversified portfolios, and case studies of balanced investment strategies.

Importance of Bonds for Portfolio Stability

Bonds are often considered the bedrock of a stable investment portfolio. They provide a steady stream of income through interest payments and are generally less volatile than stocks. This makes them particularly valuable during periods of market turbulence. Bonds can act as a cushion, smoothing out the fluctuations in a portfolio's value, which is crucial for investors who seek consistency and lower risk.

Bonds also play a defensive role in a portfolio. When stock markets decline, bonds often perform better or remain stable, helping to offset losses. This inverse relationship between bonds and stocks is fundamental to their role in diversification. By including bonds in your portfolio, you can achieve a more balanced risk-return profile.

Balancing Bonds with Stocks and Other Assets
Effective portfolio diversification involves balancing bonds with stocks and other asset classes. Each asset class has its unique characteristics and responds differently to market conditions. Here's how to achieve a balanced portfolio:

Stocks: Stocks are essential for growth. They offer higher potential returns but come with greater risk. Including a mix of large-cap, mid-cap, and small-cap stocks, as well as international stocks, can enhance diversification.

Bonds: Bonds provide stability and income. A mix of government, corporate, and municipal bonds, as well as bonds with varying maturities and credit qualities, can create a well-rounded bond allocation.

Other Assets: Adding other assets such as real estate, commodities, and cash can further diversify your portfolio. Real estate and commodities can provide inflation protection, while cash offers liquidity and security.

Strategies for Bond Allocation
Determining the right bond allocation depends on your investment goals, risk tolerance, and time horizon. Here are some strategies to consider:

Age-Based Allocation: A common approach is to allocate bonds based on your age. For instance, a simple rule of thumb is to subtract your age from 100 to determine the percentage of your portfolio to invest in stocks, with the remaining percentage in bonds. A 30-year-old might have 70% in stocks and 30% in bonds, while a 60-year-old might have 40% in stocks and 60% in bonds.

Risk Tolerance: If you have a lower risk tolerance, you might allocate a higher percentage to bonds. Conversely, if you can tolerate more risk, you might allocate more to stocks.

Investment Horizon: Your time horizon affects your bond allocation. If you're investing for a short-term goal, you might prioritize bonds to preserve capital. For long-term goals, a higher allocation to stocks might be appropriate, with bonds providing balance.

Bond Types and Maturities: Diversify within your bond allocation by including different types of bonds (government, corporate, municipal) and varying maturities (short-term, intermediate-term, long-term). This can help manage interest rate risk and credit risk.

Let's look at some practical examples of diversified portfolios:

Conservative Portfolio:

- **30% Stocks**: Primarily large-cap, dividend-paying stocks for income and stability.
- **60% Bonds**: A mix of government and high-quality corporate bonds.
- **10% Cash and Cash Equivalents**: For liquidity and security.

Balanced Portfolio:

- **50% Stocks**: A mix of large-cap, mid-cap, and small-cap stocks, including international exposure.

- **40% Bonds:** A diverse mix of government, corporate, and municipal bonds with varying maturities.
- **10% Real Estate and Commodities**: For additional diversification and inflation protection.

Aggressive Portfolio:

- **70% Stocks**: A diverse mix of domestic and international stocks across various sectors and market capitalizations.
- **20% Bonds**: Mainly corporate and high-yield bonds for income with some risk.
- **10% Alternative Investments**: Including real estate, commodities, and emerging markets for growth potential.

Case Studies of Balanced Investment Strategies

Conservative Investor:
Emily, a 55-year-old nearing retirement, prioritized capital preservation and income. She allocated 30% to a mix of dividend-paying stocks and 60% to a combination of government and high-quality corporate bonds. The remaining 10% was kept in cash equivalents. This strategy provided her with a steady income stream and protected her portfolio from significant market downturns.

Young Professional:
Jake, a 30-year-old professional, was focused on long-term growth. He allocated 70% to a diversified mix of stocks, including international and small-cap stocks, for growth. He invested 20% in corporate and high-yield bonds to balance risk and income.

The remaining 10% was in real estate and commodities, providing additional diversification and inflation protection. This aggressive strategy aimed to maximize growth while maintaining a degree of stability through bonds and alternative investments.

Balanced Approach:
Sophia, a 40-year-old with a moderate risk tolerance, chose a balanced portfolio. She allocated 50% to a mix of large-cap, mid-cap, and small-cap stocks, ensuring diversification across sectors and regions. She invested 40% in a combination of government, corporate, and municipal bonds, spreading risk across different types and maturities. The remaining 10% was allocated to real estate and commodities. This balanced approach provided growth potential while maintaining a solid foundation of income and stability.

Tools for Evaluating and Selecting Bonds
Selecting the right bonds for your investment portfolio requires careful analysis and access to reliable tools and resources. Bonds, though generally perceived as safer investments compared to stocks, come with their own set of risks and considerations. This section will explore resources for bond research and analysis, understanding bond ratings and reports, practical examples of bond selection, tools for tracking bond investments, and case studies of bond evaluation tools.

Effective bond investing begins with thorough research. Several resources can aid in evaluating bonds, providing crucial information about their performance, risk, and potential returns. Financial news websites, such as Bloomberg, CNBC, and Reuters, offer up-to-date information on bond markets and individual bonds. These platforms often provide insights from experts and analysts, which can be invaluable for making informed decisions.

Bond-specific databases and tools, like FINRA's Bond Center, provide comprehensive data on various bonds, including their prices, yields, and historical performance. Morningstar and Moody's Analytics also offer detailed research reports and analysis tools that help investors assess the quality and potential of different bonds.

Understanding Bond Ratings and Reports

Bond ratings are critical for evaluating the creditworthiness of a bond issuer. Ratings agencies such as Moody's, Standard & Poor's (S&P), and Fitch assign ratings that indicate the risk of default. These ratings range from high-grade (AAA or AA) to speculative (BB or lower). High-grade bonds are considered safer but offer lower yields, while lower-rated bonds provide higher yields but come with increased risk.

Understanding these ratings is essential. A bond with a AAA rating is deemed very secure, implying a low risk of default. Conversely, a bond rated BB or lower, often called a "junk bond," carries a higher risk but might attract investors with its potential for higher returns.

In addition to ratings, reports from these agencies provide detailed analyses of the issuer's financial health, industry conditions, and economic factors that might affect the bond's performance. Reviewing these reports can offer deeper insights into the risks and opportunities associated with a bond.

Practical Examples of Bond Selection

Selecting bonds involves balancing risk, return, and portfolio goals. Here's a practical example: suppose you are a young professional looking to diversify your investment portfolio.

You might start by allocating a portion of your portfolio to government bonds, which are considered safe and provide stable returns. Within this category, you could choose U.S. Treasury bonds, known for their security and liquidity.

Next, you might consider corporate bonds to enhance returns. Here, you could look at bonds issued by well-established companies with solid credit ratings (e.g., AA or higher). For instance, bonds from a company like Apple Inc., which has a strong financial standing, might be an attractive choice.

To diversify further, you could add some municipal bonds, particularly if they offer tax advantages in your state. For example, if you live in California, investing in California municipal bonds could provide tax-free income.

Tools for Tracking Bond Investments

Tracking your bond investments is crucial for managing your portfolio effectively. Several tools can assist in this task. Portfolio management software allows you to track all your investments, including bonds, in one place. These platforms offer features to monitor performance, analyze asset allocation, and review transaction history. More specialized tools, such as BondView and Morningstar's Bond Portfolio Manager, provide detailed tracking and analysis of bond investments. These tools can help you stay informed about interest rate changes, price fluctuations, and other factors that affect your bonds' performance.

Case Studies of Bond Evaluation Tools

Let’s consider a case study of an investor using Morningstar’s Bond Portfolio Manager. John, a mid-career professional, aims to create a balanced portfolio that includes a significant bond component.

Using Morningstar's tool, he inputs his bond holdings and reviews the comprehensive analysis provided. The tool offers insights into each bond's credit rating, yield, maturity, and performance metrics. John can see how his bonds are performing relative to market benchmarks and make informed decisions about buying or selling specific bonds.

Another case study involves an investor using FINRA's Bond Center. Sarah, a retiree, wants to ensure her investments provide stable income with minimal risk. She uses the Bond Center to search for municipal bonds from her home state, which offer tax-free income. The platform provides detailed information about each bond, including its yield, maturity date, and credit rating. By comparing different bonds, Sarah can select those that meet her income needs and risk tolerance.

Lastly, consider an investor using Bloomberg's financial news and analysis platform. Michael, a young entrepreneur, is interested in high-yield corporate bonds. He uses Bloomberg to access the latest market news, expert analyses, and detailed reports on various corporate bonds. This information helps him identify bonds that offer attractive yields while being mindful of the associated risks. By staying updated on market trends and issuer developments, Michael can make informed investment choices.

Practical Steps to Invest in Bonds

Investing in bonds can be a key component of a diversified investment strategy, providing a stable income stream and reducing overall portfolio risk. Understanding the practical steps to buy and sell bonds, setting up a bond ladder, and implementing strategies for regular bond investing is essential for achieving financial goals. In this section, we will explore these aspects in detail, offering practical tips for monitoring bond investments and sharing case studies of successful bond investing.

How to Buy and Sell Bonds

Buying and selling bonds can be straightforward once you understand the process and available platforms. Bonds can be purchased directly from the issuer, through a broker, or via bond funds.

Direct Purchase: Investors can buy bonds directly from the issuer. For example, U.S. Treasury bonds can be purchased through the TreasuryDirect website. This method usually involves no intermediary fees, making it cost-effective.

Through a Broker: Many investors use brokerage accounts to buy and sell bonds. Brokers such as Charles Schwab, Fidelity, and E*TRADE offer access to a wide range of bonds, including government, corporate, and municipal bonds. Brokers provide research tools and expert advice, but they may charge commissions or fees.

Bond Funds and ETFs: For those who prefer a more hands-off approach, bond mutual funds and exchange-traded funds (ETFs) are excellent options. These funds pool money from multiple investors to purchase a diversified portfolio of bonds, managed by professional fund managers.

When selling bonds, the process is similar. Investors can sell bonds through their broker or on the open market. It's important to be aware of the bond's market value, which can fluctuate based on interest rates and other economic factors.

Setting Up a Bond Ladder

A bond ladder is a strategy where an investor purchases bonds with different maturity dates, creating a steady income stream and reducing interest rate risk. Here's how to set up a bond ladder:

Choose the Ladder Length: Decide on the range of maturities for your bond ladder. For example, you might choose bonds maturing in one, two, three, four, and five years.

Select Bonds: Purchase bonds that mature at regular intervals. This way, you will have bonds maturing every year, providing liquidity and reinvestment opportunities.

Reinvest Proceeds: As each bond matures, reinvest the principal in a new bond with the longest maturity in your ladder. This maintains the ladder's structure and takes advantage of current interest rates.

For instance, if you start with a five-year bond ladder, when the one-year bond matures, reinvest in a new five-year bond. This approach ensures a continuous flow of income and mitigates the impact of interest rate fluctuations.

Example

Suppose an investor has $100,000 to invest, and due to his awareness of the **bond ladder portfolio** approach, he has made the following investment regime:

Year	0	1	2	3	4	5	6	7	8	9	10
Coupon Rate		5%	6%	7%	8%	9%	10%	11%	12%	13%	14%
Bond A	-10,000.00	10,500.00									
Bond B	-10,000.00	600.00	10,600.00								
Bond C	-10,000.00	700.00	700.00	10,700.00							
Bond D	-10,000.00	800.00	800.00	800.00	10,800.00						
Bond E	-10,000.00	900.00	900.00	900.00	900.00	10,900.00					
Bond F	-10,000.00	1,000.00	1,000.00	1,000.00	1,000.00	1,000.00	11,000.00				
Bond G	-10,000.00	1,100.00	1,100.00	1,100.00	1,100.00	1,100.00	1,100.00	11,100.00			
Bond H	-10,000.00	1,200.00	1,200.00	1,200.00	1,200.00	1,200.00	1,200.00	1,200.00	11,200.00		
Bond I	-10,000.00	1,300.00	1,300.00	1,300.00	1,300.00	1,300.00	1,300.00	1,300.00	1,300.00	11,300.00	
Bond J	-10,000.00	1,400.00	1,400.00	1,400.00	1,400.00	1,400.00	1,400.00	1,400.00	1,400.00	1,400.00	11,400.00
Total Investment	-100,000.00										

- We assume that the bonds are selling at par, so the initial investment is $10,000 in each bond, and as it is a cash outflow, it is represented by a negative number

- All bonds give annual coupons and, on the maturity dates, repay the principal
- Bonds with longer maturity pay higher coupon rates due to greater interest rate risk
- Once any of the bonds mature, they are reinvested for a different maturity per the current interest rate environment.
- The appearance of the portfolio above is like a ladder, and that is why this strategy is so named.

Dollar-Cost Averaging: This strategy involves investing a fixed amount in bonds at regular intervals, regardless of market conditions. It helps reduce the impact of market volatility and averages the purchase price over time.

Reinvestment of Interest: Automatically reinvest interest payments to buy more bonds. This compounding effect can significantly boost your investment returns over time.

Diversification: Spread your investments across different types of bonds (government, corporate, municipal) and varying credit qualities to minimize risk and maximize returns.

Stay Informed: Regularly review economic indicators and interest rate trends to make informed decisions about buying and selling bonds.

Practical Tips for Monitoring Bond Investments

Monitoring bond investments is crucial for ensuring they align with your financial goals and risk tolerance. Here are some practical tips:

- Platforms like Bloomberg, Morningstar, and brokerage websites offer tools for tracking bond performance, yields, and market conditions. Utilize these resources to stay updated on your investments.

- Schedule regular reviews of your bond portfolio, at least quarterly, to assess performance and make necessary adjustments. Check for any changes in the issuer's credit rating or market conditions that might impact your bonds.

- Ensure your bond portfolio remains diversified across different issuers, sectors, and maturities. This helps spread risk and avoid significant losses from any single bond defaulting.

- Revisit your bond investments when significant life events occur, such as retirement or changes in income. Adjust your strategy to ensure it continues to meet your financial needs.

To illustrate these principles, let's examine some case studies of successful bond investing.

Building a Bond Ladder for Retirement

Emma, a 60-year-old nearing retirement, wanted a stable income stream. She created a bond ladder with five-year maturities. Each year, she invested in bonds maturing from one to five years. As each bond matured, she reinvested in a new five-year bond. This strategy provided her with a predictable income and reduced the impact of interest rate fluctuations.

Dollar-Cost Averaging in Corporate Bonds

John, a 35-year-old professional, aimed to diversify his investment portfolio with corporate bonds. He allocated $500 monthly to purchase a mix of high-quality corporate bonds. By dollar-cost averaging, he spread his investments over time, reducing the risk of buying at a market peak. Over ten years, his disciplined approach yielded a robust bond portfolio with steady returns.

Diversification Across Bond Types

Sophia, a young entrepreneur, sought to balance her stock-heavy portfolio with bonds. She invested equally in U.S. Treasury bonds, high-rated corporate bonds, and municipal bonds. This diversification strategy provided her with stability, tax advantages, and higher yields than solely relying on government bonds.

Monitoring and Rebalancing

David, a 50-year-old investor, used online tools to monitor his bond investments regularly. He set alerts for any changes in credit ratings or significant market movements. When one of his corporate bonds was downgraded, he sold it and reinvested in a higher-rated bond. His proactive monitoring ensured his portfolio remained high quality and aligned with his risk tolerance.

Adapting to Life Changes

Lily, a 45-year-old investor, initially focused on high-yield bonds for growth. As she approached her children's college years, she shifted her strategy towards safer municipal bonds to secure their education fund. This adjustment provided stability and tax-free income, ensuring her investment goals were met.

In conclusion, investing in bonds can be a rewarding strategy for achieving financial stability and diversification.

Chapter 8
Exploring Real Estate Investment Trusts (REITs)

Definition and Basics of REITs

Real Estate Investment Trusts (REITs) offer a compelling way to invest in real estate without the need to directly purchase properties. A REIT is a company that owns, operates, or finances income-producing real estate across a range of property sectors. These companies pool the capital of numerous investors, making it possible for individual investors to earn dividends from real estate investments without buying, managing, or financing any properties themselves.

REITs are traded on major stock exchanges, similar to stocks. This feature provides liquidity, allowing investors to buy and sell shares with ease. Additionally, REITs must distribute at least 90% of their taxable income to shareholders annually in the form of dividends, providing a consistent income stream.

Types of REITs: Equity, Mortgage, and Hybrid

There are three primary types of REITs:

1. **Equity REITs**: These REITs own and operate income-producing real estate. Their revenues come primarily from leasing space and collecting rents on the properties they own. Equity REITs are typically involved in various property sectors, including residential, commercial, industrial, and retail.

2. **Mortgage REITs (mREITs)**: Mortgage REITs provide financing for income-producing real estate by purchasing or originating mortgages and mortgage-backed securities. Their income is generated from the interest earned on the mortgage loans.

3. **Hybrid REITs**: These REITs combine the investment strategies of both equity REITs and mortgage REITs. They own properties and invest in mortgages, thereby diversifying their income streams.

How REITs Work and Generate Income

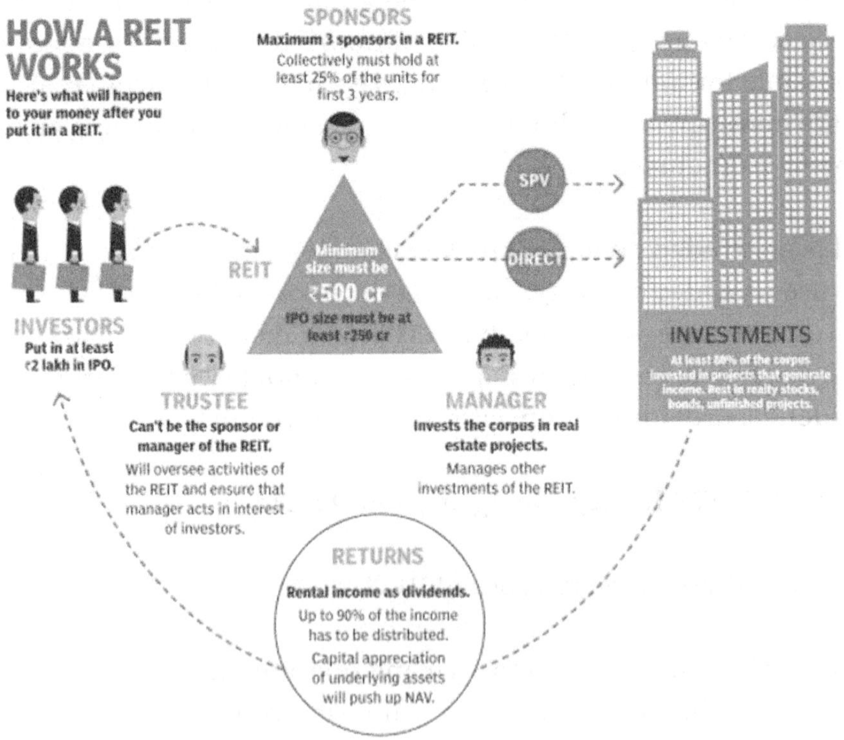

REITs generate income through the rental income from their properties and the interest income from the mortgages they own. The income is then distributed to shareholders as dividends. Equity REITs, for instance, earn rental income from tenants.

This income, after deducting operating expenses, is distributed to shareholders. Mortgage REITs earn income through the interest on their mortgage loans and mortgage-backed securities.

Investors benefit from both regular dividend income and the potential for capital appreciation if the value of the underlying properties or mortgages increases.

Practical Examples of REIT Investments

Example 1: Simon Property Group (Equity REIT) Simon Property Group, one of the largest equity REITs, specializes in retail properties like shopping malls. By investing in Simon Property Group, investors gain exposure to a portfolio of high-quality retail spaces without having to purchase any property themselves.

Example 2: Annaly Capital Management (Mortgage REIT) Annaly Capital Management is a significant player in the mortgage REIT space. It invests in various mortgage-backed securities, providing investors with exposure to the mortgage market and interest income from these investments.

Case Studies of REIT Portfolios

Case Study 1: Diversified Equity REIT Portfolio An investor allocates 30% of their portfolio to equity REITs, focusing on diversification across various property sectors. They invest in:

- Residential REITs: AvalonBay Communities, which owns apartment communities.
- Commercial REITs: Boston Properties, which owns office buildings.
- Industrial REITs: Prologis, specializing in logistics facilities.

- Retail REITs: Simon Property Group, focusing on shopping centers.

This diversified approach helps mitigate sector-specific risks and provides exposure to the broader real estate market.

Case Study 2: Focused Mortgage REIT Portfolio Another investor prefers the income potential of mortgage REITs and allocates 20% of their portfolio to:

- Residential Mortgage-Backed Securities: Annaly Capital Management.
- Commercial Real Estate Loans: Blackstone Mortgage Trust.

By investing in these mREITs, the investor gains exposure to the mortgage market and benefits from regular interest income.

Advantages of REIT Investments

- Regular Income: REITs are required to distribute a significant portion of their earnings as dividends, providing a steady income stream.

- Diversification: REITs allow investors to diversify their portfolios by adding real estate exposure without the need for direct property ownership.

- Liquidity: REIT shares are traded on major stock exchanges, offering high liquidity compared to direct real estate investments.

- Professional Management: REITs are managed by experienced professionals, reducing the burden on individual investors to manage properties.

Risks of REIT Investments

- **Market Risk**: Like any publicly traded security, REITs are subject to market fluctuations, which can impact share prices.

- **Interest Rate Risk**: REITs are sensitive to changes in interest rates. Rising interest rates can increase borrowing costs and make alternative income investments more attractive, potentially reducing the appeal of REITs.

- **Property-Specific Risk**: The performance of REITs is linked to the performance of their underlying properties. Economic downturns, changes in property values, and tenant defaults can negatively impact REIT income.

Practical Tips for Mitigating REIT Risks

- **Diversify Your REIT Holdings**: Invest in REITs across different sectors and geographic locations to reduce exposure to any single market.
- **Monitor Interest Rates**: Keep an eye on interest rate trends and understand how they can affect REIT performance.
- **Research Property Portfolios**: Investigate the properties within a REIT's portfolio to ensure they are diversified and located in economically stable areas.
- **Assess Management Quality**: Look at the experience and track record of the REIT's management team to gauge their ability to navigate market challenges.

Case Study: Risk Management Through Diversification

An investor allocates 25% of their portfolio to REITs, spreading investments across residential, commercial, and industrial sectors.

By diversifying their REIT holdings, they reduce the risk of a downturn in any one sector significantly impacting their overall returns.

Role of REITs in Portfolio Diversification

REITs play a crucial role in diversification by providing exposure to the real estate market, which often has a low correlation with stocks and bonds. This low correlation helps reduce overall portfolio volatility and enhances long-term returns.

Strategies for REIT Allocation

- **Percentage Allocation:** Allocate a specific percentage of your portfolio to REITs based on your risk tolerance and investment goals. A common allocation ranges from 5% to 20%.

- **Sector Diversification**: Spread your REIT investments across different property sectors to mitigate sector-specific risks.

- **Geographic Diversification**: Invest in REITs with properties in various geographic regions to reduce location-specific risks.

Practical Examples of Diversified Portfolios with REITs

Example 1: Conservative Portfolio

A conservative investor allocates 10% of their portfolio to REITs, focusing on well-established equity REITs with a history of stable dividends. The rest of the portfolio includes:

- 50% Bonds: Providing income and stability.
- 30% Blue-Chip Stocks: Offering growth potential with lower volatility.
- 10% Cash: For liquidity and emergency needs.

Example 2: Aggressive Portfolio

An aggressive investor allocates 20% of their portfolio to REITs, including both equity and mortgage REITs. The rest of the portfolio includes:

- 60% Stocks: Including a mix of growth and value stocks for high returns.
- 15% Bonds: For income and risk mitigation.
- 5% Alternatives: Such as commodities or private equity for additional diversification.

Key Resources for REIT Analysis

Effective REIT investment requires thorough research. Key resources include:

REIT Websites: Most REITs have detailed websites with financial reports, property information, and management insights.

- **Financial News Platforms**: Websites like Bloomberg, Reuters, and MarketWatch provide updates on REIT performance and industry trends.
- **Analyst Reports**: Brokerage firms and financial analysts often publish reports and ratings on REITs.
- **Industry Associations**: Organizations like the National Association of Real Estate Investment Trusts (NAREIT) offer valuable data and resources.

Chapter 9

Exploring Tax Liens and Tax Deeds

Tax liens and tax deeds present unique investment opportunities that differ significantly from traditional real estate and stock market investments. These methods offer the potential for high returns by targeting delinquent property taxes. When property owners fail to pay their taxes, local governments have the authority to sell tax liens or tax deeds to recover the owed amounts. Investors can then earn interest, penalties, or potentially acquire the property itself.

A tax lien represents a legal claim against a property due to unpaid property taxes. When an investor purchases a tax lien, they pay the outstanding taxes on behalf of the property owner. In return, the investor earns interest on the amount paid. If the property owner fails to pay the taxes plus interest within a specified period, the investor may initiate foreclosure proceedings to acquire the property.

A tax deed, on the other hand, involves the outright purchase of the property at a tax sale auction. When taxes remain unpaid, the government can sell the property to recover the debt. The winning bidder receives the deed to the property, often at a price significantly below market value.

The legal framework for tax lien and tax deed investing varies by state, with specific rules governing the process. Generally, the steps include:

Identification: Investors identify properties with unpaid taxes by reviewing county tax records.

Auction: Properties with tax liens or deeds are auctioned publicly, either in person or online.

Bidding: Investors bid on tax liens or deeds, with the highest bidder winning the auction.

Payment: The winning bidder pays the owed taxes (for liens) or the auction price (for deeds).

Redemption Period: Property owners have a redemption period to repay the owed amount plus interest (for liens). If not repaid, the investor can foreclose on the property.

Deed Acquisition: Deed Acquisition: For tax deeds, the investor gains ownership of the property immediately after the auction. Most tax deeds are sold by the county with extinguished mortgages and liens, excluding state or county liens.

Practical Examples of Tax Lien and Deed Investments

Example 1: Tax Lien Investment

An investor purchases a tax lien certificate for $5,000 on a residential property. The annual interest rate on the lien is 10%. The property owner repays the debt, including the interest, after one year. The investor receives $5,500 ($5,000 principal + $500 interest), earning a $500 profit.

Example 2: Tax Deed Investment

An investor buys a tax deed for $50,000 at an auction for a property valued at $150,000. After acquiring the deed, the investor decides to renovate and sell the property.

After renovations costing $20,000, the property sells for $180,000. The investor's profit is $110,000 ($180,000 sale price - $50,000 purchase price - $20,000 renovation cost).

Case Studies of Tax Lien and Deed Portfolios

Case Study 1: Diversified Tax Lien Portfolio

An investor builds a diversified tax lien portfolio by purchasing liens on various residential and commercial properties across different counties. By spreading investments, they reduce the risk of any single lien failing to pay off. Over five years, the investor earns an average annual return of 12%, significantly enhancing their overall investment returns.

Case Study 2: Strategic Tax Deed Acquisition

An investor focuses on acquiring tax deeds in up-and-coming neighborhoods. They purchase several properties at below-market prices, renovate them, and either sell or rent them out. This strategy results in substantial profits from property sales and consistent rental income, showcasing the potential of tax deed investments.

Tax lien and deed investing offer several potential benefits:

- **High Returns**: Interest rates on tax liens can be significantly higher than traditional investments.

Tax deeds can be purchased below market value, providing opportunities for substantial profits.

- **Diversification:** These investments add diversity to a portfolio, reducing overall risk by not being directly correlated with stock market performance.

- **Property Acquisition**: Investors have the potential to acquire properties at a fraction of their market value, especially through tax deeds.

- **Risks Involved**: Foreclosure, Legal Issues, Property Conditions

Despite the benefits, there are risks to consider:

- **Foreclosure**: With tax liens, if the property owner does not repay the debt, the investor must foreclose on the property, which can be a lengthy and costly process.

- **Legal Issues**: Navigating the legal framework for tax liens and deeds requires understanding state-specific laws and regulations. Legal missteps can lead to significant losses.

- **Property Conditions**: Investors may acquire properties in poor condition, requiring substantial renovation costs. Conducting thorough due diligence is crucial.

Balancing tax lien and deed investments with other assets can mitigate risks and enhance overall portfolio stability. Integrating these investments with stocks, bonds, and real estate can provide diversification and potential for higher returns.

Practical Tips for Mitigating Risks

- **Thorough Research:** Investigate the property's condition, market value, and potential issues before investing.

- **Legal Understanding:** Familiarize yourself with state-specific laws and regulations regarding tax liens and deeds.

- **Diversification:** Spread investments across various properties and locations to reduce risk.

- **Budget for Costs**: Allocate funds for potential renovation and legal costs associated with foreclosures or property improvements.

Case Studies of Successful Risk Management

Comprehensive Due Diligence
An investor conducts extensive research before purchasing tax liens, including property inspections and legal checks. This approach helps them avoid problematic properties and focus on high-potential investments, resulting in consistent returns and minimal losses.

Diversified Tax Deed Strategy
A wise investor diversifies their tax deed investments across residential and commercial properties in multiple states. This strategy reduces the impact of any single investment performing poorly and leverages different real estate market conditions for overall stability and growth.

Tools and Resources for Researching Properties
Effective tax lien and deed investing require comprehensive research. Key resources include:

- **County Tax Records:** Local government websites provide information on properties with unpaid taxes.
- **Property Assessment Sites:** Websites like Zillow and Realtor.com offer property value estimates and market trends.
- **Auction Platforms:** Online auction sites list available tax liens and deeds and provide auction details.
- **Legal Resources**: State and county websites offer information on legal requirements and procedures.

Assessing the value and condition of a property is crucial for successful investing. Consider the following steps:

- Market Analysis: Compare similar properties in the area to determine market value.
- Physical Inspection: If possible, visit the property to assess its condition and identify potential repair costs.
- Title Search: Conduct a title search to uncover any liens or legal issues that may affect the property's value.

Practical Examples of Due Diligence

Example 1: In-Depth Market Analysis
An investor identifies a tax lien on a residential property and conducts a market analysis. They compare recent sales of similar properties in the area, assessing average prices and market trends. This research helps them determine the property's potential value and make an informed investment decision.

Example 2: Property Inspection and Title Search
Before purchasing a tax deed, an investor inspects the property and performs a title search. They discover the property requires minor repairs and confirm there are no other outstanding liens. This due diligence ensures the investor makes a well-informed bid at the auction.

Strategies for Identifying Promising Investments

To identify promising tax lien and deed investments, consider these strategies:

1. **Focus on High-Growth Areas**: Target properties in regions with strong economic growth and rising property values.
2. **Analyze Historical Data**: Review historical auction results and lien redemptions to identify patterns and high-performing areas.
3. **Network with Local Experts**: Engage with local real estate professionals, attorneys, and investors to gain insights and recommendations.

Case Studies of Thorough Property Evaluation

Case Study 1: High-Growth Area Focus
An investor focuses on purchasing tax liens in a rapidly growing city. By targeting properties in high-demand areas, they experience high redemption rates and significant interest earnings, leading to consistent profits.

Case Study 2: Networking and Expert Insights
Another investor builds relationships with local real estate agents and attorneys. These connections provide valuable information on promising tax deed opportunities and potential pitfalls, enhancing the investor's success rate and profitability.

Navigating the Auction Process

Understanding Auction Procedures and Rules
Navigating the auction process requires understanding the specific procedures and rules governing tax lien and deed auctions. These can vary by state and county but generally include:

Registration: Investors must register to participate in auctions, often requiring proof of funds.

- **Bidding Rules**: Auctions may be competitive (bidding up the interest rate or purchase price) or non-competitive (fixed interest rates or prices).

- **Payment Requirements**: Winning bidders typically need to pay immediately or within a specified period.

Preparation is key to successful auction participation. Steps include:

Research and Due Diligence: Identify and evaluate properties before the auction.

Budgeting: Set a budget and determine maximum bid amounts for each property.

Financing: Ensure you have the necessary funds available for bidding and potential post-auction expenses.

Practical Tips for Successful Bidding

Set Limits: Establish maximum bid amounts based on property value and potential returns.

Stay Informed: Monitor auction updates and changes to procedures or available properties.

Be Disciplined: Stick to your budget and avoid overbidding due to competition.

Managing Post-Auction Processes

After winning a bid, managing the post-auction process involves:

- Payment: Complete the payment within the required timeframe.
- Documentation: Obtain and file necessary documents, such as tax lien certificates or deeds.
- Property Management: For tax deeds, plan for property management, including potential renovations or sales strategies.

Case Studies of Auction Experiences

Disciplined Bidding Strategy

An investor sets strict bidding limits based on thorough research and sticks to them during the auction. By avoiding overbidding, they secure tax liens with attractive interest rates and successfully redeem several liens, earning substantial returns.

Post-Auction Property Management

After acquiring a tax deed, an investor quickly arranges for property inspections and necessary renovations. They successfully sell the improved property at a significant profit, demonstrating the importance of efficient post-auction management.

Setting Up a Tax Lien and Deed Investment Plan

A structured investment plan helps achieve financial goals. Key components include:

- **Define Objectives**: Determine whether you seek income, property acquisition, or diversification.
- **Set Allocation Targets**: Decide on the portion of your portfolio to allocate to tax liens and deeds.
- **Develop Criteria**: Establish criteria for selecting investments, such as property type, location, and minimum return rates.

For those new to tax lien and deed investing, consider these initial steps:

- **Educate Yourself**: Learn about the legal framework, auction processes, and due diligence requirements.
- **Start Small**: Begin with a few smaller investments to gain experience and build confidence.
- **Seek Guidance**: Consult with experienced investors or professionals to navigate the complexities of tax lien and deed investing.

Practical Tips for Building a Portfolio

- **Diversify**: Invest in a variety of properties and locations to spread risk.
- **Reinvest Earnings**: Use interest earnings or profits from property sales to reinvest and grow your portfolio.

Monitor Performance: Regularly review your investments and adjust your strategy based on performance and market conditions.

Monitoring and Managing Investments

Effective monitoring and management that are crucial for success include:

Track Redemptions: Keep detailed records of lien redemptions and interest payments.

Manage Properties: For acquired properties, plan for maintenance, renovations, or sales.

Adjust Strategies: Adapt your investment strategy based on market trends and individual investment performance.

Case Studies of Beginner Investors

Starting Small and Learning
A beginner investor starts with a few small tax lien investments, focusing on learning the process and understanding the market. Over time, they build knowledge and confidence, gradually increasing their investment size and achieving consistent returns.

Guided Investment Approach
Another beginner seeks guidance from experienced investors and attends workshops on tax lien and deed investing. By leveraging expert advice and starting with well-researched investments, they build a successful portfolio and avoid common pitfalls.

Ultimately, investing in tax liens and tax deeds offers a unique and potentially lucrative opportunity for those willing to conduct thorough research and navigate the complexities of the process.

Chapter 10
FOREX INVESTING

The Foreign Exchange Market, often abbreviated as FOREX or FX, is a global decentralized market where currencies are traded. It is by far the largest and most liquid financial market in the world, with a daily trading volume surpassing $6 trillion. This figure dwarfs the trading volumes of all other financial markets, including the stock market. The FOREX market operates 24 hours a day, five days a week, reflecting its global nature. Unlike traditional financial markets, which have set trading hours, the FOREX market is constantly active, driven by the overlapping trading sessions in major financial hubs across different time zones.

The Global Nature of FOREX Trading

The FOREX market is truly global, encompassing various regions and time zones. Major trading centers include London, New York, Tokyo, and Sydney, with each center playing a crucial role in maintaining the market's continuous operation. The market's decentralized structure means there is no single exchange where all currency transactions occur. Instead, trading happens over-the-counter (OTC) through a network of financial institutions, corporations, governments, and individual traders.

The 24-hour operation of the FOREX market is one of its most attractive features, especially for traders who require flexibility. The market begins in Sydney, Australia, and moves across the globe with the time zones, passing through Tokyo, London, and finally New York. This round-the-clock operation allows traders to react to news, economic events, and market developments as they happen, without being constrained by market hours.

Daily Trading Volume Comparison: FOREX vs. Stock Market

To fully appreciate the scale of the FOREX market, it's essential to compare its daily trading volume with that of the stock market. On average, the daily trading volume in the FOREX market is more than $6 trillion, while the combined trading volume of global stock markets is around $200 billion. This comparison highlights the massive liquidity in the FOREX market, making it easier to enter and exit positions quickly without significantly impacting prices.

Introduction to Currency Pairs

In FOREX trading, currencies are always traded in pairs. This means that when you buy one currency, you are simultaneously selling another. The two currencies involved in a transaction are called the base currency and the quote currency. The base currency is the first currency listed in the pair, while the quote currency is the second. For example, in the EUR/USD currency pair, the euro (EUR) is the base currency, and the U.S. dollar (USD) is the quote currency.

The price of a currency pair is expressed as the amount of the quote currency needed to purchase one unit of the base currency. For instance, if the EUR/USD pair is quoted at 1.20, it means that 1 euro can be exchanged for 1.20 U.S. dollars. If the price of the EUR/USD pair rises to 1.25, the euro has strengthened relative to the dollar, meaning it now takes more dollars to buy one euro.

Currency pairs are typically divided into three categories: majors, minors, and exotics. The major pairs all include the U.S. dollar and are the most traded in the market. Examples include EUR/USD, GBP/USD, and USD/JPY. Minor pairs do not include the U.S. dollar but involve other major currencies like the euro, yen, or British pound. Examples include EUR/GBP and EUR/JPY. Exotic pairs involve one major currency and one currency from an emerging or smaller economy, such as USD/TRY (U.S. dollar and Turkish lira).

How Currency Pairs are Quoted

Understanding how currency pairs are quoted is fundamental to FOREX trading. When you see a currency pair quote, it typically consists of two prices: the bid price and the ask price. The bid price is the highest price that a buyer is willing to pay for the base currency, while the ask price is the lowest price at which a seller is willing to sell the base currency. The difference between these two prices is known as the spread, which represents the transaction cost for the trade.

For example, if the EUR/USD pair is quoted as 1.2050/1.2053, it means that you can sell 1 euro for 1.2050 U.S. dollars (bid price) or buy 1 euro for 1.2053 U.S. dollars (ask price). The spread in this case is 3 pips (1.2053 - 1.2050), which is the cost you incur for the transaction.

The spread can vary depending on the currency pair, market conditions, and the broker. Majors, which are more liquid, tend to have tighter spreads compared to exotic pairs, which are less liquid and more volatile.

The Role of Market Participants

The FOREX market is made up of a diverse group of participants, each with different motives for trading currencies. These participants include:

Central Banks: Central banks, such as the Federal Reserve (Fed) or the European Central Bank (ECB), play a crucial role in the FOREX market. They intervene in the market to stabilize or devalue their currencies as part of their monetary policies. Central banks also use the FOREX market to influence their country's economic performance by adjusting interest rates.

Commercial Banks: Large commercial banks facilitate most of the daily transactions in the FOREX market. These banks trade on behalf of their clients, which include businesses, governments, and institutional investors. Commercial banks also engage in proprietary trading, where they trade currencies to profit from market fluctuations.

Hedge Funds and Investment Managers: Hedge funds and institutional investors like pension funds and mutual funds are significant players in the FOREX market. They use the market to hedge against currency risk or to speculate on currency movements to generate profits.

Corporations: Multinational corporations participate in the FOREX market to manage the risks associated with foreign currency fluctuations.

For example, a U.S. company that imports goods from Europe may buy euros in the FOREX market to pay for its imports, thereby locking in a favorable exchange rate.

Retail Traders: Retail traders, including individual investors, have become increasingly active in the FOREX market. These traders use online trading platforms provided by brokers to speculate on currency movements. While retail traders make up a small portion of the market in terms of volume, their numbers have grown significantly over the years.

Key Features of the FOREX Market

Several key features distinguish the FOREX market from other financial markets, making it unique and attractive to traders:

Liquidity: The FOREX market is the most liquid market in the world, with the ability to execute large orders with minimal price movement. This high level of liquidity ensures that traders can enter and exit positions quickly and at competitive prices.

Leverage: One of the most attractive aspects of FOREX trading is the availability of leverage. Leverage allows traders to control large positions with a relatively small amount of capital. However, while leverage amplifies potential profits, it also increases the risk of significant losses.

Volatility: Currency prices can be highly volatile, leading to rapid and substantial price movements. This volatility creates opportunities for traders to profit from short-term price fluctuations but also presents risks, especially when trading with leverage.

Low Transaction Costs: Compared to other financial markets, the transaction costs in the FOREX market are relatively low. The primary cost associated with trading is the spread, which can be as low as a fraction of a pip for major currency pairs.

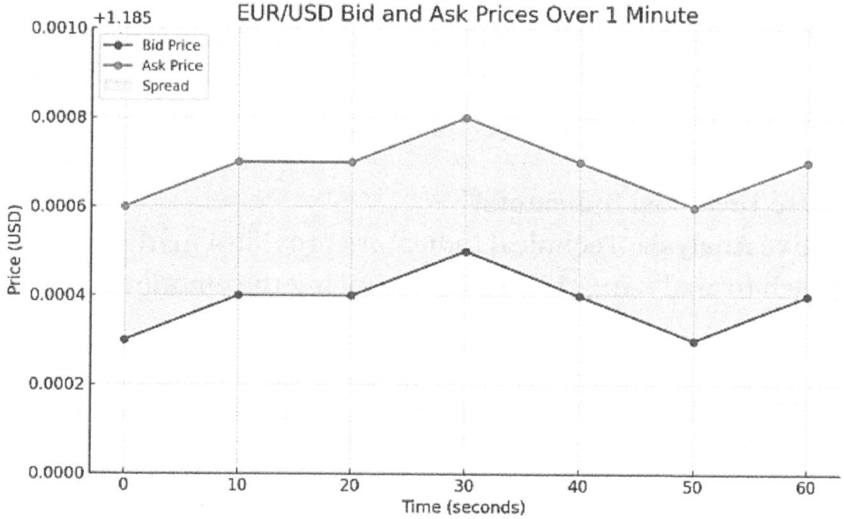

The graph above compares the bid and ask prices of the EUR/USD currency pair over a 1-minute period. The shaded area between the two lines represents the spread, highlighting the difference between the bid and ask prices.

Understanding and Using Technical Indicators

In the world of FOREX trading, technical indicators are powerful tools that help traders make informed decisions. Unlike fundamental analysis, which focuses on economic data and news, technical analysis relies on historical price data and various mathematical calculations to predict future market movements. This section will guide you through some of the most popular technical indicators and how they can be used to improve your trading strategy.

Introduction to Technical Indicators
Technical indicators are statistical tools that traders use to analyze past market data, such as prices and volumes, to forecast future price movements. These indicators are vital because they help traders identify trends, reversals, and potential entry and exit points in the market. Understanding how to use these indicators effectively can give traders an edge in the competitive FOREX market.

Why Use Technical Indicators?
Objective Analysis: Technical indicators provide a mathematical approach to analyzing the market, reducing the emotional impact of trading.

Trend Identification: Indicators can help identify whether a market is trending upwards, downwards, or is in a range.

Timing: They can assist traders in finding the best times to enter or exit trades.

Moving Averages: Smoothing Out the Noise
One of the most widely used technical indicators is the moving average (MA). A moving average smooths out price data by creating a constantly updated average price over a specific period. This helps traders see the general direction of the market without getting distracted by short-term fluctuations.

Types of Moving Averages

Simple Moving Average (SMA):
The SMA is calculated by adding up the prices over a certain period and dividing by the number of periods. For example, a 50-day SMA is the average of the closing prices of the last 50 days.
Use Case: The SMA is often used to identify long-term trends.

A common strategy is to look for "crossovers," where a short-term SMA crosses above a long-term SMA (a bullish signal) or below it (a bearish signal).

Exponential Moving Average (EMA):
The EMA gives more weight to recent prices, making it more responsive to new information. This makes the EMA more sensitive to recent price changes compared to the SMA.

Use Case: The EMA is favored by traders looking for quicker signals. It's commonly used in strategies that require timely decision-making, such as day trading.

Golden Cross and Death Cross
Two popular terms associated with moving averages are the "Golden Cross" and the "Death Cross."

Golden Cross: This occurs when a short-term moving average (like the 50-day SMA) crosses above a long-term moving average (like the 200-day SMA). It's considered a bullish signal, indicating that the market may be entering an uptrend.

Death Cross: The opposite of the Golden Cross, the Death Cross happens when a short-term moving average crosses below a long-term moving average. This is a bearish signal, suggesting that the market could be heading into a downtrend.

Here is a chart illustrating the impact of the 50-day and 200-day moving averages on trade decisions across different quarters. This visual representation highlights how the Golden Cross and Death Cross could affect the number of buy/sell signals.

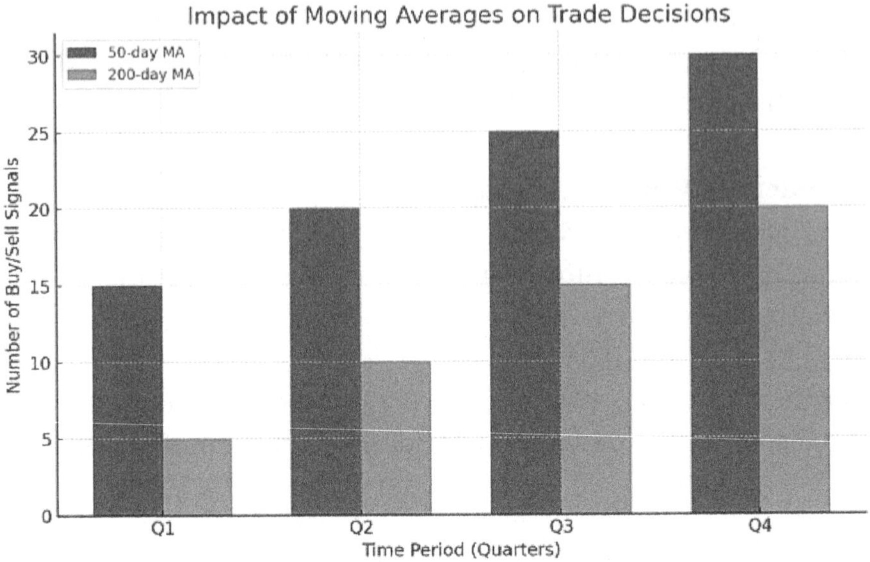

Relative Strength Index (RSI): Gauging Market Momentum
The Relative Strength Index (RSI) is another essential technical indicator. It measures the speed and change of price movements to determine whether a currency pair is overbought or oversold. The RSI is plotted on a scale of 0 to 100 and typically uses a 14-day period for its calculation.

Understanding the RSI Scale
Overbought Condition (Above 70): When the RSI rises above 70, it suggests that the currency pair might be overbought and due for a correction or pullback. This can be a signal to sell or consider tightening stop-losses.

Oversold Condition (Below 30): When the RSI falls below 30, it indicates that the currency pair might be oversold and could be due for a bounce or reversal. This can be a signal to buy or to prepare for a potential price increase.

Divergence: A Powerful RSI Signal

RSI divergence occurs when the price of a currency pair is moving in the opposite direction to the RSI. This can be a powerful signal of a potential reversal:

Bullish Divergence: Occurs when the price makes a lower low, but the RSI makes a higher low. This suggests that the downtrend might be weakening, and a reversal to the upside could be on the horizon.

Bearish Divergence: Occurs when the price makes a higher high, but the RSI makes a lower high. This suggests that the uptrend might be losing momentum, and a reversal to the downside could be imminent.

How to Use RSI in Trading
Traders often use the RSI in conjunction with other indicators to confirm signals. For instance, if the RSI shows an overbought condition and a bearish divergence at a resistance level, it might be a strong signal to sell.

Example: Applying RSI in a Trade

Imagine you're trading the EUR/USD pair. The RSI has climbed above 70, indicating an overbought condition. At the same time, the price is approaching a known resistance level. You notice that the RSI is also showing a bearish divergence, as it begins to fall while the price continues to rise. Based on this, you decide to enter a short position, expecting the price to drop.

Bollinger Bands: Measuring Market Volatility

Bollinger Bands are a technical indicator that consists of a simple moving average (usually 20 periods) and two standard deviation lines plotted above and below the moving average. These bands expand and contract based on market volatility, providing insights into potential breakout points.

Understanding Bollinger Bands

Upper Band: Represents a level that is two standard deviations above the moving average. If the price touches or exceeds the upper band, it might indicate that the asset is overbought.

Lower Band: Represents a level that is two standard deviations below the moving average. If the price touches or falls below the lower band, it might indicate that the asset is oversold.

The Squeeze: A Precursor to Breakouts

One of the key features of Bollinger Bands is the "squeeze," which occurs when the bands narrow due to reduced volatility. A squeeze often precedes a significant price move, but it does not predict the direction of the move.

Breakout Strategy: When a squeeze occurs, traders watch for a breakout above or below the bands as a signal to enter a trade. For example, if the price breaks above the upper band after a squeeze, it could be a signal to buy.

Using Bollinger Bands with RSI

Combining Bollinger Bands with the RSI can provide more reliable trading signals. For instance, if the price breaks above the upper band and the RSI is in overbought territory, it might be a strong signal to sell.

Case Study: Using Technical Indicators in Real-World Trades
Let's apply what we've learned to real-world case studies to see how these indicators can be used in actual trading situations.

Example 1: George Soros and the Bank of England
George Soros's legendary short trade against the British pound in 1992 is a classic example of combining fundamental analysis with technical indicators.

Using Moving Averages: During the lead-up to Black Wednesday, the pound's price showed signs of weakness. A trader using technical analysis might have observed a Death Cross, where the 50-day SMA crossed below the 200-day SMA, signaling a strong downtrend.

Using RSI: The RSI likely showed overbought conditions before the pound began its descent, providing an additional signal to sell.

Example 2: Stanley Druckenmiller and the German Mark
Stanley Druckenmiller's trade on the German mark during the 1992 ERM crisis is another example where technical indicators could have played a crucial role.

Using Bollinger Bands: Before the mark surged, a trader might have noticed a squeeze in the Bollinger Bands, indicating a potential breakout. Once the price broke above the upper band, it would have been a strong signal to buy.

Using RSI: The RSI might have shown oversold conditions just before the mark began its rise, providing a signal to enter a long position.

Let's delve into four prominent trading strategies: **Trend Following, Range Trading, Swing Trading, and Day Trading**. Each strategy will be discussed with practical examples and a focus on risk management techniques, including the use of stop-loss orders and leverage.

Overview of Different Trading Strategies

Trend Following

Trend Following is a strategy based on the principle that markets tend to move in trends. This strategy involves identifying and trading in the direction of the current market trend. The key to successful trend following is to enter a trade when the trend is established and ride it until there are signs of reversal.

How to Implement Trend Following:

Identify the Trend: Use technical indicators such as moving averages (MA) or trendlines to determine the current market trend. For instance, if the 50-day moving average is above the 200-day moving average, the market is in an uptrend.

Entry Points: Enter a trade when the price breaks above a resistance level in an uptrend or below a support level in a downtrend.

Exit Points: Exit the trade when the trend shows signs of reversal. This can be identified using indicators like the Relative Strength Index (RSI) or moving average crossovers.

Example: Suppose the EUR/USD pair has been in an uptrend for the past three weeks. The 50-day MA is consistently above the 200-day MA. You decide to enter a long position when the price breaks above a previous resistance level of 1.1050. You set a stop-loss order at 1.1000 and aim to exit when the price reaches 1.1150.

Range Trading

Range Trading involves identifying levels of support and resistance and trading within that range. This strategy works best in a market that is moving sideways rather than trending.

How to Implement Range Trading:

Identify the Range: Look for price levels where the market has repeatedly reversed direction. Draw horizontal lines to mark these support and resistance levels.

Entry Points: Buy at the support level and sell at the resistance level. Use technical indicators like the Stochastic Oscillator to confirm overbought or oversold conditions.

Exit Points: Exit the trade when the price approaches the opposite boundary of the range.

Example: Consider the USD/JPY pair trading between 110.00 (support) and 112.00 (resistance). You decide to buy at 110.10 and set a stop-loss at 109.80. You plan to sell when the price reaches 111.90.

Swing Trading

Swing Trading aims to capture short- to medium-term gains in a stock (or currency pair) over a period of days to weeks. It involves identifying the highs and lows of the market and taking advantage of price swings.

How to Implement Swing Trading:

Identify Swing Points: Look for recent highs and lows on the price chart. Use indicators like the Moving Average Convergence Divergence (MACD) to spot potential reversal points.

Entry Points: Enter trades when the price pulls back to a support level in an uptrend or a resistance level in a downtrend.

Exit Points: Exit when the price shows signs of reversing direction or when a predetermined target is reached.

Example: If the GBP/USD pair is experiencing a short-term pullback after reaching a high of 1.3050, you might buy at 1.2950 with a target price of 1.3100. Set a stop-loss order at 1.2900 to manage risk.

Day Trading

Day Trading involves buying and selling financial instruments within the same trading day, with the goal of profiting from short-term price movements. This strategy requires quick decision-making and a good understanding of market dynamics.

How to Implement Day Trading:

Identify Short-Term Trends: Use intraday charts and indicators like Bollinger Bands and RSI to identify short-term price movements.

Entry Points: Enter trades based on short-term trends and patterns. For example, buy when a breakout occurs or sell when a reversal pattern forms.

Exit Points: Exit trades based on predefined targets or stop-loss levels. Day traders often set tight stop-loss orders to minimize losses.

Example: Suppose the AUD/USD pair is showing a bullish trend on a 15-minute chart. You decide to buy at 0.6800 and set a profit target at 0.6830. You place a stop-loss order at 0.6780 to protect against adverse movements.

Chapter 11
THE POWER OF DOLLAR COST AVERAGING

Understanding Dollar Cost Averaging as an Investment Strategy

Dollar Cost Averaging (DCA) is an investment strategy that involves regularly investing a fixed amount of money into a particular asset, such as stocks, bonds, or mutual funds, regardless of the asset's price. This systematic approach helps investors mitigate the impact of market volatility and avoid the pitfalls of trying to time the market. By spreading out investments over time, DCA reduces the risk of making large investments at inopportune moments.

For example, if an investor commits to investing $500 monthly into a mutual fund, they will purchase more shares when prices are low and fewer shares when prices are high. Over time, this can result in a lower average cost per share compared to making a one-time lump-sum investment.

How It Works in Different Market Conditions

Dollar Cost Averaging is effective in various market conditions:

Bull Markets: In a rising market, the investor buys shares at increasing prices, potentially leading to higher overall portfolio value. Although the average cost per share may be higher compared to a one-time investment at the market's start, the investor still benefits from overall market growth.

Bear Markets: In a declining market, DCA allows the investor to buy more shares at lower prices. This strategy can significantly reduce the average cost per share and position the investor for substantial gains when the market eventually recovers

Sideways Markets: In a market with little movement, DCA helps maintain discipline and consistency. The investor continues to accumulate shares without worrying about short-term price fluctuations, ensuring a steady growth of their investment over time.

Practical Examples and Illustrations

Consider two investors: Alex and Jordan. Alex invests $6,000 as a lump sum at the beginning of the year, while Jordan invests $500 monthly over the same year. Let's see how their investments fare in different market conditions:

Example 1: Bull Market

Imagine Investor A starts with $10,000 and invests it all in a bull market. Over the course of the year, the market grows consistently, and by the end of the year, the share price increases by 20%. Investor A ends up with a portfolio valued at $12,000. With no additional investments made, the number of shares purchased initially remains constant.

Example 2: Bear Market

Now, consider Investor B, who also starts with $10,000 but invests it in a bear market. Over the same one-year period, the market experiences declines, and share prices drop.

Investor B continues to invest regularly, purchasing more shares at the lower prices throughout the year. By the end of the year, even though the portfolio value might have dropped to $9,000, Investor B has accumulated a significantly higher number of shares.

Comparing the Two Investors

Here's where the strategy shines. If no additional investments are made in the following year, and the bear market returns to a bull market, Investor B, with more shares, will experience a stronger portfolio recovery. As the share prices rise, the value of Investor B's portfolio will surpass that of Investor A. This is because Investor B had more shares accumulated at the end of the first year, giving them a larger base to benefit from the market rebound.

The graph below shows the share accumulation of Investor A, who invests in a Bull Market, and Investor B, who invests in a Bear Market over 1 year. Despite both starting with the same investment amount, Investor B accumulates more shares due to lower share prices in the Bear Market.

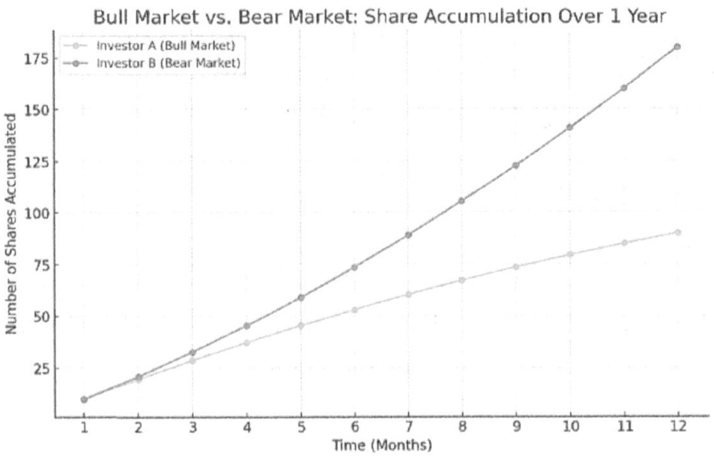

This bar chart compares the portfolio values of Investor A and Investor B at the end of Year 1. Despite accumulating more shares, Investor B's portfolio value is lower than Investor A's due to the market conditions.

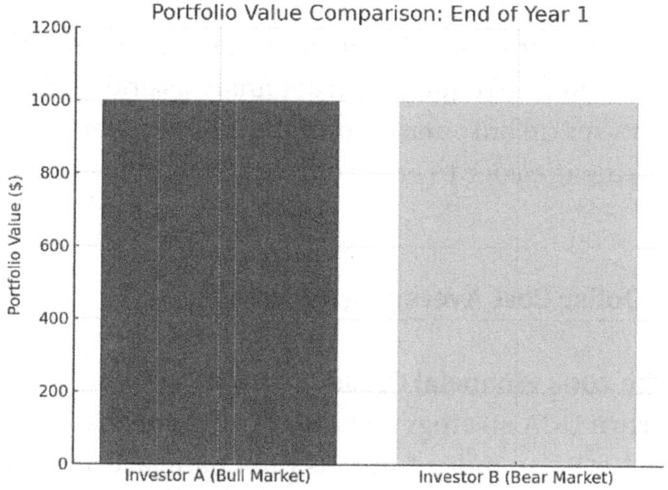

The line graph below illustrates how the portfolio values of Investor A and Investor B progress during Year 2, with the market recovering to a Bull Market. Investor B's portfolio surpasses Investor A's, demonstrating the long-term benefits of investing during a Bear Market.

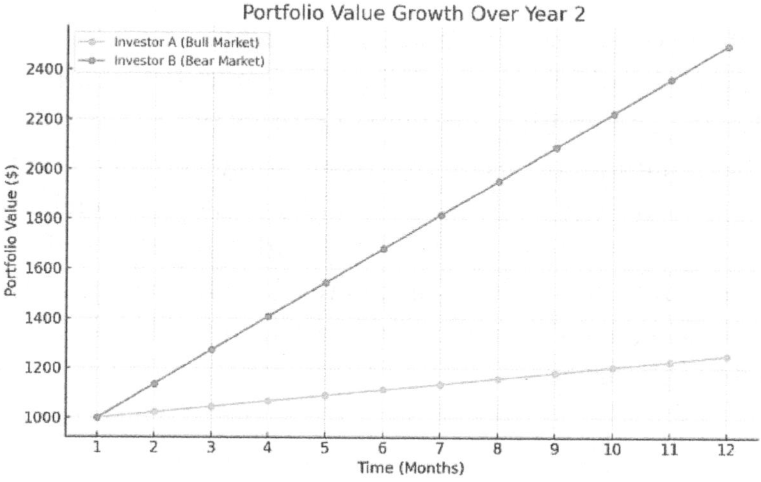

Encourages Long-Term Perspective: DCA aligns with a long-term investment strategy. By regularly investing over months and years, investors benefit from the potential for compound growth and the overall upward trend of the market.

Simplifies Investment Process: This strategy simplifies investing by removing the need for frequent market analysis and decision-making. Investors set up automatic contributions and let the process run, making it easier to stay committed to their financial goals.

Case Studies of Dollar Cost Averaging Success

Case Study 1: The 2008 Financial Crisis

An investor starts a DCA strategy in January 2007, investing $500 monthly into an S&P 500 index fund. As the financial crisis hits, the market declines significantly through 2008 and early 2009. Despite the downturn, the investor continues to invest $500 each month. During the market's lowest points, the investor buys more shares at reduced prices. By 2013, the market recovers, and the investor's portfolio sees substantial gains, benefiting from the low average cost per share accumulated during the crisis.

Case Study 2: Long-Term Retirement Savings

Starting in their mid-20s, an individual commits to investing $200 monthly into a diversified portfolio of mutual funds. Over 40 years, they maintain this strategy, weathering various market conditions, including the dot-com bubble, the 2008 financial crisis, and the COVID-19 pandemic. By consistently investing and reinvesting dividends, they accumulate a significant retirement fund, benefiting from compounded growth and a disciplined investment approach.

Case Study 3: Technology Sector Investment
An investor uses DCA to invest in a technology-focused mutual fund starting in 2010. Despite the volatility in the tech sector, including rapid rises and falls in stock prices, the investor consistently invests $1,000 monthly. Over a decade, the tech sector experiences substantial growth, and the investor's disciplined approach results in impressive returns, with the average cost per share significantly lower than the current market value.

Dollar Cost Averaging (DCA) is a powerful investment strategy that harnesses the potential for long-term growth. By investing a fixed amount of money at regular intervals, investors can accumulate significant wealth over time. This method is particularly advantageous for those who may not have a large sum of money to invest all at once but want to build their portfolio steadily.

Compounding Effect: One of the key benefits of DCA is the compounding effect. As investors consistently invest over the years, they earn returns on their initial investments and on the returns generated by those investments. This snowball effect can lead to substantial growth, especially over extended periods.

Consistent Investment: DCA encourages consistent investing, which is crucial for long-term growth. By maintaining a disciplined approach, investors can benefit from the overall upward trend of the market, regardless of short-term fluctuations.

Example: Suppose an investor commits to investing $200 monthly into an S&P 500 index fund. Over 30 years, with an average annual return of 7%, their investment can grow significantly. This consistent investment strategy not only builds wealth but also fosters good financial habits.

Reducing the Impact of Market Volatility

Market volatility is a common concern for investors. DCA mitigates the impact of market swings by spreading investments over time. Instead of investing a lump sum and risking a poor entry point, DCA smooths out the purchase price over many transactions.

Lower Average Cost: When markets decline, DCA allows investors to buy more shares at lower prices, reducing the average cost per share. Conversely, in rising markets, investors buy fewer shares at higher prices, balancing the overall cost.

Emotional Buffer: By adhering to a predetermined investment schedule, investors are less likely to make emotional decisions based on market highs and lows. This disciplined approach helps prevent panic selling during downturns and overenthusiastic buying during booms.

Example: During the 2008 financial crisis, investors who continued their DCA strategy were able to purchase shares at significantly lower prices. When the market recovered, these shares contributed to substantial portfolio gains.

Historical Performance and Analysis

Historical data supports the effectiveness of DCA in building wealth and managing risk. Let's look at a few key points from historical performance:

S&P 500 Analysis: Analyzing the S&P 500 over the past several decades, investors who adopted a DCA strategy typically fared well.

Even through periods of significant volatility, such as the dot-com bubble, the 2008 financial crisis, and the COVID-19 pandemic, DCA investors who maintained their strategy saw their investments grow over time.

Steady Growth: Historically, markets have shown a tendency to recover from downturns and continue growing. DCA leverages this recovery by continuously investing, allowing investors to benefit from long-term market growth.

Reduced Risk: By investing over time, DCA reduces the risk of making poor investment decisions based on market timing. Investors avoid the pitfalls of investing large sums at market peaks, instead benefiting from the average performance of the market.

Practical Tips for Maximizing Benefits

To maximize the benefits of DCA, consider the following practical tips:

Set a Realistic Budget: Determine an amount you can consistently invest without straining your finances. The key is consistency, so choose a comfortable amount that you can maintain over the long term.

Automate Investments: Set up automatic contributions to your investment account. This ensures you stick to your investment schedule and reduces the temptation to skip contributions.

Diversify Investments: Spread your investments across different asset classes, such as stocks, bonds, and mutual funds. Diversification helps manage risk and enhances potential returns.

Stay Committed: Market fluctuations can be unsettling, but it's important to stay committed to your DCA strategy. Remember that DCA is designed to navigate volatility and capitalize on long-term growth.

Review and Adjust: Periodically review your investment portfolio and make adjustments as needed. Ensure your investments align with your financial goals and risk tolerance.

Applying the Strategy to Stocks, ETFs, and Mutual Funds

Dollar Cost Averaging (DCA) is a versatile strategy that can be applied to various investment vehicles, including stocks, Exchange-Traded Funds (ETFs), and mutual funds. By investing a fixed amount of money at regular intervals, investors can mitigate the impact of market volatility and build a diversified portfolio over time.

Stocks: Applying DCA to individual stocks allows investors to gradually build positions in companies they believe in without worrying about short-term price fluctuations. For instance, if an investor wants to invest in a blue-chip stock like Apple, they can commit to purchasing $200 worth of Apple shares every month. This approach helps reduce the risk of buying a large number of shares at a peak price.

ETFs: ETFs are a popular choice for DCA because they offer diversification within a single investment. By investing in ETFs, investors can gain exposure to a broad range of assets, such as equities, bonds, or commodities. For example, an investor might decide to invest $150 monthly in an S&P 500 ETF. This allows them to benefit from the overall performance of the market while reducing the impact of volatility on their investment.

Mutual Funds: Mutual funds pool money from multiple investors to buy a diversified portfolio of stocks, bonds, or other securities. Using DCA with mutual funds simplifies the investment process, as investors can contribute a fixed amount to their chosen fund each month. For instance, an investor might allocate $100 monthly to a growth mutual fund, gradually increasing their stake and taking advantage of professional management and diversification.

Practical Examples of Investment Plans

To illustrate how DCA can be implemented across different investment vehicles, let's consider a few practical examples:

Example 1: Stock Investment Plan

An investor aims to build a portfolio of high-quality tech stocks. They select three companies: Apple, Microsoft, and Google. They allocate $300 monthly, with $100 directed to each stock. Over time, this approach helps them accumulate shares in these leading tech companies without being overly exposed to short-term market volatility.

Example 2: ETF Investment Plan

An investor decides to diversify their portfolio by investing in ETFs. They choose three ETFs: an S&P 500 ETF, an international equity ETF, and a bond ETF. They allocate $600 monthly, with $200 directed to each ETF. This strategy provides exposure to different markets and asset classes, enhancing diversification and reducing risk.

Example 3: Mutual Fund Investment Plan

An investor prefers mutual funds for their professional management and diversification.

They select three funds: a growth fund, a balanced fund, and an income fund. They allocate $450 monthly, with $150 directed to each fund. This approach allows them to benefit from different investment strategies and objectives, building a well-rounded portfolio over time.

Tools and Platforms for Automated Investing

Implementing DCA can be made easier with the help of various tools and platforms that offer automated investing. These platforms can help investors stick to their investment plans without the need for constant manual intervention.

Robo-Advisors: Robo-advisors are digital platforms that provide automated, algorithm-driven financial planning services with little to no human supervision. They can automatically invest and rebalance portfolios based on the investor's goals and risk tolerance. Popular robo-advisors include **Betterment**, **Wealthfront**, and **Ellevest**.

Brokerage Accounts: Many brokerage firms offer automated investment plans that allow investors to set up recurring contributions to their chosen investments. Firms like **Vanguard**, **Fidelity**, and **Charles Schwab** provide tools for automatic investing in stocks, ETFs, and mutual funds.

Employer-Sponsored Retirement Plans: For those with access to employer-sponsored retirement plans like 401(k)s, automatic contributions can be set up to invest a portion of each paycheck into selected funds. This ensures consistent investing and leverages the benefits of DCA.

Monitoring and Adjusting the Strategy
While DCA is a relatively hands-off strategy, it's important to periodically monitor and adjust your investments to ensure they align with your financial goals and risk tolerance. Here are some tips for effective monitoring and adjustment:

Regular Reviews: Conduct regular reviews of your portfolio to assess performance and ensure it's on track to meet your goals. Quarterly or annual reviews are a good practice.

Rebalancing: Over time, the allocation of your portfolio may drift from your target due to market movements. Rebalancing involves adjusting your holdings to bring them back in line with your desired allocation. This can be done manually or automatically through your investment platform.

Adjust Contribution Levels: As your financial situation changes, you may need to adjust the amount you're investing each month. For example, if you receive a raise, you might increase your monthly contributions to accelerate your investment growth.

Stay Informed: Keep up with market trends, economic developments, and changes in your personal financial situation. This knowledge can help you make informed decisions about your investment strategy.

Case Studies of Diverse Investment Applications

Case Study 1: Tech Stock Investment

A young professional starts a DCA strategy focusing on the tech sector. They allocate $400 monthly to buy shares in Apple, Amazon, and Microsoft.

Over five years, they continue their regular investments, regardless of market conditions. By the end of this period, they have built a substantial portfolio of tech stocks, benefiting from the sector's growth and innovation. Their average cost per share is lower than it would have been with lump-sum investments, highlighting the effectiveness of DCA in a volatile sector.

Case Study 2: ETF Diversification

An investor with a moderate risk tolerance decides to use DCA to build a diversified portfolio of ETFs. They invest $500 monthly, splitting the amount equally between a total market ETF, an international equity ETF, and a bond ETF. Over ten years, they consistently contribute, reaping the benefits of global diversification and balanced risk. Despite market ups and downs, their disciplined approach results in a robust portfolio that balances growth and stability.

Case Study 3: Retirement Fund Growth

A couple in their early 30s begins a DCA strategy with their retirement accounts. They each set up automatic contributions to their 401(k) plans, investing $200 monthly into a target-date retirement fund. Over 25 years, their regular contributions grow significantly, boosted by employer matching and market gains. By retirement, they have built a solid nest egg, demonstrating the power of DCA and compounding over the long term.

Case Study 4: Balanced Mutual Fund Portfolio

An investor interested in mutual funds implements a DCA strategy, allocating $600 monthly to three funds: a growth fund, a balanced fund, and an income fund.

Over 15 years, they consistently invest, taking advantage of professional management and diversification. The balanced approach helps mitigate risk and capture gains from different market segments, leading to steady portfolio growth.

Common Pitfalls and Misconceptions

Dollar Cost Averaging (DCA) is a straightforward and effective investment strategy, but it's not without its potential pitfalls and misconceptions. Understanding and avoiding these can help ensure that investors maximize the benefits of DCA.

Mistake 1: Inconsistent Contributions

One of the most common mistakes is failing to maintain consistent contributions. DCA relies on regular investments to average out the cost of shares over time. Skipping contributions or making them irregularly can undermine the strategy's effectiveness.

Mistake 2: Ignoring Market Conditions

While DCA is designed to mitigate the impact of market volatility, completely ignoring market conditions can be a mistake. It's important to stay informed about major economic events and trends that could affect your investments, even though DCA reduces the need for active market timing.

Mistake 3: Over-diversification

While diversification is key to managing risk, over-diversifying can dilute potential returns. Spreading investments too thinly across too many assets or funds can lead to suboptimal performance. It's important to find a balance that offers diversification without compromising potential gains.

Mistake 4: Emotional Reactions
Reacting emotionally to short-term market movements can derail a DCA strategy. Panic selling during market downturns or getting overly enthusiastic during market booms can disrupt the regular investment schedule and negatively impact long-term returns.

Mistake 5: Setting Unrealistic Expectations
Investors sometimes expect immediate or outsized returns from their DCA strategy. It's important to remember that DCA is a long-term approach designed to build wealth gradually. Patience and realistic expectations are crucial for success.

Importance of Consistency and Discipline
Consistency and discipline are the cornerstones of a successful DCA strategy. By adhering to a regular investment schedule, investors can harness the power of compounding and mitigate the impact of market volatility.

Consistency: Regular contributions, regardless of market conditions, help smooth out the average cost of investments. This steady approach reduces the risk of making poor investment decisions based on short-term market fluctuations.

Discipline: Staying disciplined means resisting the urge to alter the investment plan based on emotional reactions or market news. It involves sticking to the strategy during both market highs and lows, understanding that DCA is designed to work over the long term.

Practical Examples of Mistake Avoidance

Example 1: Maintaining Regular Contributions
An investor commits to investing $200 monthly into a diversified mutual fund. Despite market fluctuations and personal financial changes, they ensure the contributions are made consistently. Over time, this disciplined approach helps them build a substantial portfolio, demonstrating the importance of regular contributions.

Example 2: Balanced Diversification
Another investor initially spreads their investments across 20 different funds, leading to over-diversification and mediocre returns. Recognizing this, they consolidate their portfolio into five well-chosen funds, balancing diversification with potential returns. This adjustment leads to improved performance while maintaining risk management.

Example 3: Avoiding Emotional Reactions
During a market downturn, an investor is tempted to halt their DCA contributions and sell their holdings to avoid further losses. Instead, they remind themselves of the long-term benefits of DCA and continue their regular investments. When the market recovers, their portfolio benefits from the shares purchased at lower prices, highlighting the importance of sticking to the plan.

Strategies for Maintaining the Investment Plan

Automate Contributions: One of the most effective ways to ensure consistency is by automating contributions. Setting up automatic transfers from your bank account to your investment account helps maintain regular investments without requiring manual intervention.

Set Realistic Goals: Establish clear, realistic financial goals that align with your DCA strategy. Having specific objectives, such as retirement savings or funding a child's education, can provide motivation and focus.

Regularly Review Progress: Periodically reviewing your investment progress can help you stay on track and make necessary adjustments. Regular reviews also reinforce the importance of consistency and provide reassurance during market volatility.

Educate Yourself: Continuously educating yourself about investing and financial markets can help you stay committed to your DCA strategy. Understanding how DCA works and its long-term benefits can strengthen your resolve during challenging times.

Seek Professional Advice: Consulting with a financial advisor can provide personalized guidance and support. An advisor can help you develop a robust investment plan, monitor your progress, and offer advice on adjustments when necessary.

Chapter 12

Leveraging IULs and Velocity Banking for Financial Freedom

Overview of IULs and Velocity Banking

In today's dynamic financial landscape, finding strategies that not only build wealth but also provide protection, flexibility, and long-term security is crucial. Among the many financial tools available, Indexed Universal Life Insurance (IULs) and Velocity Banking stand out as powerful methods for achieving these goals. Both strategies offer unique advantages, and when used together, they can create a robust system for wealth accumulation, debt management, and financial independence.

Understanding Indexed Universal Life Insurance (IULs):

Indexed Universal Life Insurance (IUL) is a type of permanent life insurance that provides both a death benefit and a cash value component. Unlike traditional whole life insurance, where the cash value grows at a fixed interest rate, the cash value in an IUL is tied to the performance of a stock market index, such as the S&P 500. This means that the cash value can grow based on the upward movement of the index, although it is also protected from losses due to a market downturn through a floor rate, which ensures that the cash value never decreases below a certain level.

An IUL offers several key benefits:

1. Lifetime Coverage: As a form of permanent life insurance, an IUL provides coverage for the policyholder's entire life, as long as premiums are paid.

This ensures that beneficiaries will receive a death benefit, regardless of when the policyholder passes away.

Cash Value Growth: The cash value in an IUL can grow significantly over time, thanks to the indexed interest feature. This growth can be tax-deferred, meaning you won't pay taxes on the cash value increase until you withdraw it.

Flexibility: IULs offer flexible premium payments, allowing policyholders to adjust their contributions based on their financial situation. Additionally, policyholders can access the cash value through loans or withdrawals, offering financial flexibility when needed.

Potential for Higher Returns: By tying the cash value growth to a market index, IULs provide the potential for higher returns compared to traditional fixed-rate insurance products, while still offering downside protection.

Understanding Velocity Banking:
Velocity Banking is a financial strategy that leverages lines of credit, such as Home Equity Lines of Credit (HELOCs), to accelerate debt payoff and increase cash flow. The core idea behind Velocity Banking is to use a line of credit as a primary account for managing income and expenses, which allows for the rapid reduction of interest costs on debt and the freeing up of cash flow that can be redirected toward wealth-building activities.

Key elements of Velocity Banking include:
Debt Acceleration: By using a line of credit to make large lump-sum payments toward a mortgage or other debts, individuals can reduce the principal balance more quickly, thereby lowering the amount of interest paid over time.

Cash Flow Management: Velocity Banking emphasizes managing cash flow efficiently by funneling all income into the line of credit. This reduces the average daily balance, which in turn lowers interest charges.

Strategic Use of Credit: Instead of relying on traditional checking and savings accounts, Velocity Banking advocates for the strategic use of a HELOC or other revolving credit lines. This approach provides greater flexibility and the potential to save on interest.

Continuous Reinvestment: As debts are paid off and cash flow increases, the freed-up funds can be reinvested into other wealth-building opportunities, such as investments or additional debt reduction.

Combining IULs and Velocity Banking for Maximum Impact:

When IULs and Velocity Banking are combined, they create a powerful financial system that offers both protection and growth. The IUL provides a safe, tax-advantaged environment for accumulating wealth, while Velocity Banking maximizes cash flow and accelerates debt reduction. Together, these strategies can help individuals achieve financial independence, protect their wealth, and create a lasting legacy.

The Concept of "*Be Your Own Bank*"

One of the most compelling aspects of using IULs in conjunction with Velocity Banking is the concept of "Be Your Own Bank." This idea revolves around the ability to leverage the cash value accumulated within an IUL policy as a personal financing tool. By using the cash value as collateral, policyholders can take out loans from the insurance company to fund significant expenses, such as buying a home, purchasing a car, or starting a business.

This approach allows individuals to bypass traditional lending institutions and enjoy the benefits of borrowing from themselves.

How IULs Facilitate the "Be Your Own Bank" Strategy:

The "Be Your Own Bank" strategy hinges on the unique features of IULs that make them ideal for personal banking purposes:

Cash Value Accumulation: Over time, the cash value within an IUL policy grows, providing a substantial reserve of funds that can be accessed when needed. This growth is enhanced by the indexed interest feature, which allows the cash value to benefit from market gains while being protected from losses.

Tax-Free Loans: When a policyholder takes out a loan against the cash value of their IUL, the loan is not considered taxable income. This is because the policyholder is borrowing against their own assets rather than receiving a distribution. As long as the loan is repaid, the policyholder can continue to borrow against the cash value without triggering tax liabilities.

Uninterrupted Cash Value Growth: One of the most significant advantages of borrowing against an IUL is that the cash value continues to grow as if no money was withdrawn. This is because the loan is taken from the insurance company, not from the cash value itself. The insurance company places a "hold" on the portion of the cash value that is being borrowed, but the full cash value remains intact and continues to earn interest.

Flexible Repayment: Policyholders have the flexibility to repay the loan on their terms. There is no set repayment schedule, and the loan can be repaid with interest at the policyholder's convenience.

If the loan is not repaid, the outstanding balance will be deducted from the death benefit.

Practical Applications of the "Be Your Own Bank" Strategy:
The "Be Your Own Bank" strategy can be applied in various scenarios, providing financial flexibility and control:

Purchasing a Home: Instead of taking out a traditional mortgage, a policyholder can borrow against the cash value of their IUL to fund a home purchase. By doing so, they avoid the strict requirements and interest rates associated with conventional lenders. Additionally, the policyholder can structure the loan repayment in a way that fits their financial situation.

Buying a Car: Similarly, an IUL loan can be used to purchase a vehicle. The policyholder can borrow the necessary funds, buy the car outright, and then repay the loan on a flexible schedule. This approach eliminates the need for car loans with potentially high-interest rates and rigid terms.

Starting a Business: For aspiring entrepreneurs, accessing capital is often a significant hurdle. By leveraging the cash value of an IUL, individuals can obtain the necessary funds to start or grow a business without going through traditional financing channels. This approach allows the entrepreneur to retain control of their business and avoid the debt burdens typically associated with business loans.

Paying for Education: Higher education can be a substantial expense. An IUL loan can provide a tax-free source of funds for college tuition or other educational expenses, giving the policyholder a flexible and cost-effective way to finance education.

Illustrating the "Be Your Own Bank" Concept:

To better understand how the "Be Your Own Bank" strategy works, consider a visual illustration showing the flow of money within an IUL policy. The illustration can depict the cash value growing over time, the process of taking out a loan, and how the full cash value continues to grow despite the loan. A side-by-side comparison with traditional borrowing methods can also highlight the benefits of using an IUL for personal financing.

Key Benefits of Using IULs and Velocity Banking

The combined use of IULs and Velocity Banking offers several key benefits that make them an attractive option for those looking to build and protect wealth while maintaining financial flexibility.

1. Tax Advantages:

One of the most significant benefits of using an IUL is the tax advantages it provides. The cash value within the policy grows on a tax-deferred basis, meaning that no taxes are owed on the growth until the funds are withdrawn. Furthermore, when the policyholder takes out a loan against the cash value, the loan proceeds are tax-free. This feature allows for tax-efficient access to funds, whether for retirement, major purchases, or other financial needs.

Additionally, the death benefit provided by an IUL is typically paid out to beneficiaries tax-free. This ensures that the policyholder's loved ones receive the full value of the death benefit without the burden of estate taxes.

2. Potential for Higher Returns:

The indexed interest feature of an IUL allows for the potential of higher returns compared to traditional fixed-interest savings or insurance products. By tying the cash value growth to the performance of a stock market index, policyholders can benefit from market gains without being directly exposed to market risks. This feature offers a balance of growth potential and security, making IULs an appealing option for long-term wealth accumulation.

3. Flexibility in Premium Payments and Loan Repayment:

IULs offer flexibility in premium payments, allowing policyholders to adjust their contributions based on their financial situation. This feature is particularly beneficial during periods of financial uncertainty, as it provides the option to reduce or increase premium payments as needed.

The flexibility extends to loan repayment as well. Unlike traditional loans with fixed repayment schedules, IUL loans can be repaid on a timeline that suits the policyholder. There is no requirement to make monthly payments, and the loan can be repaid in full or in part at any time. This flexibility makes IUL loans an attractive option for those who need access to funds but want to avoid the constraints of traditional borrowing.

How Cash Value Builds in an IUL

Indexed Universal Life Insurance (IUL) policies are unique financial instruments that blend the benefits of life insurance with the potential for cash value accumulation.

One of the most compelling aspects of an IUL is its ability to build cash value over time, providing policyholders with a flexible, tax-advantaged source of funds that can be leveraged for various financial needs.

The Mechanics of Cash Value Growth:

The cash value in an IUL grows through a combination of premium payments and interest credited based on the performance of a selected stock market index, such as the S&P 500. Here's how it works:

Premium Allocation:

When you pay your IUL premiums, a portion goes toward the cost of insurance (COI) and administrative fees, while the remaining portion is allocated to the policy's cash value account.
The cash value portion is then credited with interest based on the performance of the chosen index, but with important safeguards in place.

Indexed Interest Crediting:

The cash value in an IUL can grow through interest credited based on the upward movement of a stock market index. However, your cash value is never directly invested in the market. Instead, the insurance company tracks the index's performance and credits your account with a portion of the gains.

IUL policies often have a "cap rate," which is the maximum interest rate that can be credited to the cash value. For example, if the cap rate is 10% and the index performs at 12%, your cash value would be credited at the cap rate of 10%.

Additionally, IULs have a "floor rate," typically set at 0% or 1%, which protects your cash value from negative index performance. This means that even if the market experiences a downturn, your cash value won't decrease due to market losses.

Tax-Deferred Growth:

The cash value in an IUL grows on a tax-deferred basis, meaning you don't pay taxes on the gains as they accumulate. This allows your money to compound over time without the drag of annual taxes, which can significantly enhance the growth of your cash value.

Practical Example of Cash Value Growth:
Let's consider a practical example of how cash value might build in an IUL policy:

Initial Setup: Sarah, a 35-year-old professional, purchases an IUL with an annual premium of $10,000. She selects the S&P 500 as her index, with a cap rate of 10% and a floor rate of 0%.

Year 1: The S&P 500 performs well, with a 12% gain. However, due to the cap rate, Sarah's cash value is credited with 10% interest. Her cash value at the end of the year, after accounting for the cost of insurance and fees, grows to $9,500.

Year 2: The market experiences a slight downturn with a -3% return. Thanks to the floor rate of 0%, Sarah's cash value does not decrease. Instead, it remains steady at $9,500.

Year 5: After five years of consistent premium payments and positive market performance, Sarah's cash value has grown to $55,000, providing a substantial reserve of funds she can access if needed.

The graph below represents the cash value growth in Sarah's IUL policy over five years, based on the given scenario. It shows the impact of market performance, including the cap and floor rates, on the cash value.

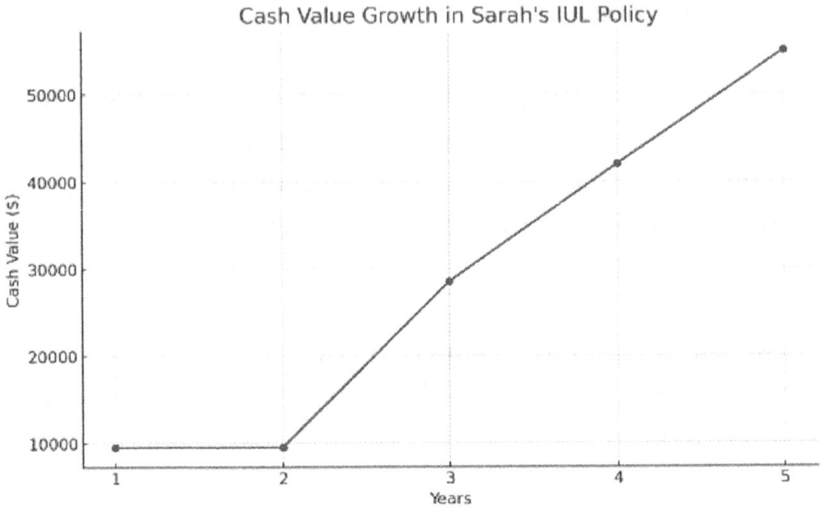

Accessing the Cash Value

One of the most powerful features of an IUL is the ability to access the cash value through loans or withdrawals. Unlike traditional savings accounts or retirement plans, accessing funds from an IUL offers unique advantages, particularly when it comes to tax efficiency and maintaining the policy's growth potential.

Taking Out a Loan Against the Cash Value:

When you need to access funds from your IUL, you can take out a loan against the cash value. This loan is not a withdrawal but rather a loan from the insurance company using your cash value as collateral. Here's how it works:

Loan Process:

You request a loan from the insurance company, specifying the amount you wish to borrow. Typically, you can borrow up to 90% of the cash value, though the exact amount may vary depending on the policy and the insurance company's rules.

The insurance company places a "hold" on the portion of the cash value you've borrowed against, but the full cash value remains intact and continues to earn interest as if no money was withdrawn.

Tax-Free Access:

One of the most significant advantages of taking out a loan against your IUL is that the loan proceeds are tax-free. Since you are borrowing against your own cash value, the IRS does not consider this as taxable income.

This feature makes IUL loans an attractive option for accessing funds during retirement, making major purchases, or covering unexpected expenses without triggering tax liabilities.

Loan Repayment:

You have the flexibility to repay the loan on your terms. There is no fixed repayment schedule, and you can repay the loan in full or in part whenever you choose. If you decide not to repay the loan, the outstanding balance will be deducted from the death benefit when the policy pays out to your beneficiaries.

The loan accrues interest, which is typically lower than the interest rates on traditional loans. This interest is added to the outstanding loan balance if not repaid.

Practical Applications of IUL Loans:

IUL loans offer a versatile financial tool that can be applied to various life situations, providing policyholders with the means to achieve their financial goals without the constraints of traditional borrowing. Here are some practical applications:

Purchasing a Home:

Traditional homebuyers often rely on mortgages, which come with strict lending criteria, fixed repayment schedules, and potentially high-interest rates. With an IUL, policyholders can borrow against their cash value to fund a home purchase, bypassing the conventional mortgage process.

This approach provides the flexibility to structure loan repayments according to the policyholder's financial situation, avoiding the pressure of monthly mortgage payments.

Additionally, because the loan does not reduce the policy's cash value, the policyholder continues to benefit from the tax-deferred growth of their IUL.

Buying a Car:

Cars are significant purchases that often require financing. Instead of taking out a car loan with potentially high-interest rates and strict repayment terms, policyholders can use an IUL loan to purchase a vehicle.

By borrowing against the cash value, the policyholder avoids the interest costs associated with traditional car loans while maintaining control over repayment.

The flexibility of an IUL loan allows the policyholder to pay off the loan at their own pace, ensuring that the car purchase does not strain their finances.

Starting or Expanding a Business:

Entrepreneurship often requires significant upfront capital, and accessing financing can be challenging. Traditional business loans come with interest rates, collateral requirements, and rigid repayment schedules. By leveraging an IUL loan, entrepreneurs can access the capital needed to start or grow their business without the hurdles of conventional lending.

The flexibility of an IUL loan allows business owners to invest in their ventures with confidence, knowing that they have control over repayment terms. Furthermore, because the IUL cash value continues to grow despite the loan, the policyholder benefits from the continued accumulation of wealth.

Paying for Education:

Higher education is a substantial expense, and student loans can be burdensome, often with high-interest rates and long repayment periods. An IUL loan provides an alternative method of financing education, offering tax-free access to funds without the need for traditional student loans.

This approach allows parents or students to borrow against the IUL's cash value to cover tuition, fees, and other educational expenses. With the flexibility to repay the loan over time, the policyholder can manage the cost of education in a way that aligns with their financial situation.

Emergency Expenses:

Life is unpredictable, and unexpected expenses can arise at any time. Whether it's a medical emergency, home repair, or other unforeseen costs, having access to funds is crucial. An IUL loan provides a ready source of funds that can be accessed quickly and tax-free.

By borrowing against the cash value, policyholders can cover emergency expenses without the need to liquidate investments or incur high-interest debt. The flexibility of an IUL loan ensures that repayment can be managed on a schedule that works for the policyholder.

To fully appreciate the benefits of using IUL loans, it's essential to understand the loan mechanism and how it affects the policy's overall performance. Unlike traditional loans, where the borrowed amount is directly deducted from the principal, IUL loans work differently, ensuring that the policyholder's cash value continues to grow uninterrupted.

How the Loan Mechanism Works:

Loan from the Insurance Company:
When you take out a loan against your IUL, you are not actually withdrawing money from your cash value. Instead, you are borrowing money from the insurance company, which uses your cash value as collateral for the loan. The insurance company places a "hold" on the portion of your cash value equivalent to the loan amount.

Despite this hold, the entire cash value continues to participate in the index-linked growth.

This means that even though you have borrowed funds, your cash value still earns interest as if no loan was taken.

The unique feature of IUL loans is that the loan does not directly impact the growth of the cash value. Because the loan is from the insurance company and not a withdrawal from your cash value, the cash value remains intact and continues to benefit from any indexed gains.

This mechanism allows policyholders to leverage their cash value without compromising the long-term growth of their IUL. As a result, the policyholder can enjoy the benefits of borrowing while still building wealth within the policy.

Loan Interest and Repayment:
The insurance company charges interest on the loan, which accrues over time. The interest rate on IUL loans is generally lower than traditional loan rates, making it an attractive borrowing option.

Policyholders have the flexibility to repay the loan on their terms, with no fixed repayment schedule.

Repayment can be made in full or in part at any time. If the loan is not repaid, the outstanding balance, including accrued interest, will be deducted from the death benefit when the policyholder passes away.

Indexed Universal Life Insurance (IUL) policies are not only powerful tools for accumulating wealth and accessing funds through loans, but they also offer significant tax advantages and serve as an effective vehicle for wealth transfer.

In this section, we will explore how IULs provide tax-free growth, retirement income, and facilitate seamless wealth transfer to beneficiaries. We will also discuss how these features can be leveraged in long-term financial and estate planning.

Tax-Free Growth and Retirement Income

Understanding Tax-Free Growth in an IUL:
One of the most appealing aspects of an IUL is its ability to grow cash value on a tax-deferred basis. This means that the interest credited to the cash value—based on the performance of a stock market index—is not subject to annual income taxes. Instead, the cash value grows over time without the drag of taxes, allowing for more substantial accumulation of wealth.

The Mechanics of Tax-Deferred Growth:

Premium Payments and Cash Value Accumulation:
When you pay premiums on your IUL, a portion of those payments is allocated to the policy's cash value account after accounting for the cost of insurance and administrative fees. The remaining cash value is then credited with interest based on the performance of the chosen stock market index, such as the S&P 500.

The cash value grows tax-deferred, meaning you won't pay taxes on the growth as long as the money remains within the policy. This allows the cash value to compound over time, resulting in potentially significant growth.

Indexed Interest and Cap Rates:

The interest credited to the cash value is tied to the performance of the chosen index, subject to a cap rate (the maximum interest rate that can be credited) and a floor rate (the minimum rate that ensures your cash value doesn't lose money during market downturns).

This combination of upside potential and downside protection enhances the growth potential while safeguarding your wealth.

Because the growth is tax-deferred, the entire amount credited to the cash value remains within the policy, further compounding the growth in subsequent years.

Tax Implications:

Since the cash value grows tax-deferred, you won't need to report the growth on your annual tax return. This is a significant advantage over other investment vehicles, such as taxable brokerage accounts, where you may be subject to taxes on dividends, interest, and capital gains each year.

Additionally, you can access the cash value through policy loans without triggering a taxable event. As long as the loan is repaid, the money borrowed remains tax-free.

Using IULs for Tax-Free Retirement Income:

As retirement approaches, many individuals seek ways to convert their accumulated assets into a reliable income stream while minimizing taxes. IULs offer a unique solution by allowing policyholders to access their cash value through loans and withdrawals, providing tax-free income during retirement.

Strategies for Generating Tax-Free Retirement Income:

Policy Loans:
One of the most popular strategies for generating tax-free retirement income from an IUL is to take out policy loans against the cash value. These loans are not considered taxable income because they are loans rather than withdrawals from the cash value.

You can use these tax-free loans to supplement your retirement income, pay for living expenses, travel, or cover healthcare costs. The flexibility of IUL loans allows you to tailor your income strategy to your specific needs.

Structured Withdrawals:
Another strategy is to take structured withdrawals from the cash value, ensuring that the withdrawals do not exceed the total amount of premiums paid (the "basis" in the policy). As long as the withdrawals are within the basis, they are not subject to income tax.

After the basis is exhausted, you can switch to taking policy loans, which continue to provide tax-free income. This approach allows you to maximize the tax efficiency of your IUL.

Combination Strategy:
Many retirees opt for a combination strategy, where they take tax-free withdrawals up to the basis amount and then transition to policy loans for the remaining income needs. This approach ensures that they can draw on their accumulated wealth in the most tax-efficient manner possible.

Comparing IULs to Other Retirement Accounts:
To appreciate the benefits of using IULs for retirement income, it's helpful to compare them to other common retirement accounts, such as traditional IRAs, Roth IRAs, and 401(k)s:

Traditional IRAs/401(k)s:
Contributions to traditional IRAs and 401(k)s are typically tax-deferred, meaning you don't pay taxes on contributions or growth until you withdraw the funds in retirement. However, when you take distributions, they are subject to ordinary income tax, which can be a significant tax burden if you're in a higher tax bracket during retirement.

Required Minimum Distributions (RMDs) also force you to start taking taxable withdrawals at age 73, regardless of whether you need the income.

Roth IRAs:
Contributions to Roth IRAs are made with after-tax dollars, but the growth and qualified withdrawals in retirement are tax-free. However, Roth IRAs have contribution limits, and eligibility is phased out for higher-income individuals.

While Roth IRAs offer tax-free income similar to IULs, they lack the additional benefits of life insurance protection and flexible loan options that IULs provide.

IULs:
IULs offer the best of both worlds: tax-deferred growth like traditional IRAs and tax-free income like Roth IRAs. However, they go a step further by providing a death benefit, flexible premium payments, and the ability to access cash value through loans without triggering taxes.

Unlike traditional retirement accounts, IULs do not have contribution limits or RMDs, giving you more control over your financial planning.

Estate Planning and Wealth Transfer Using IULs

The Role of IULs in Estate Planning:
Estate planning is a critical component of wealth management, ensuring that your assets are transferred to your beneficiaries according to your wishes while minimizing taxes and administrative burdens. IULs play a vital role in estate planning by providing tax-efficient wealth transfer options and protecting your legacy for future generations.

Tax-Free Death Benefit:
One of the primary advantages of IULs in estate planning is the tax-free death benefit. When the policyholder passes away, the death benefit is paid out to the beneficiaries without being subject to federal income tax. This ensures that the full value of the policy is transferred to your loved ones without the erosion of taxes.

Preserving Wealth for Heirs:
The tax-free nature of the death benefit helps preserve the wealth you've accumulated, allowing your heirs to receive the maximum benefit from your estate. This is particularly important for high-net-worth individuals who may be subject to estate taxes, as the IUL can help offset these liabilities.

For families with significant assets, the IUL's death benefit can be used to pay estate taxes or other expenses, ensuring that your heirs don't have to liquidate other assets to cover these costs.

Avoiding Probate:

Another advantage of IULs is that the death benefit typically bypasses probate, the legal process of distributing a deceased person's estate. Probate can be time-consuming, costly, and subject to public scrutiny. By avoiding probate, the IUL's death benefit is paid directly to the beneficiaries, ensuring a quicker and more private transfer of wealth.

Equalizing Inheritances:

In some cases, families may wish to equalize inheritances among heirs. For example, if one child inherits a family business or a significant piece of real estate, an IUL can provide a death benefit to other children, ensuring that each heir receives an equitable share of the estate.

This strategy helps prevent potential conflicts among heirs and ensures that your estate is distributed according to your wishes.

Creating a Legacy with IULs:

IULs can also be used to create a lasting legacy, whether through charitable giving, funding future generations, or supporting causes that are important to you.

Charitable Giving:

Many individuals use IULs to fund charitable donations after their passing. By designating a charity as the beneficiary of the death benefit, you can make a significant impact on the causes you care about while enjoying potential tax benefits during your lifetime.

Charitable giving through IULs can be structured in various ways, including through charitable remainder trusts or donor-advised funds, allowing you to tailor your legacy to your specific goals.

Funding Future Generations:
IULs can be an effective way to fund the education, housing, or business ventures of future generations. By leaving a tax-free death benefit to your children or grandchildren, you provide them with the financial resources they need to pursue their dreams and achieve long-term success.

This approach not only helps your descendants financially but also instills the values of financial responsibility and long-term planning.

Supporting Family Businesses:
For families with closely-held businesses, IULs can provide liquidity to support business succession plans. The death benefit can be used to buy out non-family members, pay off business debts, or fund the transition of leadership to the next generation.

This ensures that the family business remains intact and can continue to thrive, preserving your legacy for future generations.
Long-Term Wealth Building Strategy with IULs
The Power of Consistent Funding:

To maximize the benefits of an IUL, it's essential to consistently fund the policy over time. Regular premium payments contribute to the growth of the cash value, which in turn increases the potential for tax-free loans, retirement income, and wealth transfer.

Chapter 13

The Entrepreneurial Journey: Starting and Growing a Business

Understanding Benefits and Challenges of Entrepreneurship

Rewards of Starting a Business

Embarking on the entrepreneurial journey offers numerous rewards that can significantly enhance your professional and personal life. The primary benefit is the opportunity to create something from scratch—building a business that reflects your vision, values, and goals. This creation process can be incredibly fulfilling and offers a sense of accomplishment that few other endeavors can match.

Financial Independence: One of the most compelling rewards is the potential for financial independence. Successful entrepreneurs often achieve significant financial returns, allowing them to enjoy a lifestyle that aligns with their aspirations and desires.

The graph on the next page illustrates the correlation between time commitment and financial returns over five years. Entrepreneurs A, B, and C invest different amounts of capital and time, leading to varying financial outcomes. Entrepreneur C, who dedicates the most time, experiences higher returns despite the lowest initial investment.

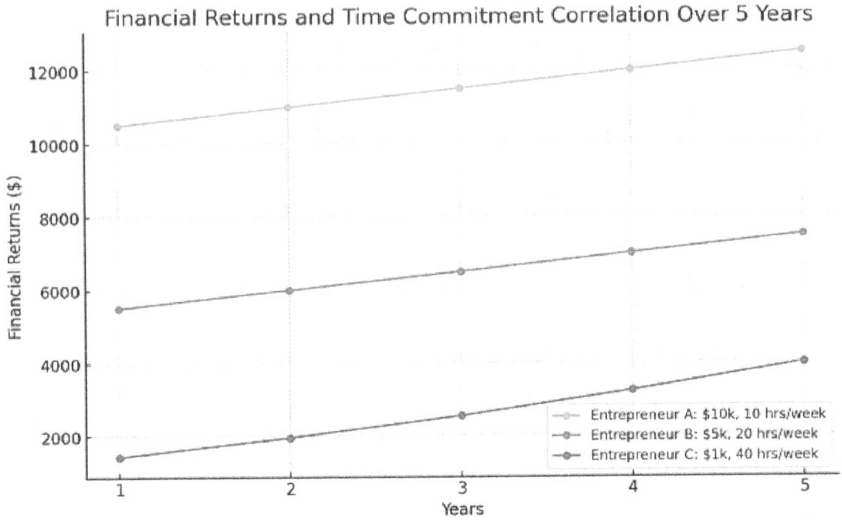

Personal Growth: Entrepreneurship fosters personal growth. The challenges and responsibilities involved in running a business force you to develop a wide range of skills, from leadership and decision-making to problem-solving and resilience.

Flexibility and Autonomy: Running your own business gives you the flexibility to set your schedule and make strategic decisions that align with your values. This autonomy can lead to a more balanced and satisfying work-life dynamic.

Impact and Legacy: Entrepreneurs have the opportunity to make a substantial impact on their industry, community, or even the world. Whether through innovative products, job creation, or philanthropic efforts, you can leave a lasting legacy.

Common Challenges Faced by Entrepreneurs

While the rewards are significant, the path of entrepreneurship is fraught with challenges. Recognizing these obstacles and preparing to navigate them is crucial for long-term success.

Financial Risk: Starting a business often requires a substantial financial investment, and there is always the risk that the venture may not generate the expected returns. Managing cash flow and securing funding can be ongoing challenges.

Uncertainty and Stress: The uncertainty inherent in starting and running a business can be a significant source of stress. Market fluctuations, competitive pressures, and changing consumer preferences require constant vigilance and adaptability.

Time Commitment: Entrepreneurship demands a considerable time investment. Balancing business responsibilities with personal life can be challenging, and many entrepreneurs struggle with work-life balance, especially in the early stages.

Skill Gaps: Entrepreneurs often need to wear many hats, from marketing and sales to finance and operations. Identifying and addressing skill gaps—either through learning or hiring—can be a critical aspect of building a successful business.

Market Competition: Competing with established players in the market can be daunting. Developing a unique value proposition and differentiating your business from competitors is essential for attracting and retaining customers.

Practical Steps to Launch and Grow a Business

Starting a business requires a clear roadmap to navigate from concept to reality. Here's a comprehensive step-by-step guide to help you through this journey:

Begin by brainstorming business ideas that align with your interests, skills, and market needs.

Validate your idea by researching potential demand, identifying your target audience, and gathering feedback through surveys or focus groups.

Conduct thorough market research to understand your industry, competitors, and customer preferences. Use this data to refine your business concept, develop a unique selling proposition (USP), and identify your competitive advantage.

Create a detailed business plan outlining your vision, mission, objectives, market analysis, marketing strategy, operational plan, and financial projections. A solid business plan serves as a roadmap for your business and is essential for securing funding.

Buying an Established Business

One alternative to starting a business from scratch is buying an established one. This approach can provide immediate cash flow, a customer base, and established brand recognition.

Where to Find Them

Business Brokers: Specialized agents who connect buyers with sellers.

Online Marketplaces: Websites like BizBuySell, BusinessesForSale, and LoopNet list businesses available for purchase.

Networking: Industry events, local chambers of commerce, and personal networks can also lead to opportunities.

The evaluation process involves:

Due Diligence: Review financial statements, business operations, customer relationships, and legal matters.

Valuation: Assess the business's worth using methods like the earnings multiple or discounted cash flow analysis.

Negotiation and Purchase: Work with legal and financial advisors to negotiate terms and finalize the purchase.

Example:
Sarah, an entrepreneur passionate about health, found an established organic grocery store through a business broker. After thorough due diligence, she purchased the business and immediately started generating revenue.

Financing Options for Startups:

Explore various financing options, including personal savings, loans, angel investors, venture capital, crowdfunding, and grants. Evaluate each option based on your business needs, growth potential, and the terms and conditions involved.

Buying a Franchise Aligned with Your Values

Purchasing a franchise offers the advantage of operating under a proven business model with brand recognition and ongoing support from the franchisor.

Where to Find Franchises:

- **Franchise Directories**: Websites like Franchise Direct, Franchise Gator, and the International Franchise Association list franchise opportunities.

- **Franchise Expos**: Events where franchisors showcase their businesses to potential franchisees.

-

- **Franchise Consultants**: Experts who can help match you with a franchise that aligns with your goals.

Evaluation Process:

1. Assess the franchise's history, success rates, and market demand.
2. Review the Franchise Disclosure Document (FDD) document carefully to understand the obligations, costs, and support provided.
3. After evaluating the opportunity and securing financing, you can proceed with the franchise agreement.

Example: John, who loves fitness, purchased a franchise from a well-known gym chain. He found the opportunity on Franchise Gator, conducted thorough research, and successfully aligned the franchise's mission with his personal goals.

Legal and Administrative Setup:

Choose an appropriate business structure (e.g., sole proprietorship, partnership, corporation, LLC) based on your needs and goals.

Register your business with the relevant government authorities, obtain necessary licenses and permits, and set up a business bank account.

Building Your Team:

Identify key roles and hire individuals who complement your skills and share your vision.

Foster a positive work culture that encourages collaboration, innovation, and continuous learning.

Product Development and Testing:
Develop a minimum viable product (MVP) or prototype and test it with a select group of customers.

Use their feedback to refine your product, address any issues, and ensure it meets market expectations.

Launch and Marketing:
Plan your launch strategy, including marketing campaigns, public relations, and events.

Utilize digital marketing tools such as social media, email marketing, and search engine optimization (SEO) to reach your target audience effectively.

Monitoring and Scaling:
Continuously monitor your business performance through key performance indicators (KPIs) and customer feedback.

Identify opportunities for growth and scaling, such as expanding product lines, entering new markets, or forming strategic partnerships.

Importance of Market Research and Planning
Market research and planning are critical components of a successful business launch. They provide valuable insights into your industry, help identify opportunities and threats, and guide strategic decision-making.

Understanding the Market:
Market research helps you understand your industry's dynamics, including trends, customer needs, and competitor activities. This knowledge enables you to position your business effectively and identify gaps in the market.

Informed Decision-Making:
A well-researched business plan allows you to make informed decisions, allocate resources efficiently, and set realistic goals. It also helps you anticipate challenges and develop strategies to overcome them.

Investor Confidence:
Investors and lenders require a comprehensive business plan to assess the viability of your business. Demonstrating thorough market research and planning increases your chances of securing funding and gaining investor confidence.

Financing Options for Startups
Securing adequate funding is a major hurdle for many startups. Here are some common financing options:

Personal Savings:
Using personal savings is a common way to fund a startup. It involves minimal risk to external parties but can be financially stressful if the business does not succeed.

Loans:
Bank loans, Small Business Administration (SBA) loans, and microloans are traditional financing options. They require a solid business plan and collateral but offer competitive interest rates.

Angel Investors:
Angel investors are individuals who provide capital in exchange for equity or convertible debt. They often offer mentorship and industry connections, which can be invaluable for early-stage startups.

Venture Capital:
Venture capital firms invest in high-growth potential startups in exchange for equity. They provide significant funding but expect a substantial return on investment and may influence business decisions.

Crowdfunding:
Platforms like **Kickstarter** and **Indiegogo** allow entrepreneurs to raise funds from a large number of people. Successful campaigns can validate your business idea and generate early customer interest.

Grants:
Government and private grants provide funding without the need for repayment. They are often competitive and require a thorough application process.

Building a Strong Business Foundation

Creating a Solid Business Plan
A well-crafted business plan is the cornerstone of a successful business. It serves as a roadmap, guiding your strategy and decision-making processes.

Executive Summary:
Provide a brief overview of your business, including your mission statement, product/service offerings, and objectives.

Market Analysis:
Detail your market research, including industry trends, target market, and competitive analysis. Identify your unique value proposition and competitive advantage.

Marketing and Sales Strategy:
Outline your marketing and sales approach, including pricing, distribution channels, promotional tactics, and customer acquisition strategies.

Operational Plan:
Describe your business operations, including location, facilities, technology, and logistics. Highlight key milestones and timelines.

Financial Projections:
Provide detailed financial forecasts, including income statements, cash flow statements, and balance sheets. Include funding requirements and potential revenue streams.

Management Team:
Introduce your management team, highlighting their skills, experience, and roles within the company. Strong leadership is crucial for investor confidence.

Key Person Policy and Its Importance

A Key Person policy is a type of life insurance designed to protect your business in the event of the unexpected loss of a critical team member. This policy provides financial support to help the business navigate the transition period, covering expenses such as hiring and training a replacement, addressing potential revenue loss, and maintaining investor confidence.

Why is the Key Person policy needed? If a key person leaves due to unforeseen circumstances like death or disability, the business could face significant challenges. The Key Person policy ensures the business can continue operating smoothly while addressing the gap left by the individual's departure.

Implementation would involve identifying critical personnel whose absence would most impact the business. Work with an insurance provider to establish a policy that covers the necessary financial aspects, ensuring that the business remains stable during such a crisis.

Importance of Legal and Financial Structures

Establishing the right legal and financial structures is essential for protecting your business and ensuring compliance with regulations.

Legal Structures:
Choose a business structure that aligns with your goals and offers the appropriate level of liability protection. Common structures include sole proprietorship, partnership, corporation, and LLC.

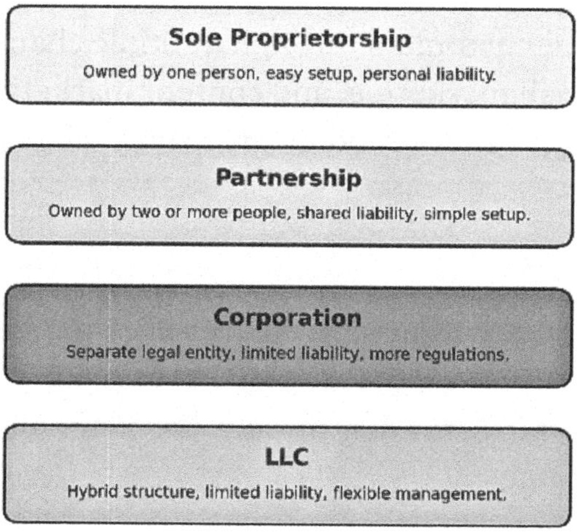

Financial Management:
Implement robust financial management practices, including accurate bookkeeping, budgeting, and financial reporting. Use accounting software to streamline processes and ensure transparency.

Compliance:
Ensure your business complies with all relevant laws and regulations, including tax obligations, employment laws, and industry-specific regulations. Seek legal counsel if necessary to navigate complex requirements.

Strategies for Effective Branding and Marketing

Building a strong brand and effective marketing strategy is crucial for attracting and retaining customers.

Brand Identity:
Develop a compelling brand identity that reflects your values, mission, and unique selling proposition. This includes your logo, tagline, and overall visual aesthetic.

Customer Engagement:
Engage with your customers through multiple channels, including social media, email marketing, and content marketing. Build a community around your brand by providing value and fostering interaction.

Digital Marketing:
Leverage digital marketing tools such as SEO, pay-per-click advertising, and social media advertising to reach your target audience. Use analytics to measure performance and adjust your strategy accordingly.

Public Relations:
Build relationships with the media and industry influencers to generate positive publicity. Press releases, interviews, and events can help increase your brand's visibility and credibility.

Practical Tips for Building a Loyal Customer Base

Customer Service:
Provide exceptional customer service to build trust and loyalty. Respond promptly to inquiries, address concerns effectively, and go the extra mile to exceed customer expectations.

Loyalty Programs:
Implement loyalty programs to reward repeat customers. Discounts, exclusive offers, and referral bonuses can incentivize continued patronage and attract new customers.

Feedback and Improvement:
Actively seek customer feedback and use it to improve your products or services. Show customers that their opinions matter by making tangible changes based on their suggestions.

Community Involvement:
Engage with your local community through events, sponsorships, and partnerships. Building strong community ties can enhance your brand's reputation and foster customer loyalty.

Scaling and Expanding the Business

Strategies for Scaling Operations
Scaling a business involves expanding its capacity to grow and increase revenue without compromising performance or losing quality.

To achieve this, entrepreneurs must implement strategic approaches to handle increased demand and operational complexity.

1. Streamline Processes:

Analyze current operations to identify bottlenecks and inefficiencies.

Implement automation tools and software to improve efficiency and reduce manual tasks.

Standardize procedures to ensure consistency and scalability.

2. Invest in Technology:

Leverage technology to enhance productivity and support growth. This can include CRM systems, project management tools, and e-commerce platforms.

Adopt cloud-based solutions for scalability and flexibility.

3. Strengthen the Team:

Hire skilled professionals who can contribute to the company's growth. Focus on building a team with diverse skills and expertise. Provide training and development opportunities to ensure your team evolves with the company's needs.

4. Expand Market Reach:

Explore new markets and customer segments. This can involve geographic expansion or targeting different demographics.

Utilize digital marketing strategies to reach a broader audience.

5. Diversify Product Offerings:

Introduce new products or services that complement your existing offerings.

Conduct market research to identify gaps and opportunities for diversification.

6. Build Strategic Partnerships:

Form alliances with other businesses to leverage their strengths and resources. This can include partnerships for distribution, marketing, or product development.

Collaborate with industry influencers and thought leaders to enhance your brand's credibility and reach.

Importance of Innovation and Adaptability

Innovation and adaptability are crucial for sustaining growth and staying competitive in a dynamic market.

Embrace Change:
Stay open to new ideas and be willing to adapt your business model as needed.

Encourage a culture of innovation within your team, where creativity and new solutions are valued.

Invest in Research and Development:
Allocate resources to research and development to keep your products and services relevant.

Stay ahead of industry trends and technological advancements to maintain a competitive edge.

Customer-Centric Approach:
Continuously gather customer feedback to improve your offerings.

Adapt your products and services based on customer needs and preferences.

Risk Management:
Anticipate potential risks associated with scaling and have contingency plans in place.

Stay agile and ready to pivot if necessary.

Practical Examples of Business Expansion

Example 1: E-Commerce Business
A small online retailer decides to scale by expanding its product line and entering international markets. They streamline operations by adopting an advanced inventory management system and partnering with global logistics providers. By leveraging digital marketing strategies, including social media advertising and SEO, they successfully attract customers from new regions, significantly increasing their revenue.

Example 2: Service-Based Business
A digital marketing agency plans to scale by offering new services such as web development and data analytics. They hire experts in these fields and invest in training existing staff. By promoting their expanded service offerings through targeted marketing campaigns, they attract larger clients and projects, resulting in substantial business growth.

Managing Growth and Maintaining Quality

As a business scales, maintaining quality is crucial to sustaining success and customer satisfaction.

Quality Control Systems:

Implement robust quality control systems to ensure consistent product or service standards.

Regularly review and update quality assurance processes.

Customer Service:

Maintain high standards of customer service by training staff and using customer feedback to make improvements.

Scale customer support operations to handle increased demand efficiently.

Operational Efficiency:

Continuously optimize operations to handle growing volumes without sacrificing quality.

Monitor key performance indicators (KPIs) to track efficiency and identify areas for improvement.

Brand Integrity:

Stay true to your brand values and mission as you grow. Consistency in brand messaging and customer experience is vital for long-term success.

Sustaining Long-term Business Success

Long-term business success requires a commitment to continuous improvement and learning. Staying competitive in a dynamic market involves regularly evaluating and enhancing your business practices.

Continuous Learning:
Encourage lifelong learning for yourself and your team. Attend workshops, conferences, and training sessions to stay updated on industry trends and best practices.

Foster a culture of curiosity and innovation within your organization.

Process Improvement:
Regularly assess and refine your business processes to improve efficiency and effectiveness.

Implement feedback loops to gather insights from employees and customers, and use this data to drive improvements.

Technology Adoption:
Embrace new technologies that can enhance your operations and customer experience.

Stay informed about technological advancements relevant to your industry and be proactive in integrating them into your business.

Strategies for Maintaining Competitive Advantage
Innovation:

Continuously innovate your products, services, and business model to stay ahead of competitors.

Invest in research and development to explore new opportunities and improve existing offerings.

Customer Focus:
Keep your customers at the center of your business strategy. Understand their needs and preferences and adapt your offerings accordingly.

Provide exceptional customer service and build strong relationships to foster loyalty and repeat business.

Brand Building:
Strengthen your brand identity and consistently communicate your value proposition.

Engage with your audience through various channels, including social media, content marketing, and public relations.

Employee Engagement:
Invest in your employees' growth and development. Engaged and motivated employees are more productive and contribute to the company's success.

Create a positive work environment that encourages collaboration and innovation.

Practical Tips for Long-term Sustainability
Financial Management:

Maintain sound financial practices, including budgeting, forecasting, and cash flow management.

Diversify revenue streams to reduce dependency on a single source of income.

Sustainability Practices:
Implement sustainable business practices to minimize environmental impact and appeal to eco-conscious consumers. Explore ways to reduce waste, conserve resources, and promote sustainability within your operations.

Adaptability:
Stay agile and ready to adapt to changing market conditions and customer demands.

Monitor industry trends and be prepared to pivot your strategy when necessary.

Risk Management:
Identify potential risks and develop contingency plans to mitigate them.

Regularly review and update your risk management strategies to address emerging threats.

Balancing Business Growth with Personal Goals
Achieving long-term business success also involves balancing professional ambitions with personal goals. Striking this balance ensures sustainable growth and personal well-being.

Work-Life Balance:
Prioritize work-life balance to avoid burnout and maintain overall well-being.

Set boundaries and allocate time for personal activities, family, and relaxation.

Personal Development:
Invest in personal development to enhance your skills and knowledge.

Pursue hobbies and interests outside of work to maintain a well-rounded life.

Delegation:
Delegate tasks and responsibilities to trusted team members to avoid overburdening yourself.

Empower your team to take ownership and make decisions, allowing you to focus on strategic aspects of the business.

Goal Alignment:
Align your business goals with your personal values and aspirations.

Regularly reassess your goals to ensure they remain relevant and achievable.

Chapter 14

Navigating Challenges and Risks in Wealth Building

Wealth management involves various financial activities, from saving and investing to budgeting and risk management. However, many people fall into common traps that can hinder their financial growth and stability. Understanding these mistakes is the first step toward avoiding them.

1. Lack of a Clear Financial Plan:
Without a well-defined financial plan, it is difficult to set and achieve financial goals. Many individuals fail to outline their income, expenses, savings, and investment strategies, leading to missed opportunities for wealth accumulation.

2. Insufficient Emergency Savings:
Failing to maintain an adequate emergency fund can result in financial distress during unexpected events such as job loss, medical emergencies, or major repairs. An emergency fund acts as a financial buffer, preventing the need to dip into investments or incur debt.

3. Over-Reliance on Debt:
Excessive use of credit cards and loans can lead to high-interest payments and financial strain. Relying too heavily on debt can erode savings and limit investment potential.

4. Neglecting Retirement Savings:
Postponing retirement savings can significantly impact one's financial future.

Starting early with consistent contributions to retirement accounts, such as 401(k) plans or IRAs, is crucial for building a secure retirement fund.

5. Ignoring Inflation:
Not accounting for inflation in financial planning can diminish the purchasing power of savings and investments over time. It's essential to choose investments that outpace inflation to preserve wealth.

Impact of Overspending and Lack of Diversification
Overspending

Living beyond one's means can quickly deplete savings and increase debt. Overspending often stems from lifestyle inflation, where increased income leads to higher spending rather than increased savings or investments. This behavior can derail financial goals and lead to long-term financial instability.

Lack of Diversification:
Investing heavily in a single asset or market exposes one to significant risks. Lack of diversification can result in substantial losses if that asset or market underperforms. Diversifying investments across different asset classes, industries, and geographies helps mitigate risk and stabilize returns.

Practical Examples of Financial Pitfalls

Example 1: Lifestyle Inflation
Sarah received a substantial raise at her job and decided to upgrade her lifestyle by purchasing a luxury car and a larger home. Despite her higher income, her increased spending left her with little savings.

When faced with an unexpected medical expense, Sarah struggled to cover the costs, highlighting the consequences of lifestyle inflation.

Example 2: Undiversified Investment
John invested all his savings in a single tech stock, confident it would continue to rise. However, the company faced a major scandal, causing the stock price to plummet. John's lack of diversification resulted in a significant financial loss, emphasizing the importance of spreading investments.

Strategies for Avoiding Common Mistakes

1. Create a Comprehensive Financial Plan
Outline clear financial goals, including short-term, mid-term, and long-term objectives. Track income, expenses, and savings to ensure adherence to the plan. Regularly review and adjust the plan to reflect changes in financial circumstances.

2. Build an Emergency Fund
Aim to save three to six months' worth of living expenses in a liquid, easily accessible account. This fund provides a safety net during unexpected financial setbacks.

3. Manage Debt Wisely
Use credit responsibly and avoid accumulating high-interest debt. Pay off outstanding balances promptly and consider debt consolidation options if necessary.

4. Prioritize Retirement Savings
Contribute regularly to retirement accounts and take advantage of employer-sponsored plans and matching contributions.

The power of compound interest makes early and consistent saving critical.

5. Diversify Investments
Spread investments across various asset classes, such as stocks, bonds, real estate, and mutual funds. Diversification reduces risk and enhances the potential for stable returns.

Case Studies of Overcoming Financial Challenges

Rebuilding After Financial Setbacks
Emma faced significant debt due to medical expenses and overspending. She created a strict budget, cut unnecessary expenses, and prioritized debt repayment. By consolidating her debt and negotiating lower interest rates, she gradually regained financial stability. Emma also started an emergency fund to prevent future setbacks.

Successful Diversification
Mark initially invested heavily in the real estate market. Recognizing the risks, he diversified his portfolio to include stocks, bonds, and international assets. When the real estate market experienced a downturn, his diversified investments provided stability and continued growth.

Implementing Strategies for Risk Mitigation and Wealth Preservation

Importance of Risk Management in Wealth Building
Risk management is a fundamental aspect of wealth building. It involves identifying potential risks, assessing their impact, and implementing strategies to mitigate them. Effective risk management protects assets and ensures sustainable financial growth.

1. Protecting Capital

Preserving the principal amount of investments is crucial. By managing risks, investors can protect their initial capital and prevent significant losses.

2. Ensuring Consistent Returns

Risk management helps stabilize returns by minimizing the impact of market volatility and unforeseen events. A well-diversified portfolio is less likely to suffer substantial losses from a single adverse event.

3. Enhancing Financial Security

Implementing risk management strategies enhances overall financial security, allowing individuals to focus on long-term wealth accumulation without constant worry about potential setbacks.

Strategies for Asset Allocation and Diversification

- **Strategic Asset Allocation**

Asset allocation involves dividing investments among different asset classes, such as stocks, bonds, real estate, and cash. The allocation should align with the investor's risk tolerance, time horizon, and financial goals.

- **Diversification Across Asset Classes**

Diversify investments within each asset class. For example, within the stock portfolio, invest in various industries and sectors to reduce risk.

Similarly, in the bond portfolio, include government, corporate, and municipal bonds with varying maturities.

- **Geographic Diversification**

Spread investments across different geographic regions to mitigate country-specific risks. Investing in both domestic and international markets can enhance portfolio resilience.

- **Regular Portfolio Rebalancing**

Periodically review and rebalance the portfolio to maintain the desired asset allocation. This involves selling overperforming assets and buying underperforming ones to keep the portfolio aligned with the investment strategy.

Practical Examples of Wealth Preservation

Example 1: Diversified Investment Portfolio
Lisa's investment portfolio includes a mix of stocks, bonds, real estate, and commodities. This diversified approach reduces her exposure to market volatility. During a stock market downturn, her bonds and real estate investments provide stability, preserving her overall wealth.

Example 2: Use of Insurance
David invests in life insurance and disability insurance to protect his family's financial future. In the event of his untimely death or disability, these insurance policies ensure that his family remains financially secure, preserving their wealth and lifestyle.

Tools for Managing Financial Risks

1. Financial Planning Software

Use financial planning software to create detailed financial plans, track progress, and simulate different scenarios. These tools provide insights into potential risks and help develop strategies to mitigate them.

2. Risk Assessment Tools

Utilize risk assessment tools to evaluate the risk profile of individual investments and the overall portfolio. These tools help identify high-risk areas and suggest appropriate risk mitigation strategies.

3. Professional Financial Advisors

Consult with financial advisors to gain expert insights into risk management and wealth preservation. Advisors can provide personalized strategies based on individual financial situations and goals.

4. Insurance Products

Invest in various insurance products, such as life insurance, health insurance, and property insurance, to protect against unexpected events. Insurance acts as a financial safety net, preserving wealth in the face of adversity.

Developing a Long-term Wealth Management Plan

Creating a comprehensive financial plan is the cornerstone of successful wealth management. A well-thought-out plan acts as a roadmap, guiding your financial decisions and helping you navigate the complexities of wealth building.

Creating a Comprehensive Financial Plan

A comprehensive financial plan encompasses several critical components: budgeting, savings, investment strategies, retirement planning, tax planning, and estate planning. Start by assessing your current financial situation, including income, expenses, debts, and assets. This assessment forms the baseline for your plan.

Next, establish a budget that aligns with your financial goals. Allocate a portion of your income to savings and investments, ensuring you live within your means. Consider using financial software or apps to track your expenses and manage your budget efficiently.

Importance of Setting Long-term Goals

Long-term goals provide direction and motivation. Whether it's buying a home, funding your children's education, or achieving a comfortable retirement, having clear objectives helps prioritize your financial decisions. Break down these goals into manageable milestones, and set timelines for achieving them.

For example, if your goal is to retire at 65 with a specific amount of savings, calculate how much you need to save annually to reach that goal. Use retirement calculators and projections to help with this process. Regularly review your progress and adjust your savings rate or investment strategy as needed.

Practical Examples of Strategic Planning

Consider a young professional, Jane, who wants to buy a house in five years and retire comfortably by 60. Jane starts by creating a detailed financial plan.

She sets a budget that allows her to save a portion of her income each month. Jane invests in a diversified portfolio of stocks and bonds, focusing on growth for her long-term goals and stability for her down payment savings.

Jane reviews her plan annually, adjusting her investment allocations based on market conditions and her evolving risk tolerance. By maintaining discipline and sticking to her plan, Jane achieves her goal of buying a house and stays on track for retirement.

Regular Review and Adjustment of Plans

A financial plan is not static; it needs regular reviews and adjustments. Life events such as marriage, children, career changes, and market fluctuations can impact your financial situation. Schedule annual reviews to assess your progress and make necessary adjustments.

For example, if an economic downturn affects your investments, you might need to reassess your risk tolerance and adjust your portfolio to protect your assets. Similarly, if you receive a salary increase, consider increasing your savings rate to accelerate your progress towards your goals.

Leveraging Professional Financial Advice

Working with financial advisors can provide valuable insights and expertise, helping you navigate the complexities of wealth management.

Financial advisors offer several benefits, including personalized advice, comprehensive financial planning, and ongoing support.

They can help you develop a tailored financial plan, optimize your investment strategy, and provide guidance on tax planning, retirement planning, and estate planning.

Advisors also offer an objective perspective, helping you make informed decisions and avoid emotional reactions to market fluctuations. Their expertise can be particularly beneficial during significant life events, such as marriage, divorce, inheritance, or retirement.

Choosing the right advisor is crucial. Look for advisors with relevant qualifications, such as Certified Financial Planner (CFP) or Chartered Financial Analyst (CFA) credentials. Consider their experience, areas of expertise, and client reviews.

Interview multiple advisors to find one who understands your financial goals and aligns with your values. Discuss their fee structure, whether it's a flat fee, hourly rate, or percentage of assets under management. Transparency in fees and services is essential for a successful partnership.

Practical Tips for Effective Collaboration

Effective collaboration with your advisor involves clear communication and active participation. Be transparent about your financial situation, goals, and concerns. Regularly update your advisor on any changes in your circumstances, such as income, expenses, or life events.

Set realistic expectations and establish a plan for regular check-ins, whether quarterly or annually. Use these meetings to review your progress, discuss any adjustments, and address any questions or concerns. Stay engaged in the process and make informed decisions based on your advisor's recommendations.

Continuously educating yourself about personal finance enhances your ability to make informed decisions. Stay updated on financial trends, investment strategies, and economic developments. Read books, attend workshops, and follow reputable financial news sources.

An informed investor is better equipped to understand the advice provided by their advisor and to make strategic decisions that align with their goals. Ongoing education also helps you adapt to changes in the financial landscape and seize new opportunities.

Discipline and focus are critical for long-term financial success. Consistently adhering to your financial plan and staying motivated can help you achieve your goals despite challenges and market volatility.

Discipline in financial management involves regular saving, prudent spending, and strategic investing. It requires sticking to your budget, avoiding impulsive purchases, and making consistent contributions to your savings and investment accounts.

For instance, automated savings plans can ensure regular contributions without the temptation to spend that money elsewhere. Setting up automatic transfers to retirement accounts, emergency funds, and investment portfolios can reinforce disciplined saving habits.

Maintaining focus on long-term goals can be challenging, especially during periods of market volatility or personal financial stress. To stay motivated, regularly remind yourself of your financial objectives and the benefits of achieving them.

Visualize your goals and the positive impact they will have on your life. Celebrate milestones along the way to stay motivated. For example, reaching a certain savings balance or paying off a significant portion of debt are achievements worth celebrating.

Practical Examples of Disciplined Investing

Consider an investor, Mark, who diligently contributes to his retirement account each month. Despite market downturns, Mark continues his regular contributions, understanding the long-term benefits of compounding. Over the years, his disciplined investing pays off, and he builds a substantial retirement fund.

Another example is Sarah, who sets a goal to build an emergency fund. She automates monthly transfers to a high-yield savings account, gradually reaching her target. When unexpected medical expenses arise, Sarah's emergency fund provides financial security, illustrating the importance of disciplined saving.

Tools for Tracking Progress and Staying on Track

Several tools can help you track your financial progress and stay on track with your goals. Financial apps and software, such as Personal Capital and YNAB (You Need a Budget), provide real-time tracking of income, expenses, and investments. These tools offer insights into your financial health and help you make informed decisions.

Regularly reviewing your financial statements and progress reports ensures you stay aligned with your goals. Set reminders for quarterly or annual reviews to assess your achievements, identify areas for improvement, and adjust your plan as needed.

Chapter 15

FINANCIAL PLANNING FOR LIFE TRANSITIONS

Understanding Life Transitions and Financial Impact

Life is marked by significant transitions that bring about substantial changes, not only emotionally and socially but also financially. These transitions require careful planning to ensure financial stability and the ability to meet new responsibilities and goals. Key life transitions include marriage, starting a family, career changes, and retirement, each with its own set of financial implications and planning needs.

Marriage

Marriage combines two individuals' financial lives, creating both opportunities and challenges. Couples must navigate joint finances, which involves merging incomes, expenses, savings, and debts. Effective communication and joint financial planning become essential. Couples need to set common financial goals, such as buying a home, saving for vacations, or planning for retirement. They must also decide on joint or separate bank accounts and develop a budget that reflects their shared priorities.

Starting a Family

Starting a family introduces new financial responsibilities, including childcare, education savings, and increased living expenses. Parents must budget for medical costs, childcare, and future education expenses.

Planning for parental leave and ensuring adequate health and life insurance coverage are crucial steps. Additionally, parents should consider setting up a college savings plan early to take advantage of compound growth over time.

Career Changes

Career changes, whether due to a new job, promotion, or starting a business, impact financial planning significantly. A new job might bring a higher salary, necessitating adjustments in savings and investment strategies. Conversely, starting a business involves financial risks and requires careful planning for income fluctuations. Career changes also affect retirement planning, as changes in employer-sponsored retirement plans or benefits must be addressed.

Retirement

Retirement is a major life transition that requires meticulous financial preparation. The primary focus shifts from accumulating wealth to preserving it and ensuring it lasts through the retirement years. Retirees must plan for healthcare costs, potential long-term care, and lifestyle expenses. Creating a sustainable withdrawal strategy from retirement accounts and other savings is essential to maintain financial security.

Financial Planning for Marriage and Family

When two incomes are combined, couples often have more financial flexibility, but also face the challenge of managing a larger, more complex budget. It's important to create a joint budget that accounts for all income and expenses, including fixed costs like rent or mortgage payments, utilities, and insurance, as well as variable expenses such as groceries, dining out, and entertainment.

To start, couples should list all sources of income and categorize expenses. Setting priorities and determining which expenses are essential versus discretionary can help manage spending. Establishing joint financial goals, such as saving for a home or paying off debt, provides a clear direction for budgeting. Couples should also decide on a method for managing shared expenses—whether it's pooling all their income into a joint account or maintaining individual accounts and splitting expenses proportionally.

Saving for Children's Education

Saving for children's education is a significant financial goal for many families. The cost of education continues to rise, making early planning crucial. Parents can explore various savings options, such as 529 college savings plans, which offer tax advantages and flexible investment options. Regular contributions to a 529 plan can grow significantly over time, thanks to compound interest.

It's important to set a realistic savings target based on the expected cost of education and the number of years until the child starts college. Parents should also consider other education-related expenses, such as books, supplies, and room and board. Diversifying education savings through different investment vehicles can help manage risk and maximize growth potential.

Insurance Considerations for Protecting the Family

Insurance plays a critical role in protecting the financial well-being of a family. Life insurance is essential to provide financial security in the event of the death of a primary earner.

Term life insurance is often recommended for its affordability and straightforward coverage for a specified period, such as 20 or 30 years. Whole life insurance, though more expensive, offers lifelong coverage and a cash value component.

Health insurance is another key consideration, especially with the costs of medical care rising. Families should ensure they have adequate health insurance coverage to protect against unexpected medical expenses. Disability insurance is also important, as it provides income replacement if a primary earner is unable to work due to illness or injury.

Additionally, homeowners or renters insurance protects against property loss or damage, and auto insurance is necessary for financial protection in the event of an accident. Reviewing and updating insurance coverage regularly ensures it remains adequate as the family's needs change.

Practical Examples of Strategic Planning

Example 1: Newlyweds Combining Finances

Sarah and John recently got married and decided to combine their finances. They start by listing their incomes and expenses, including student loans, car payments, rent, and groceries. They open a joint bank account for shared expenses while maintaining individual accounts for personal spending. Together, they create a budget that allocates funds for savings, investments, and their future goals, such as buying a home.

Example 2: Parents Saving for College

Emily and Mark want to save for their daughter's college education. They open a 529 college savings plan and set up automatic monthly contributions.

By starting early, they take advantage of compound growth, aiming to cover a significant portion of her future college expenses. They also diversify their savings by investing in a mix of stocks and bonds within the 529 plan to balance risk and return.

Example 3: Career Change Financial Planning

James decides to leave his corporate job to start his own business. He anticipates income fluctuations during the initial years and adjusts his financial plan accordingly. James sets up an emergency fund to cover six months of living expenses and explores health insurance options as a self-employed individual. He also continues to contribute to his retirement accounts, ensuring long-term financial stability despite the career change.

Career Changes and Financial Stability

Career changes are common in today's dynamic job market. Whether you are switching jobs, negotiating a salary increase, or considering entrepreneurship, managing your finances during these transitions is crucial for maintaining stability and achieving long-term financial goals.

Strategies for Managing Finances During Job Transitions

Transitioning between jobs can bring about periods of uncertainty, especially regarding income. To navigate these changes smoothly, start by building an emergency fund that covers three to six months of living expenses. This fund provides a financial cushion, allowing you to meet your obligations without resorting to high-interest debt.

During a job transition, it's essential to reassess your budget. Evaluate your current expenses and identify areas where you can cut back temporarily. Prioritize essential expenses such as housing, utilities, groceries, and insurance, while reducing discretionary spending on entertainment and dining out.

Health insurance is another critical consideration. If your new job does not provide immediate coverage, consider COBRA or short-term health insurance plans to bridge the gap. Additionally, review your retirement accounts and decide whether to roll over your 401(k) from your previous employer into an IRA or your new employer's plan to maintain your retirement savings continuity.

Negotiating Salary and Benefits

Negotiating salary and benefits is a key aspect of career growth and financial stability. Before entering negotiations, conduct thorough research on industry salary standards for your position and experience level. Websites like **Glassdoor** and **Payscale** can provide valuable insights into typical compensation packages.

When negotiating, articulate your value to the organization. Highlight your skills, accomplishments, and the unique contributions you can bring. Be prepared to discuss your desired salary and be open to negotiating other aspects of your compensation, such as bonuses, stock options, and benefits like health insurance, retirement contributions, and paid time off.

Remember that benefits are a significant part of your overall compensation. Evaluate the full package, including health and dental insurance, retirement plans, and other perks. Negotiating these elements can sometimes be more beneficial than focusing solely on salary.

Planning for Entrepreneurship or Career Shifts

Planning for entrepreneurship or significant career shifts requires careful financial planning and risk assessment.

Start by developing a detailed business plan that outlines your business concept, market analysis, financial projections, and funding requirements. This plan serves as a roadmap and is essential for securing financing from investors or lenders.

Building a financial safety net is crucial before making the leap into entrepreneurship. Ensure you have sufficient savings to cover personal living expenses and business costs for at least six to twelve months. Consider setting up a separate business account to manage business finances and keep them distinct from personal finances.

Diversify your income sources where possible. While focusing on your new venture, having alternative income streams, such as freelance work or part-time employment, can provide additional financial security.

Preparing for Retirement

Retirement planning is a long-term process that benefits significantly from an early start. The earlier you begin saving and investing, the more time your money has to grow through compounding, leading to greater financial security in retirement.

Starting retirement planning early allows you to take advantage of compound interest, where the interest earned on your savings also earns interest over time. This exponential growth can significantly enhance your retirement savings. For instance, if you start saving $500 a month at age 25 with an average annual return of 7%, you could accumulate over $1 million by age 65.

Early planning also provides flexibility. You can start with smaller contributions and gradually increase them as your income grows.

It also allows you to take advantage of tax-advantaged retirement accounts such as 401(k)s and IRAs, which offer tax benefits and can accelerate your savings.

Investment Strategies for Long-term Financial Security

A diversified investment strategy is essential for long-term financial security in retirement. Diversification involves spreading your investments across various asset classes, such as stocks, bonds, and real estate, to mitigate risk and optimize returns.

Stocks offer higher growth potential, making them suitable for long-term growth. Bonds provide stability and regular income, which can be beneficial as you approach retirement. Real estate investments can offer both income and potential appreciation, adding another layer of diversification.

Rebalancing your portfolio periodically ensures it remains aligned with your risk tolerance and retirement goals. As you get closer to retirement, gradually shift to more conservative investments to preserve your savings and reduce exposure to market volatility.

Estate Planning and Legacy Considerations

Estate planning is a critical component of retirement planning, ensuring that your assets are managed and distributed according to your wishes after your death. Start by creating a will, which outlines how you want your assets to be distributed and who will manage your estate.

Consider setting up a trust to provide more control over the distribution of your assets and to potentially reduce estate taxes.

Trusts can also protect your assets from creditors and provide for beneficiaries who may not be able to manage their inheritance effectively.

Healthcare directives and powers of attorney are essential estate planning tools. They ensure your medical and financial affairs are handled according to your wishes if you become incapacitated.

Navigating Unexpected Life Events

Life is unpredictable, and unexpected events can significantly impact your financial plans. Being prepared for emergencies, handling sudden financial windfalls or losses, and managing health crises are essential aspects of comprehensive financial planning.

Financial Preparedness for Emergencies

An emergency fund is your first line of defense against unexpected financial shocks. Aim to save three to six months' worth of living expenses in a readily accessible account. This fund provides a financial buffer for job loss, medical emergencies, or major home or car repairs.

In addition to an emergency fund, consider other forms of financial protection, such as disability insurance, which replaces a portion of your income if you are unable to work due to illness or injury. Life insurance is also crucial for protecting your family's financial future in the event of your untimely death.

Handling Sudden Financial Windfalls or Losses

Sudden financial windfalls, such as an inheritance, lottery win, or substantial bonus, can be both a blessing and a challenge.

Without proper planning, these windfalls can be quickly depleted. To manage a windfall wisely, take time to assess your financial situation and goals. Consider consulting a financial advisor to develop a plan that maximizes the long-term benefits of the windfall.

Allocate a portion of the windfall to pay off high-interest debt, bolster your emergency fund, and invest for future growth. Avoid making impulsive purchases and consider setting aside a discretionary amount for enjoyment, ensuring it fits within your overall financial plan.

Conversely, sudden financial losses, such as a significant market downturn or unexpected medical expenses, require a strategic response. Review your budget and adjust your spending to preserve essential financial resources. If necessary, tap into your emergency fund to cover immediate needs, and develop a plan to rebuild your savings over time.

Impact of Health Crises on Financial Planning

Health crises can have a profound impact on your financial well-being. Medical expenses, reduced income, and the need for long-term care can strain finances. Health insurance is vital for mitigating the costs of medical care. Review your coverage regularly to ensure it meets your needs, and consider supplemental insurance if necessary.

Long-term care insurance can provide financial support for extended care needs, such as nursing homes or in-home care, which are not typically covered by health insurance or Medicare. This coverage can protect your savings and provide peace of mind for you and your family.

Creating a healthcare directive and assigning a durable power of attorney for healthcare ensures your medical decisions are made according to your wishes if you are unable to make them yourself. These documents are essential components of a comprehensive financial plan, particularly as you age.

BEHAVIORAL FINANCE

Financial decision-making is as much about psychology as it is about numbers and data. Behavioral finance is a field that explores how psychological factors and emotional biases influence financial decisions, often leading to irrational behaviors. These behaviors can have a significant impact on wealth accumulation, long-term financial health, and decision-making during volatile markets.

In this chapter, we will explore how key biases like loss aversion, overconfidence, and herding affect financial choices. We'll also introduce strategies for overcoming these psychological traps, providing a blend of practical financial advice and Biblical wisdom.

Understanding Behavioral Finance and Key Biases

What is Behavioral Finance?

Behavioral finance examines how emotions and psychological factors influence people's financial decisions. Traditional finance assumes that individuals make rational decisions aimed at maximizing financial returns. However, real-world decisions are often influenced by cognitive biases, leading individuals to act irrationally at times, even when they possess the financial knowledge to do otherwise.

Consider this example: during a market downturn, a rational investor would hold their position and trust in the long-term trajectory of their investments. However, many investors panic and sell their holdings, locking in losses due to fear. This reaction stems from emotional and psychological factors, not financial knowledge.

The Role of Psychology in Financial Behavior

Several psychological forces drive financial decision-making. Two key forces include:

Emotions: Fear, greed, and anxiety play a powerful role in influencing financial choices. For example, fear may cause an investor to sell assets prematurely, while greed may lead to excessive risk-taking during market booms.

Mental Shortcuts (Heuristics): People often rely on mental shortcuts to make complex decisions simpler. These shortcuts, however, can sometimes lead to poor decision-making. For instance, recency bias, which is the tendency to focus on recent events, may cause an investor to expect future market performance to mirror recent trends.

Cognitive Biases in Financial Decisions

Behavioral finance identifies several key biases that frequently influence financial decisions. Understanding these biases is the first step toward avoiding their negative impact. Below are some of the most common biases:

Loss Aversion

Loss aversion refers to the human tendency to fear losses more intensely than we appreciate gains. Behavioral economists have demonstrated that the pain of losing money is psychologically twice as powerful as the pleasure of gaining an equivalent amount.

This bias often leads to risk-averse behavior, even when taking calculated risks could result in long-term financial gains.

For example, an investor who experiences a small loss during a market downturn might sell their stocks out of fear that the market will continue to decline. However, if they had held onto the stocks, they could have benefited from the eventual market recovery.

Matthew 6:34 reminds us, "*Do not worry about tomorrow, for tomorrow will worry about itself.*" Loss aversion is driven by fear of future losses, but placing trust in God's provision can help alleviate the need to act out of fear. Long-term stewardship and trust in God's plan should guide our financial decisions.

Overconfidence Bias

Overconfidence occurs when individuals overestimate their financial knowledge and ability to predict future outcomes. This bias often leads to excessive trading, risky investments, and an overestimation of one's ability to outperform the market. Investors may believe they have superior knowledge or insights, causing them to take unnecessary risks.

For instance, an investor might frequently trade stocks based on short-term market trends, confident that they can "time the market." However, research consistently shows that frequent traders tend to underperform compared to those who follow long-term strategies, due to transaction costs and poor timing.

Proverbs 16:18 states, "*Pride goes before destruction, a haughty spirit before a fall.*" Overconfidence is closely linked to pride, which can lead to financial ruin.

Humility, recognizing that we do not control or fully understand market forces, is a key to wise investing. Seeking counsel and being humble enough to admit what we don't know can protect us from poor financial choices.

Herding Behavior
Herding occurs when individuals follow the actions of others, believing that the crowd must have valuable insights. This behavior is often seen during asset bubbles when investors rush to buy overvalued assets simply because everyone else is doing so. Herding behavior can lead to speculative bubbles, where asset prices rise far beyond their intrinsic value, followed by a sharp decline when the bubble bursts.

A classic example of herding is the dot-com bubble of the late 1990s. Investors flocked to invest in internet-based companies without understanding the underlying fundamentals of those businesses. When the bubble burst, stock prices plummeted, leading to massive financial losses for those who had followed the herd.

Romans 12:2 warns, "*Do not conform to the pattern of this world, but be transformed by the renewing of your mind.*" Herding behavior reflects the desire to conform to what everyone else is doing. Instead of following the crowd, Christians are encouraged to use discernment, applying God's wisdom to their decisions rather than blindly following popular trends.

Anchoring Bias
Anchoring occurs when people rely too heavily on specific reference points when making decisions, even when those reference points are no longer relevant.

For instance, an investor may refuse to sell a stock that has decreased in value, anchoring their decision on the price they initially paid for the stock, rather than the current market conditions or future prospects of the company.

This bias prevents rational decision-making because it focuses on past information that has little bearing on future outcomes. As a result, investors may hold onto poor-performing investments for too long or miss out on opportunities to reallocate their portfolio to better-performing assets.

Strategies to Overcome Behavioral Biases

Recognizing these behavioral biases is an important first step, but it's equally critical to develop strategies to overcome them. By incorporating both practical techniques and Biblical wisdom, investors can make better financial decisions that align with long-term goals.

- **Build Awareness of Biases**

The first step to overcoming biases is to be aware of them. By understanding that emotional and cognitive biases influence decision-making, individuals can pause before acting impulsively and reflect on whether their decisions are truly rational or driven by emotions.

Practical Tip: Keep a decision journal. Write down the reasons behind each major financial decision you make. Periodically review these entries to identify patterns or biases in your behavior. This reflective practice can help you spot instances where emotions, such as fear or greed, may have influenced your choices.

Proverbs 4:7 tells us, "*The beginning of wisdom is this: Get wisdom. Though it cost all you have, get understanding.*" Awareness and understanding are the first steps in making wise financial decisions. Seeking God's wisdom and taking the time to understand the motivations behind our choices can help us avoid acting out of fear, pride, or other biases.

- **Automate Financial Decisions**

One of the best ways to remove emotions from financial decisions is to automate them. Automating savings, investments, and debt repayments can ensure that your financial goals are met consistently, regardless of market conditions or personal emotions. Automation helps you stick to a long-term plan and prevents impulsive decisions based on short-term market movements.

For example, setting up automatic contributions to a retirement account, such as a 401(k) or an IRA, ensures that you are consistently saving for the future without being swayed by day-to-day market fluctuations. Similarly, using a strategy like dollar-cost averaging—investing a fixed amount of money at regular intervals—can help mitigate the effects of market volatility.

Chapter 16

CULTIVATING A HEART OF GRATITUDE AND CONTENTMENT

The pursuit of wealth often stems from the belief that financial success will lead to happiness and fulfillment. While financial stability can provide comfort and security, studies and personal experiences reveal that beyond a certain point, increasing wealth does not equate to increasing happiness. True joy and satisfaction often come from deeper, more meaningful sources.

The Bible addresses this in several passages. Ecclesiastes 5:10 states, "Whoever loves money never has enough; whoever loves wealth is never satisfied with their income. This too is meaningless." This verse highlights the futility of seeking fulfillment solely through material wealth.

Jesus emphasized prioritizing spiritual wealth over material possessions in Matthew 6:19-21, where He advises, "Do not store up for yourselves treasures on earth... But store up for yourselves treasures in heaven." While this warns against letting wealth dominate our lives, it doesn't mean that money is bad. Figures like Abraham and Job were wealthy but used their riches responsibly. The key is not letting wealth control you but using it to build eternal treasures—helping the poor, caring for the sick, and giving generously in secret, as Jesus taught. Wealth becomes meaningful when it serves God's purpose.

Importance of Spiritual and Relational Fulfillment

Cultivating a relationship with God, nurturing family bonds, and building meaningful connections with others can provide a sense of purpose and joy that material possessions cannot match.

Developing a relationship with God involves regular prayer, studying the Bible, and seeking to live according to His teachings. The Holy Spirit guides believers, providing comfort, wisdom, and strength. Galatians 5:22-23 describes the fruits of the Spirit, including love, joy, peace, and kindness, which contribute to a fulfilling life.

Relational fulfillment comes from investing time and energy in family and friendships. Strong relationships provide emotional support, companionship, and shared experiences that enrich our lives. Ecclesiastes 4:9-10 highlights the value of companionship: "Two are better than one because they have a good return for their labor: If either of them falls down, one can help the other up."

Practical Examples of Finding Joy Beyond Materialism

Consider the story of John, a successful entrepreneur who amassed considerable wealth but felt a lingering sense of emptiness. Seeking deeper fulfillment, John began volunteering at his church and mentoring young professionals. He found immense joy in helping others grow and succeed, which provided a sense of purpose beyond his business achievements.

Another example is Sarah, who, after experiencing the pressures of corporate success, chose to prioritize her family and community. She reduced her work hours to spend more time with her children and became actively involved in local charitable activities.

Sarah discovered that the joy and satisfaction she gained from these relationships far surpassed any material rewards.

Strategies for Cultivating Gratitude

Gratitude is a powerful practice that enhances well-being and contentment. Cultivating gratitude involves recognizing and appreciating the blessings in your life, both big and small.

Daily Gratitude Journal: Keep a journal where you write down three things you are grateful for each day. This practice shifts your focus from what you lack to the abundance in your life.

Prayer and Meditation: Spend time in prayer and meditation, thanking God for His blessings and seeking a deeper connection with Him.

Expressing Appreciation: Regularly express gratitude to others, acknowledging their contributions and support. This strengthens relationships and fosters a positive environment.

Mindfulness: Practice mindfulness to stay present and fully appreciate each moment. This helps you recognize the simple joys and beauty in everyday life.

Overcoming Temptations of Greed and Materialism

Common Challenges Associated with Wealth Accumulation
Accumulating wealth can bring temptations of greed and materialism, leading to a constant desire for more and a focus on possessions over meaningful experiences and relationships. This pursuit can cause stress, dissatisfaction, and strained relationships.

The Bible warns against the dangers of greed. In Luke 12:15, Jesus says, "Watch out! Be on your guard against all kinds of greed; life does not consist in an abundance of possessions."

This verse reminds us that true life and fulfillment are not found in material wealth.

Practical Tips for Resisting Greed and Envy

Set Meaningful Goals: Focus on goals that align with your values and bring lasting fulfillment, such as personal growth, helping others, and building strong relationships.

Practice Generosity: Regularly give to those in need. Acts of generosity shift your focus from accumulating wealth to making a positive impact. Proverbs 11:25 states, "A generous person will prosper; whoever refreshes others will be refreshed."

Contentment: Learn to be content with what you have. Philippians 4:11-13 highlights the Apostle Paul's contentment in all circumstances through Christ who strengthens him. Embrace a mindset of gratitude and sufficiency.

Avoid Comparisons: Resist the urge to compare yourself with others. Comparisons can fuel envy and dissatisfaction. Instead, focus on your unique journey and celebrate your progress and blessings.

Strategies for Maintaining a Balanced Perspective

Maintaining a balanced perspective involves recognizing the true source of fulfillment and keeping material pursuits in their proper place.

Regular Reflection: Take time to reflect on your life, values, and priorities. Assess whether your actions and goals align with your core beliefs.

Spiritual Practices: Engage in regular spiritual practices, such as prayer, Bible study, and attending church. These activities help you stay grounded in your faith and connected to God's purpose for your life.

Life Balance: Strive for a balance between work, family, and personal time. Ensure that you allocate time and energy to nurturing relationships and personal growth.

Accountability: Surround yourself with a supportive community that shares your values. Accountability partners or small groups can provide encouragement and help you stay focused on what truly matters.

Importance of Contentment in Financial Well-being

Contentment is crucial for financial well-being and overall happiness. It involves appreciating what you have and finding joy in non-material aspects of life. Contentment reduces stress and promotes a healthier, more fulfilling approach to wealth and possessions.

The Apostle Paul's words in 1 Timothy 6:6-8 emphasize the value of contentment: "But godliness with contentment is great gain. For we brought nothing into the world, and we can take nothing out of it. But if we have food and clothing, we will be content with that." This passage highlights the importance of focusing on essential needs and maintaining a grateful heart.

Practicing Mindfulness and Gratitude in Daily Life

Mindfulness and gratitude are powerful practices that can profoundly impact daily life, including financial decisions and overall well-being. Incorporating these practices can help entrepreneurs and professionals maintain balance and perspective, fostering a healthier relationship with money and success.

Techniques for Mindfulness and Gratitude

Mindfulness involves being fully present and engaged in the current moment, while gratitude is the practice of recognizing and appreciating the positive aspects of life. Several techniques can help cultivate these practices:

Mindful Breathing: Take a few minutes each day to focus on your breath. Inhale deeply, hold for a few seconds, and exhale slowly. This simple practice helps calm the mind and center your thoughts.

Gratitude Journaling: Spend a few minutes each day writing down things you are grateful for. This practice shifts your focus from what you lack to the abundance in your life.

Mindful Eating: Pay attention to the taste, texture, and aroma of your food. Eating mindfully helps you appreciate your meals and fosters a deeper connection with your body's needs.

Meditation: Set aside time for meditation, focusing on your breath or a specific mantra. Meditation helps clear the mind, reduce stress, and improve concentration.

Impact of Gratitude on Financial Decisions

Gratitude can significantly influence financial decisions by fostering a sense of contentment and reducing the desire for unnecessary material possessions. When you practice gratitude, you are less likely to make impulsive purchases driven by envy or the need to keep up with others. Instead, you make financial decisions aligned with your values and long-term goals.

The Bible encourages gratitude as a fundamental attitude. In 1 Thessalonians 5:18, it says, "Give thanks in all circumstances; for this is the will of God in Christ Jesus for you." This verse reminds us to maintain a grateful heart regardless of our financial situation, fostering a sense of peace and contentment.

Role of Mindfulness in Financial Management

Mindfulness plays a crucial role in financial management by helping individuals stay focused on their financial goals and avoid distractions. When you practice mindfulness, you are more aware of your spending habits, allowing you to identify unnecessary expenses and make intentional choices.

For instance, mindful budgeting involves regularly reviewing your income and expenses, setting clear financial goals, and making conscious spending decisions. This practice helps prevent overspending and ensures that your financial resources are allocated toward meaningful and purposeful activities.

Building Relationships and Community Through Generosity

Generosity is a powerful force for building relationships and fostering a sense of community. By giving of your time, resources, and talents, you can create positive connections and contribute to the well-being of others.

Importance of Generosity in Building Relationships

Generosity strengthens relationships by demonstrating care and concern for others. Whether through acts of kindness, charitable donations, or volunteering, generosity fosters a sense of trust and reciprocity. When you give selflessly, you create a bond with the recipient, deepening your connection and enhancing mutual respect.

The Bible emphasizes the importance of generosity in relationships. Proverbs 11:25 states, "A generous person will prosper; whoever refreshes others will be refreshed." This verse highlights the reciprocal nature of generosity and its positive impact on both the giver and the receiver.

Strategies for Community Engagement and Support

Engaging with your community and supporting those in need can be done in various ways:

Volunteering: Offer your time and skills to local organizations, charities, or community events. Volunteering not only benefits those in need but also provides a sense of fulfillment and purpose.

Charitable Giving: Consider setting aside a portion of your income for charitable donations. Supporting causes that align with your values can create a positive impact and reflect your commitment to social responsibility.

Mentorship: Share your knowledge and experience by mentoring others, whether in your industry, community, or through educational programs. Mentorship fosters personal and professional growth and helps build a supportive network.

Supporting Local Businesses: Patronize local businesses and artisans, contributing to the local economy and fostering a sense of community.

Practical Examples of Relational Wealth

Relational wealth refers to the richness of relationships and connections that bring joy and meaning to life. Consider the example of Sarah, who regularly volunteers at a local food bank. Through her volunteer work, she has built meaningful relationships with other volunteers and the individuals she serves. This sense of community provides her with a deep sense of fulfillment and purpose.

Another example is Alex, a business owner who mentors young entrepreneurs. By sharing his experiences and offering guidance, Alex has developed strong relationships with his mentees, creating a supportive network that benefits everyone involved.

Impact of Generosity on Community Well-being

Generosity has a profound impact on community well-being. When individuals and businesses engage in acts of generosity, they contribute to a culture of caring and support. This positive environment fosters social cohesion, reduces inequality, and enhances the overall quality of life.

For instance, a community that actively supports local charities and social initiatives can provide essential services to those in need, such as food, shelter, and education. This collective effort strengthens the community's resilience and creates a sense of unity.

Balancing Ambition and Contentment

This is a delicate but essential aspect of achieving a fulfilling life. While ambition drives progress and success, contentment provides peace and satisfaction, ensuring that the pursuit of goals does not lead to burnout or dissatisfaction.

Importance of Balancing Financial Ambition and Contentment

Financial ambition can motivate individuals to set and achieve significant goals, such as building a successful business, accumulating wealth, or advancing in their careers. However, without contentment, this drive can lead to an insatiable desire for more, resulting in stress, anxiety, and a constant feeling of inadequacy.

Contentment, on the other hand, allows individuals to appreciate what they have and find joy in their achievements, regardless of their financial status. It fosters a sense of gratitude and satisfaction, reducing the pressure to constantly seek more.

The Bible teaches the value of contentment in 1 Timothy 6:6-7: "But godliness with contentment is great gain. For we brought nothing into the world, and we can take nothing out of it." This passage reminds us that true wealth lies in spiritual and relational fulfillment, rather than material possessions.

Strategies for Setting Balanced Financial Goals

Setting balanced financial goals involves aligning your ambitions with your values and ensuring that your pursuit of success does not compromise your well-being. Here are some strategies to achieve this balance:

Define Your Priorities: Clearly identify what matters most to you, such as family, health, career, or personal growth. Use these priorities to guide your financial goals and decisions.

Set Realistic Goals: Establish achievable financial goals that reflect your current situation and resources. Avoid setting overly ambitious targets that may lead to unnecessary stress.

Embrace Flexibility: Be open to adjusting your goals as circumstances change. Life is unpredictable, and being flexible allows you to adapt and stay focused on your long-term vision.

Celebrate Milestones: Acknowledge and celebrate your achievements, no matter how small. This practice reinforces a positive mindset and helps you appreciate the progress you've made.

Practical Tips for Maintaining Contentment While Striving for Success

Maintaining contentment while striving for success requires intentional practices and a mindful approach. Here are some practical tips:

Practice Mindfulness: Stay present and focused on the current moment. Mindfulness helps you appreciate your journey and reduces the tendency to dwell on what you lack.

Limit Comparisons: Avoid comparing yourself to others, as this can lead to envy and dissatisfaction. Focus on your unique journey and celebrate your achievements.

Prioritize Self-Care: Take care of your physical, emotional, and mental well-being. Regular exercise, healthy eating, adequate sleep, and leisure activities contribute to overall contentment.

Nurture Relationships: Invest time and energy in building and maintaining meaningful relationships. Strong connections provide support, joy, and a sense of belonging.

Role of Faith in Achieving Balance

Faith plays a vital role in achieving balance between ambition and contentment. A strong faith foundation provides guidance, purpose, and a sense of peace, helping individuals navigate life's challenges with confidence.

The Bible encourages believers to trust in God's plan and seek His guidance in all aspects of life. Proverbs 3:5-6 advises, "Trust in the Lord with all your heart and lean not on your own understanding; in all your ways submit to him, and he will make your paths straight." This verse emphasizes the importance of relying on God's wisdom and direction.

Faith also fosters a sense of contentment, as believers recognize that true fulfillment comes from a relationship with God, rather than material possessions.

Philippians 4:12-13 illustrates this mindset: "*I know what it is to be in need, and I know what it is to have plenty. I have learned the secret of being content in any and every situation... I can do all this through him who gives me strength.*" So stop thinking God wants you to be poor. That's like a wealthy father wanting his children to be dirt poor. It makes zero sense.

Chapter 17

Leaving a Lasting Legacy: Planning for Generational Wealth Transfer

Generational wealth refers to the assets passed down from one generation to the next, creating a foundation of financial stability and opportunity. This wealth can include financial assets like stocks, bonds, and real estate, as well as businesses, intellectual property, and even valuable personal items. The transfer of generational wealth is significant because it provides future generations with a financial head start, enabling them to pursue education, start businesses, buy homes, and invest without the same financial pressures their predecessors might have faced.

Proverbs 13:22 highlights the importance of leaving a legacy: "A good person leaves an inheritance for their children's children, but a sinner's wealth is stored up for the righteous." This biblical principle emphasizes the responsibility of creating and preserving wealth not just for immediate descendants but for future generations as well.

The impact of generational wealth on future generations is profound. Financial stability provided by inherited wealth can alleviate the stress and burden of economic uncertainty, allowing individuals to focus on personal and professional growth. This stability can lead to better educational opportunities, improved health outcomes, and the ability to take calculated risks in careers and entrepreneurship.

Philippians 4:12-13 illustrates this mindset: "I know what it is to be in need, and I know what it is to have plenty.

I have learned the secret of being content in any and every situation... I can do all this through him who gives me strength."

Generational wealth also promotes social mobility. By providing financial resources, families can break the cycle of poverty and create lasting economic security. This wealth enables access to quality education, better healthcare, and the ability to live in safer, more prosperous communities.

Successful generational wealth transfer goes beyond passing down assets; it requires educating future generations on how to manage and grow that wealth. Teaching the next generation about financial responsibility ensures that they are equipped to handle what they inherit. In addition to family mentorship, professional guidance can offer critical support for making informed financial decisions.

Begin with Simple Concepts: Financial education can start in a practical way. Rather than repeating basic concepts like saving and budgeting in every family discussion, consider introducing financial decision-making opportunities. When children are old enough, include them in conversations about family investments, or allow them to take part in small decisions like choosing between saving for a larger purchase or making an immediate expense. This involvement helps them grasp the impact of financial choices early.

Professional Guidance: Family mentorship is essential, but the added value of professional advice—whether from financial advisors or estate planners—cannot be overstated. Experts can provide tailored advice on wealth transfer strategies, investment management, and tax planning, ensuring that wealth is preserved and responsibly managed across generations.

Strategies for Building and Preserving Wealth Across Generations
Estate Planning and Trusts

Estate planning is the process of arranging the management and disposal of a person's estate during their life and after death. A comprehensive estate plan includes wills, trusts, power of attorney, and healthcare directives. Trusts, in particular, are powerful tools for preserving and transferring wealth.

A trust is a fiduciary arrangement where a trustee holds assets on behalf of beneficiaries. Trusts can provide several benefits, including reducing estate taxes, protecting assets from creditors, and ensuring that the grantor's wishes are followed precisely. There are various types of trusts, such as revocable living trusts, irrevocable trusts, and charitable trusts, each serving different purposes.

Several tools can aid in preserving and transferring wealth effectively:

Wills: A will is a legal document that outlines how a person's assets should be distributed after death. It allows individuals to designate beneficiaries and appoint guardians for minor children. A well-drafted will can prevent disputes and ensure that assets are distributed according to the individual's wishes.

Life Insurance: Life insurance provides financial security for dependents after the policyholder's death. It can cover expenses such as funeral costs, debts, and living expenses, ensuring that the family's financial stability is maintained.

Retirement Accounts: Retirement accounts, such as 401(k)s and IRAs, can be designated to beneficiaries, allowing for a smooth transfer of assets.

Properly managing these accounts and understanding the tax implications are crucial for preserving their value.

Gifting: Gifting assets during one's lifetime can reduce the size of the estate and potentially lower estate taxes. Annual gifting limits allow individuals to transfer a certain amount to beneficiaries tax-free.

Family Limited Partnerships (FLPs): FLPs allow families to pool their assets and manage them collectively. This structure can provide asset protection, centralized management, and potential tax benefits.

Preparing heirs for the responsibility of managing wealth requires more than just basic financial literacy. Beyond simple concepts like saving and budgeting, it's important to introduce advanced financial principles as they grow older. Real-life experiences can be integrated to teach important lessons about managing money effectively.

For example, when making major financial decisions, such as buying a property or investing in stocks, involve younger family members in the discussion. Present them with the logic behind those decisions, including risk assessments, potential returns, and long-term impacts. This not only teaches them practical financial knowledge but also helps build a sense of responsibility and ownership over their future wealth.

Imparting Financial Wisdom and Values to Future Generations

The journey of wealth building is not just about accumulating assets but also about imparting financial wisdom and values to future generations. This responsibility ensures that the fruits of your labor continue to flourish in the hands of your heirs.

Teaching financial literacy, instilling core values, and guiding them through practical financial decisions are crucial steps in this process.

Strategies for Teaching Financial Literacy

Educating the next generation about money management should begin early and continue through different life stages. Start by introducing basic concepts such as saving, spending, and budgeting to young children. Simple activities like giving them an allowance and teaching them to save a portion can lay a strong foundation. As they grow older, delve into more complex topics such as investments, interest rates, and the importance of credit scores.

Incorporate real-life scenarios to make these lessons more relatable. For example, when making a significant purchase, involve them in the decision-making process. Discuss the costs, benefits, and potential financial impacts. Encourage questions and foster an environment where financial discussions are open and educational.

Role of Values and Principles in Wealth Management

Instilling strong values and principles is essential for responsible wealth management. Teach your heirs the importance of integrity, honesty, and stewardship in handling finances.

Biblical principles, such as those found in Proverbs, offer timeless wisdom on managing resources wisely. Proverbs 22:6 states, "Train up a child in the way he should go, and when he is old he will not depart from it." This underscores the importance of early education and consistent reinforcement of values.

Highlight the significance of generosity and helping others. Encourage them to view wealth not just as a means to personal gain but as a tool for positive impact. Sharing your own experiences and the satisfaction derived from charitable activities can inspire them to embrace a spirit of giving.

Practical Tips for Educating Heirs

Create Educational Opportunities: Set up regular family meetings to discuss financial matters. Use these gatherings to share knowledge, address questions, and make collective decisions on family investments or philanthropic efforts.

Leverage Technology: Utilize financial apps and online courses designed for young adults. These tools can make learning interactive and engaging.

Lead by Example: Demonstrate prudent financial behavior in your daily life. Children and young adults often learn best through observation.

Involve Them in Philanthropy: Encourage participation in charitable activities. Let them see firsthand the positive impact of generosity.

Mentorship plays a crucial role in imparting financial wisdom. Act as a mentor to your heirs, providing guidance and support as they navigate their financial journeys.

Share stories of your successes and failures, offering insights into the lessons learned. Encourage them to seek advice from other trusted mentors and financial professionals.

Role modeling is equally important. Live out the values you wish to impart. Demonstrate humility, diligence, and a commitment to continuous learning. Your actions will speak louder than words and leave a lasting impression on future generations.

Navigating Legal and Tax Considerations in Wealth Transfer

Wealth transfer involves a myriad of legal and tax considerations that must be navigated carefully to ensure a smooth transition and preservation of assets. Understanding these implications and employing effective strategies can significantly impact the efficiency and effectiveness of the transfer process.

Overview of Legal and Tax Implications

Transferring wealth involves several legal processes, including drafting wills, setting up trusts, and ensuring compliance with estate laws. Taxes, both federal and state, can have a substantial impact on the amount of wealth that successfully transfers to the next generation. Estate taxes, inheritance taxes, and gift taxes are among the primary concerns.

Failing to plan adequately for these taxes can result in significant portions of your estate being depleted, leaving less for your heirs. Therefore, understanding these implications and incorporating tax-efficient strategies is crucial.

Strategies for Minimizing Tax Impact

- Trusts are powerful tools for managing wealth transfer. They can help minimize estate taxes, protect assets, and ensure that your wishes are carried out. Different types of trusts, such as revocable and irrevocable trusts, offer various benefits and should be chosen based on your specific needs.

- Annual gifting allows you to transfer a portion of your wealth to your heirs tax-free. This strategy not only reduces the size of your taxable estate but also provides immediate financial support to your beneficiaries.

- Making charitable donations can reduce the taxable value of your estate. Establishing charitable trusts or foundations can align your philanthropic goals with tax planning.

- Life insurance policies can provide liquidity to pay estate taxes, ensuring that your heirs do not need to sell assets to cover these expenses.

Practical Examples of Estate Planning

Consider the case of a family business owner who wants to pass the company to their children. Setting up a family limited partnership (FLP) can be an effective strategy. By transferring business interests to the FLP, the owner can maintain control while gradually gifting partnership shares to their children, leveraging valuation discounts and reducing estate taxes.

Another example is using a generation-skipping trust (GST) to transfer wealth to grandchildren. This strategy can help avoid estate taxes at the children's level, preserving more wealth for future generations.

Importance of Professional Advice

Navigating the complexities of legal and tax considerations in wealth transfer requires professional expertise. Estate planning attorneys, tax advisors, and financial planners can provide invaluable guidance.

They ensure that your estate plan is comprehensive, up-to-date with current laws, and tailored to your unique circumstances. Seeking professional advice is not just a recommendation but a necessity for effective wealth transfer.

Building a lasting legacy goes beyond the financial assets you leave behind. It encompasses the values, principles, and spirit of generosity that you impart to future generations. Ensuring that your legacy is one of stewardship and generosity requires intentional actions and strategies.

Importance of a Values-Driven Legacy

A values-driven legacy ensures that the wealth you leave behind is managed with integrity and used to make a positive impact. Teach your heirs the importance of responsible stewardship. Proverbs 13:22 says, "A good man leaves an inheritance to his children's children," highlighting the significance of thoughtful legacy planning.

Instilling values such as humility, gratitude, and a commitment to serving others can guide your heirs in using their inheritance wisely. Encourage them to view wealth as a tool for positive change, both within the family and in the broader community.

Strategies for Fostering a Spirit of Generosity

Philanthropy as a Family Tradition: Establish charitable traditions that involve the entire family. Whether it's an annual donation drive or volunteering together, these activities can instill a sense of generosity.

Create a Family Foundation: Setting up a family foundation allows your heirs to actively participate in philanthropic efforts. It also provides a structured way to manage charitable giving and ensure it aligns with your family's values.

Share Stories of Generosity: Sharing stories of how generosity has positively impacted others can inspire your heirs. Highlighting both large-scale philanthropy and everyday acts of kindness can reinforce the importance of giving.

Practical Tips for Maintaining a Lasting Impact

- Create a legacy letter or ethical will that outlines your values, beliefs, and wishes for how your wealth should be used. This document can provide guidance and inspiration to your heirs.

- Keep the lines of communication open with your heirs. Regularly discuss your vision for the family's legacy and involve them in decision-making processes.

- Equip your heirs with the knowledge and skills they need to manage their inheritance responsibly. Offer resources, courses, and mentorship to support their financial education.

A NOTE FROM THE AUTHOR

Thank you so much for taking the time to read this book. It is my hope and prayer that the words within these pages have inspired and empowered you to pursue your dreams with renewed courage and unwavering faith. Your support means more to me than words can express, and I am deeply grateful for the time you've invested in this journey.

As you continue to walk your path, I leave you with this verse from the Bible that has always strengthened me:
"***For I know the plans I have for you," declares the Lord, "plans to prosper you and not to harm you, plans to give you hope and a future.***"
— Jeremiah 29:11

May you always trust in the plans that God has for you, even when the way seems unclear. Know that every step you take brings you closer to the purpose He has lovingly prepared for you.

Thank you once again for your support. I pray that the lessons and insights shared here will help you to flourish and succeed in all that you do. You are truly a blessing, and I look forward to seeing the incredible things you will accomplish.

With heartfelt thanks,

LeRoy L. Deal

Made in the USA
Monee, IL
04 November 2026

67385368R00174